HOW TO GET A JOB IN WASHINGTON, DC

THOMAS M. CAMDEN
KATHY STRAWSER

THE INSIDER'S GUIDE SERIES

Surrey Books
CHICAGO

HOW TO GET A JOB IN WASHINGTON, DC

Published by Surrey Books, Inc., 230 E. Ohio St., Suite 120, Chicago, IL 60611. Telephone: (312) 751-7330.

This book is manufactured in the United States of America.
2nd Edition. 1 2 3 4 5

Library of Congress Cataloging-in-Publication data:

Camden, Thomas M., 1938-
      How to get a job in Washington, D.C. / Thomas M. Camden, Kathy Strawser.—2nd ed.
     p. cm.
     Includes bibliographical references and index.
     ISBN 0-940625-50-4 (paper): $15.95
     1. Job hunting—Washington (D.C.) 2. Job vacancies—Washington (D.C.) .
3. Professions—Washington (D.C.) 4. Occupations—Washington (D.C.)
5. Washington (D.C.)—Industries—Directories. 6. Business enterprises—Washington (D.C.)—Directories.
I. Strawser, Kathy. II. Title.
HF5382.75.U62W354 1993   92-32930
650.14'09753—dc20   CIP

AVAILABLE IN THIS SERIES — $15.95 *(Pacific Rim and Europe $17.95)*

How To Get a Job in Atlanta by Diane C. Thomas, Bill Osher, Ph.D., and Thomas M. Camden.

How To Get a Job in Greater Boston by Paul S. Tanklefsky and Thomas M. Camden.

How To Get a Job in Chicago by Thomas M. Camden and Susan Schwartz.

How To Get a Job in Dallas/Fort Worth by Richard Citrin and Thomas M. Camden.

How To Get a Job in Europe by Robert Sanborn, Ed.D.

How To Get a Job in Houston by Thomas M. Camden and Robert Sanborn, Ed.D.

How To Get a Job in The New York Metropolitan Area by Thomas M. Camden and Susan Fleming-Holland.

How To Get a Job in the Pacific Rim by Robert Sanborn, Ed.D., and Anderson Brandao.

How To Get a Job in The San Francisco Bay Area by Thomas M. Camden and Evelyn Jean Pine.

How To Get a Job in Seattle/Portland by Thomas M. Camden and Robert W. Thirsk, Ed.D.

How To Get a Job in Southern California by Thomas M. Camden and Jonathan Palmer.

How To Get a Job in Washington, DC, by Thomas M. Camden and Kathy Strawser.

Single copies may be ordered directly from the publisher. Send check or money order plus $2.50 per book for postage and handling to Surrey Books at the above address. For quantity discounts, please contact the publisher.

Editorial production by Bookcrafters, Inc., Chicago.
Cover design by Hughes Design, Chicago.
Typesetting by On Track Graphics, Inc., Chicago.
"How To Get a Job Series" is distributed to the trade by Publishers Group West.

Note to Our Readers

We, the authors and editors, have made every effort to supply you with the most useful, up-to-date information to help you find the job you want, and each name, address, and phone number has been verified by our staff of fact checkers. But offices move and people change jobs, so we urge you to call before you write, and write before you visit. And, if you think we ought to include information on people or companies that we've missed, please let us know.

The publishers, authors, and editors make no guarantee that the employers listed in this book have jobs available.

Acknowledgments

The authors would like to thank Publisher Susan Schwartz, Managing Editor Gene DeRoin, Art Director Sally Hughes, and Research Assistant Dennis Sullivan for their valuable help and contributions to this book.

CONTENTS

7 How To Succeed In an Interview

Interview objective and how to prepare. Mastering the five-minute resume. The interview as a sales presentation. Steps to a successful interview. What interviewers look for. Anticipating tough questions and making sure you get your own questions answered. What to do following the interview. Books on interviewing.

8 What To Do If Money Gets Tight

Reviewing your assets and liabilites. Pros and cons of part-time and temporary work. List of selected sources for part-time work. How to sign up for unemployment benefits. Sources for emergency help.

9 Where To Turn If Your Confidence Wilts

Tips for dealing with rejection. Recognizing danger signals. Guidelines for seeking professional counseling or therapy. Selected crisis lines and mental health centers. Women in transition. What to do if you get fired. Career transition issues. Beating the job-hunt blues.

10 Selecting the Right Job for You

You don't have to jump at the first offer. What you should find out before accepting any job offer. Finding the right employment "culture." Tips on negotiating salary. How to compare job offers—sample checklist. What to do after you finally accept a job. Zeroing in on a great place to work.

How To Get the Most from This Book

So you want to get a job in the Washington, DC, area? Well, you've picked up the right book. Whether you're a recent graduate, new in town, or you know the President personally; whether or not you're currently employed; even if you're not fully convinced that you are employable—this book is crammed with helpful information.

It contains the combined wisdom of two top professionals: Tom Camden, a personnel professional and nationally known career consultant; and Kathy Strawser, a professional career consultant and job-search specialist who has already helped many people find jobs in the Washington area. She shares her knowledge of the Washington employment scene, and whether you are looking for a job in the city or along the Beltway, her extensive listings will save you hours of research time.

Dozens of other metro-area insiders have contributed tips, warnings, jokes, and observations in candid, behind-the-scenes interviews. We've done our level best to pack more useful information between these covers than you'll find anywhere else. We would love to guarantee that this book

1

is the only resource you will need to find the job of your dreams, but we are not miracle workers. This is a handbook, not a Bible. And there's just no getting around the fact that finding work takes work. *You* are the only person who can land the job you want.

What we *can* do—and, we certainly hope, have done—is to make the work of job hunting in Washington easier and more enjoyable for you. We have racked our brains, and those of many others, to provide you with the most extensive collection of local resources in print.

To get the most from this book, first browse through the Table of Contents. Acquaint yourself with each chapter's major features, see what appeals to you, and turn to the sections that interest you the most.

It may not be necessary or useful for you to read this book from cover to cover. If you're currently employed, for example, you can probably skip Chapter 8—What To Do If Money Gets Tight. If you have no interest in using a professional employment service, you'll only need to browse through Chapter 6.

There are certain parts of this book, however, that no one should overlook. One of them is Chapter 4—Researching the Washington Job Market. Unless you're a professional librarian, we'd bet money that you won't be able to read this chapter without discovering at least a few resources that you never knew existed. We've tried to make it as easy as possible for you to get the inside information that can put you over the top in an employment interview.

Chapter 5 is another "Don't Miss"—especially our unique listing of organizations that you should know about to develop your network of professional contacts. We strongly suggest that you read Chapter 7, even if you think you already know all about how to handle an interview. *Chapter 11 is completely new—a guide to help you wade through the steps in finding a job with the government.* And then, of course, there's Chapter 12—listings of the Washington area's top 1,400 employers of white-collar workers.

There's another thing you should know about in order to get the most from this book. Every chapter, even the ones you don't think you need to read, contains at least one helpful hint or insider interview that is set off from the main text. Take some time to browse through them. They contain valuable nuggets of information and many tips that have never before appeared in print.

Keep in mind that no one book can do it all for you. While we've touched on the basic tasks of any job search—self-analysis, developing a resume, researching the job market, figuring out a strategy, generating leads, interviewing, and selecting the right job—we don't have space to go into great detail on each and every one of them. What we have done is to supply suggestions for further reading. Smart users of this book will follow those suggestions when they need to know more about a particular subject.

New in town?

Have you just moved to Washington? In addition to this book, you could probably use some assistance. **The Travelers Aid Society of Washington** offers counseling and referral services for newcomers. Their offices are located at 512 C St. N.E., 202-546-3120; at Union Station, 50 Massachusetts Ave. and N. Capitol St. N.E., 202-371-1937; at National Airport, 703-684-3472; and at Dulles Airport, 703-471-9776.

The **Washington Convention and Visitors Association** (1212 New York Ave. N.W., Suite 600, 202-789-7000) provides maps and attraction guides, plus additional information that might be useful. There are several guidebooks that are particularly good at helping you learn your way around the area: *Washington DC Access*, New York: Access Press, 1992; *The Newsettler's Guide for Washington, D.C. and Communities In/Nearby Maryland and Virginia*; and *Frommer's Washington*, New York: Frommer/Pasmantier Publishers, 1992 ■

Washington in the 1990s

The Washington area's job growth rate, after experiencing an unbelievable peak in the mid-1980s, has been gradually declining over the past few years. While the area continues to create new jobs at a faster rate than the U.S. economy (3.9% vs 2.7%), the period of incredible growth is clearly over. Does this trend, coupled with proposed federal government, particularly Defense Department, budget cuts, indicate bad news for the job seeker?

"Absolutely not!" is clearly the message from the experts. According to Richard Groner, Chief of the District of Columbia Department of Employment Services, although the economy is in the bottom of a business cycle, the recession will end. "We are experiencing a fragile and weak recovery process which may not sustain itself through 1992. However, we would expect recovery to be underway later in the year or during 1993." No one expects growth in the metropolitan area to match the 1980's, but the local economy should outproduce the rest of the economy in job growth rate. Washington has this advantage due to the area's ability to combine its industrial mix with technological changes and international developments.

These factors, according to Mr. Groner, should see this economy grow well into the 21st century. Mr. Groner reminds us that even in the case of no job growth, almost 60,000 jobs per year are available. This means that the area would still require that number of workers just to replace those who leave the labor market. This is almost enough to provide employment for all of the area's job candidates!

George Greer, economist at the Greater Washington Research Center, agrees with this forecast. He says that while the job supply is down (by about 3%), this still leaves us with a lot of jobs. In fact, the local unemployment rate is almost 30% below the national average. Because the market here has been so strong for so long, a slowdown means going from incredible to extremely good. While forecasting long into the future is more difficult due to inconsistent trends, the economy appears quite stable. One of the stabilizing factors, of course, is the impact of government employment in the area. While employment in the private sector dropped slightly, federal government hiring was up slightly over the past year.

While the experts do acknowledge that Defense cuts will undoubtedly affect local companies, the move toward private sector diversification begun by many government contractors will offset the cuts to some degree. In addition, much of the work related to defense contracts is not done locally; even Martin Marietta, a major Defense Department contractor headquartered in Bethesda, MD, maintains most manufacturing facilities elsewhere.

Both Groner and Greer see the service industries as continuing their rapid growth rates, particularly computer, legal, engineering, and financial services. Newly developed technologies and applications will demand more jobs in office automation, electronics, telecommunications, and computer science. Areas most likely to experience less growth are construction, real estate, and retail trade.

Washington is certainly a mecca for entry-level people, whether their future employers be government or business. Many new college graduates either stay in DC or head here after school to find that first job. Statistics show that the 1980s belonged to the job seeker—there were more jobs than people to fill them. Our experts believe that the same will be true for the 1990s, but those job searchers might have to work harder to land that perfect job. That is what this book will help you to do.

Finding Your Way Around Washington

Washington, or the District of Columbia, is a very easy city to learn since it is divided into four quadrants (NW, NE, SW, SE), with the Capitol Building dome as the center. You must remember to observe the quadrant designators when looking for an address since some addresses can appear in four different places. Lettered (east-west) and numbered (north-south) streets make finding an address very simple; avenues, frequently named after states, run at angles across the grid pattern and often intersect at circles. By the way, ask a local resident why there is no "J" street; it will make a great conversation starter!

The adjacent counties, cities, and towns are considerably more confusing because their designs and traffic patterns are not consistent. After all, we are dealing here with two states, Virginia and Maryland, several major county organizations, and the District, which is governed both by Congress and its own internal government!

Getting around all these areas can be equally confusing. If your job hunting is restricted to the District proper, unlikely in most cases, or to those places served by Metro (the public transportation system), you can get by without a car. However, getting to many of the companies listed in Chapter 12 by public transportation would require many bus routes and changes. You might save yourself enough time to warrant the expense of renting a car for those less-central excursions. Automobile rental companies are located at all three airports serving the metropolitan area (see below) and at downtown locations. They are listed in the Yellow Pages.

Speaking of the Yellow Pages, a recent change has made it necessary to dial the area codes first before dialing numbers within the metropolitan area. (DC area code: 202; Virginia: 703; Maryland: 301). Fortunately, these are still local calls; it just takes more of your precious job-hunting time to make them!

Washington is served both by the easy-to-use Metrorail system (Metro) and the very complex Metrobus system (connecting with independent bus services in Maryland and northern Virginia). To get free timetables or help with planning your public transportation route, you may call the **Transit Information** number, 202-637-7000, or visit the Authority at 600 5th St. N.W. Phone lines are open from 6 a.m. to 11:30 p.m., but the lines are frequently busy, so plan accordingly.

Three **airports** serve the area: 1) Washington National is closest to downtown and can be reached by Metro or a $10 cab fare; 2) Dulles International, in Virginia, uses the Washington Flyer as its quasi-shuttle to downtown, 703-685-1400 (this service also connects Dulles airport with the nearest Metro station, West Falls Church, VA), and 3) Baltimore Washington International, in Maryland, has its Airport Connection service (301-441-2345). Cab rides from Dulles or BWI run about $35, much more than the bus service.

In late 1988 a truly renovated **Union Station** (50 Massachusetts Ave. N.E.) was reopened. Although many people now think of this as a shopping, restaurant, and movie spot, it is the main Amtrak station in Washington, with hourly departures and arrivals from New York. It is also a stop on the Metro's Red Line.

Greyhound Bus (110 New York Ave. N.W., 301-565-2662) serves the District. It is not an area for strolling—use taxis.

A number of **cab companies** can be found throughout the area, although the system can be confusing. DC cabs use a zone fare system; Maryland and Virginia cabs have meters. At the airports you can take any cab in the line; however Maryland and Virginia cabs can not be hailed in DC unless you are going past District lines. Yet, you can call a Virginia cab to come into the District to take you to a Virginia address, for example, to National Airport. A few hints: cabs are usually easy to hail downtown, and it is easier to phone for a cab in the suburbs than it is in the city. When calling ahead (overnight or several hours' notice) for a cab pick-up, you'll get faster service if you ask for an off-time, i.e. 6:05 or 6:20, instead of 6:00 or 6:15...everybody else calls for cabs at those times, so you may end up waiting in line or being picked up late. A few cab companies you might want to call are listed:

Barwood Taxi:	301-881-5565	(MD)
Capitol Cab:	202-546-2400	(DC)
Red Top Cab:	703-522-3333	(VA)
Yellow Cab:	202-544-1212	(DC)

Chambers of Commerce

Most major Chambers of Commerce have published material that is especially helpful to newcomers or anyone who wants to be better informed about a community. These brochures and maps are available free or for a nominal charge and provide information about area business environments, city services, transportation, public schools, utilities, and entertainment.

How to Get a Job

DC Chamber of Commerce
1411 K St. N.W.
Washington, DC 20005
202-347-7201

Alexandria Chamber of Commerce
801 N. Fairfax St., Suite 403
Alexandria, VA 22314
703-549-1000

Arlington Chamber of Commerce
2009 N. 14th St.
Arlington, VA 22201
703-525-2400

Chamber of Commerce of Montgomery County
416 Hungerford Drive, Suite 400
Rockville, MD 20850
301-424-6000

Chamber of Commerce of Prince George's County
4640 Forbes Blvd.
Lanham, MD 20706
301-731-5000

Chamber of Commerce of Rockville
600 E. Jefferson St.
Rockville, MD 20852
301-424-9300

Chamber of Commerce of Silver Spring
8601 Georgia Ave.
Silver Spring, MD 20910
301-585-6300

Fairfax County Chamber of Commerce
8391 Old Courthouse Road
Vienna, VA 22182
703-749-0400

Gaithersburg and Upper Montgomery County Chamber of Commerce
Gaithersburg, MD 20877
301-840-1400

Why businesses choose Washington

Washington, although obviously not a major industrial center, has been developing its reputation as an excellent place for corporate headquarters. This is particularly true for industries with a heavy emphasis in either regulatory businesses or government contracts. The days when executives enjoyed business travel are long gone, and the closer those executives can be to the legislators, regulators, or contract supervisors they work with, the less time is spent on the road. ■

Establishing an Objective: How To Discover What You Want to Do

One of the most common mistakes job seekers make is not establishing an *objective* before beginning the job search. Practically everyone wants a job that provides personal satisfaction, growth, good salary and benefits, prestige, and a desirable location. But unless you have a more specific idea of the kind of work you want, you probably won't find it. You wouldn't take off on your big annual vacation without a clear destination in mind. Well, you'll be spending a lot more time on the job than at the beach. As David Campbell puts it, "If you don't know where you're headed, you'll probably wind up somewhere else."

Many of our readers already have a clear objective in mind. You may want a job as a systems analyst, paralegal, sales manager, or any of a

7

thousand other occupations. (*The Dictionary of Occupational Titles* lists 40,000 jobs!) If you know what you're looking for, you're to be commended because *establishing an objective is a necessary first step in any successful job search.*

But even if you have an objective, you can benefit from a thorough self-appraisal. What follows is a list of highly personal questions designed to provide you with insights you may never have considered, and to help you answer the Big Question, "What do I want to do?"

To get the most from this exercise, write out your answers. This will take some time, but it will force you to give each question careful thought. The more effort you put into this exercise, the better prepared you'll be for the tough questions you'll be asked in any job interview. The exercise also can be the basis for constructing a winning resume—a subject we'll discuss in more detail in the next chapter.

When you've completed the exercise, consider sharing your answers with a trusted friend or relative. Self-analysis is a difficult task. Although we think we know ourselves, we seldom have the objectivity to see ourselves clearly, to outline our personal and professional strengths and weaknesses, to evaluate our needs, and to set realistic objectives. Someone who knows you well can help.

Questions About Me

1. Taking as much time as necessary—and understanding the purpose of this appraisal—honestly describe the kind of person you are. Here are some questions to get you started. Are you outgoing or are you more of a loner? How well-disciplined are you? Are you quick-tempered? Easygoing? Are you a leader or a follower? Do you tend to take a conventional, practical approach to problems? Or are you more imaginative and experimental? How sensitive are you to others?
2. Describe the kind of person others think you are.
3. What do you want to accomplish with your life? What issue or cause really motivates or excites you?
4. What role does your job play in that goal?
5. What impact do you have on other people?
6. What past experiences are you proud of? What satisfies you about them?
7. What role does money play in your standard of values?
8. Is your career the center of your life or just a part of it? Compared with your other roles, what role would you like your career to play?
9. What are your main interests?
10. What do you enjoy most?
11. What displeases you most?

Questions About My Job

1. Beginning with your most recent employment and then working back toward school graduation, describe *in detail* each job you had. Include your title, company, responsibilities, salary, achievements and successes, failures, and reason for leaving. (If you're a recent college graduate and have little or no career-related work experi-

8

ence, you may find it helpful to consider your collegiate experience, both curricular and extracurricular, as your work history for questions 1, 2, 3, 8, 9, and 11.)

2. How would you change anything in your job history if you could?
3. In your career thus far, what responsibilities have you enjoyed most? Why?
4. What kind of job do you think would be a perfect match for your talents and interests?
5. What responsibilities do you want to avoid?
6. How hard are you really prepared to work?
7. If you want the top job in your field, are you prepared to pay the price?
8. What have your subordinates thought about you as a boss? As a person?
9. What have your superiors thought about you as an employee? As a person?
10. Can your work make you happier? Should it?
11. If you have been fired from any job, what was the reason?
12. How long do you want to work before retirement?

Your answers to these highly personal questions should help you to see more clearly who you are, what you want, what your gifts are, and what you realistically have to offer. They can also reveal what you *don't* want and what you *can't* do. And if you find yourself more aware of what you *don't* like and *don't* want to do, fear not! This is a great starting place! Usually what someone really likes is just the flip-side of their dislikes. (It's kind of like looking under a rock; there's a whole other world underneath it). Take this information to heart or to a career counselor and work with it; by turning these dislikes "upside down" you just might find out what you *do* like after all!

It's important to evaluate any objective you're considering in light of your answers to these questions. If a prospective employer knew nothing about you except your answers to these questions, would she think your career objective was realistic?

People who are entering the job market for the first time, those who have been working for one company for many years, and those who are considering a career change need more help in determining their objectives. If you're still in college, be sure to take advantage of the free counseling and career planning services that are available on most campuses. Vocational analysis, also known as career planning or life planning, is much too broad a subject to try to cover here. But we can refer you to some excellent books.

BOOKS ON CAREER/LIFE PLANNING

Beatty, Richard H. *The Complete Job Search Book.* New York: John Wiley & Sons, 1988.

Bolles, Richard N. *The Three Boxes Of Life and How to Get Out Of Them.* Berkeley, CA: Ten Speed Press, 1983.

Bolles, Richard N. *The 1993 What Color Is Your Parachute?* Berkeley, CA: Ten Speed Press, 1993. The bible for job hunters and career changers, this book is revised every year and is widely regarded as the most useful and creative manual available.

How to Get a Job

Borchard, David C. *Your Career: Choices, Chances, Changes.* Dubuque, IA: Kendall-Hunt, 1988.

Camden, Thomas M. *The Job Hunter's Final Exam.* Chicago: Surrey Books, 1990.

Charland, William A., Jr. *Life Work: Meaningful Employment in a World of Change.* New York: Continuum, 1986.

Clawson, James G., et al. *Self-Assessment and Career Development.* Englewood Cliffs, NJ: Prentice-Hall, 1985.

Dail, Hilda Lee. *The Lotus and the Pool: How to Create Your Own Career.* Boston: Shambhala, 1989.

Davidson, Jeffrey P. *Blow Your Own Horn: How to Market Yourself and Your Career.* New York: Simon & Schuster, 1988.

Dyer, Sonya, and Jacqueline McMakin. *Working From the Heart.* San Diego, CA: LuraMedia, 1989.

Figler, Howard. *The Complete Job-Search Handbook.* New York: Holt, Rinehart, and Winston, 1988.

Green, Gordon W., Jr. *Getting Ahead At Work.* Washington, DC: Carol Publishing Group, 1988.

Haldane, Bernard. *Career Satisfaction and Success: A Guide to Job Freedom.* New York: AMACOM, 1982.

Jackson, Tom. *Guerrilla Tactics in the New Job Market.* New York: Bantam Books, 1991. Filled with unconventional but effective suggestions.

Kaplan, Robbie Miller. *The Whole Career Sourcebook.* New York: American Management System, 1991.

Krannich, Ronald L. *Careering and Re-Careering for the 1990's: The Complete Guide to Planning Your Future.* Manassas, VA: Impact, 1989.

Levinson, Harry. *Career Mastery.* San Francisco: Berrett-Koehler, 1992.

Lewis, Adele. *Fast Track Careers for the 90's.* New York: Scott Foresman, 1990.

Michelozzi, Betty. *Coming Alive from Nine to Five: The Career Search Handbook.* Mountain View, CA: Mayfield Publishing Co., 1988.

Miller, Arthur F., and Ralph T. Mattson. *The TRUTH About You: Discover What You Should Be Doing With Your Life.* Manassas, VA: Impact, 1990.

Munschauer, John L. *Jobs for English Majors and Other Smart People.* Princeton, NJ: Peterson's Guides, 1991.

Powell, C. Randall. *Career Planning Today.* New York: Kendall/Hunt, 1990.

Ray, Michael, and Rochelle Myers. *Creativity in Business.* New York: Doubleday Dell, 1986.

Sher, Barbara. *Wishcraft: How to Get What You Really Want.* New York: Ballantine Books, 1986.

Sinetar, Marsha. *Do What You Love, The Money Will Follow.* Mahwah, NJ: Paulist Press, 1987.

Wegmann, Robert, and Robert Chapman. *The Right Place at the Right Time.* Manassas, VA: Impact, 1990.

If you're **still in college or have recently graduated,** the following books will be of particular interest:

Baumgardner, Steve. *College and Job: Conversations With Recent Graduates.* New York: Hunt Sciences Press, 1988.

Bloch, Deborah P. *How to Get and Get Ahead on Your First Job.* New York: National Textbook, 1988.

Bloom, Bruce J. *Fast Track to the Best Job.* Manassas, VA: Impact, 1991.

Bouchard, Jerry. *Graduating to The 9-5 World.* Manassas, VA: Impact, 1991.

Briggs, James I. *The Berkeley Guide to Employment for New College Graduates.* Berkeley, CA: Ten Speed Press, 1984.

Figler, Howard. *Liberal Education and Careers Today.* Manassas, VA: Impact, 1989.

Fox, Marcia R. *Put Your Degree to Work: The New Professional's Guide to Career Planning.* New York: Norton, 1988.

10

Holton, Ed. *The M.B.A.'s Guide to Career Planning.* Princeton, NJ: Peterson's Guides, 1989.
Holton, Ed. *The New Professional.* Princeton, NJ: Peterson's Guides, 1991.
Malnig, L.R., and S.L. Morrow. *What Can I Do With a Major In...?* Ridgefield, NJ: 1984.
Osher, Bill, and Sioux Henley Campbell. *The Blue Chip Graduate: A Four Year College Plan For Career Succcess.* Atlanta: Peachtree Publishers, 1987.

For those of you involved in a **mid-life career change**, here are some books that might prove helpful:

Anthony, Rebecca, and Gerald Roe. *Over 40 and Looking for Work? A Guide for Unemployed, Underemployed and Unhappily Employed.* Holbrook, MA: Bob Adams, 1991.
Bardwick, Judith M. *The Plateauing Trap.* New York: AMACOM, 1987.
Bicker, C.E. *Executive Reemployment, Out Not Down...A Positive Approach.* Hawthorne, NJ: Career Press, 1989.
Bird, Caroline. *Second Careers: New Ways to Work After 50.* 1992.
Birsner, E. Patricia. *The Forty-Plus Job Hunting Guide: Official Handbook of the 40-Plus Club.* New York: Facts on File, 1990.
Goldstein, Dr. Ross, and Diana Landau. *Fortysomething.* Manassas, VA: Impact, 1991.
Hardy, Karen. *Fifty and Starting Over: Career Strategies for Success.* Newcastle, 1991.
Hecklinger, Fred J., and Bernadette M. Black. *Training for Life: A Practical Guide to Career and Life Planning.* New York: Kendall-Hunt, 1991.
Hyatt, Carole. *Shifting Gears: How to Master Career Change and Find the Work That's Right for You.* New York: Simon & Schuster, 1990.
Montana, Patrick J. *Stepping Out, Starting Over.* New York: National Center for Career Life Planning, 1988.
Simon, Dr. Sidney B. *Getting Unstuck.* Manassas, VA: Impact, 1988.

For workers who are nearing **retirement age** or have already reached it, here are a few books that might be useful:

Connor, J. Robert. *Cracking the Over-50 Job Market.* New York: Plume, 1992.
Morgan, John S. *Getting a Job After Fifty.* Princeton, NJ: Petrocelli, 1988.
Myers, Albert, and Christopher P. Anderson. *Success Over Sixty.* New York: Summit Books, 1984.
Strasser, Stephen, and John Sena. *Transitions: Successful Strategies from Mid-Career to Retirement.* Hawthorne, NJ: Career Press, 1990.

And for **handicapped** job seekers, these title could prove helpful:

Bolles, Richard N. *The 1993 What Color Is Your Parachute?* Berkeley, CA: Ten Speed Press, 1993.
Hoffa, Helynn, and Gary Morgan. *Yes You Can.* Manassas, VA: Impact, 1990.
Lewis, Adele, and Edith Marks. *Job Hunting for the Disabled.* Woodbury, NY: Barrons, 1987.
Lobodinski, Jeanine, McFadden, Deborah, and Arlene Markowicz. *Marketing Your Abilities: A Guide for the Disabled Job-Seeker.* Mainstream, 1984.
Rabbi, Rami, and Diane Croft. *Take Charge: A Strategic Guide for Blind Job Seekers.* Boston, MA: National Braille Press, 1989.

How to Get a Job

For **women** in the work force, these titles will be of interest:

Berryman, Sue E. *Routes Into the Mainstream: Career Choices of Women and Minorities.* New York: National Center for Research in Vocational Education, 1988.

Betz, Nancy E., and Louise Fitzgerald. *The Career Psychology of Women.* Orlando: Academic Press, 1987.

Gutek, Barbara, and Laurie Larwood, eds. *Women's Career Development.* Newbury Park, CA: Sage, 1987.

Jaffe, Betsy. *Altered Ambitions.* New York: Donald A. Fine, 1991.

Lunnenborg, Patricia. *Women Changing Work.* New York: Bergin & Garvey, 1990.

Morrow, Jodie B., and Myrna Lebov. *Not Just a Secretary: Using the Job to Get Ahead.* New York: Wiley & Sons, 1984.

Nivens, Beatrice. *The Black Woman's Career Guide.* New York: Anchor Books, 1987.

Scollard, Jeannette. *Risk to Win: A Woman's Guide to Success.* New York: Macmillan, 1989.

Thomas, Marian. *Balancing Career and Family.* Manassas, VA: Impact, 1991.

Thompson, Charlotte E. *Single Solutions—An Essential Guide for the Single Career Woman.* Brookline Village, MA: Branden, 1990.

Working mothers create their own resource and referral service

In 1984 several working mothers in the Washington area, frustrated by the difficulty of finding information on available child care, formed their own non-profit resource, Metropolitan Mothers at Work. In the years that followed they have provided counseling, workshops, and seminars for a number of private companies and government agencies, as well as individuals.

A few years ago they brought out a great publication, useful for any working parents: *Metropolitan Mothers at Work Book; Complete Guide to Child Care in Metropolitan Washington, Maryland and Virginia.* It is available in local bookstores or can be ordered from Metropolitan Mothers at Work, 8512 Cedar Street, Silver Spring, MD 20910 (301-585-2268). The book costs $14.95 plus $3.00 for postage. Addendum available monthly. ∎

Professional Vocational Analysis

It would be great if there were some psychological test that would confirm without a doubt who you are and precisely what job, career, or field best suits you. Unfortunately, there isn't. Professionals in vocational planning have literally dozens of tests at their disposal designed to assess personality and aptitude for particular careers.

The test most commonly used is probably the Strong-Campbell Interest Inventory (SCII). This multiple-choice test takes about an hour to administer and is scored by machine. The SCII has been around since 1933. The most recent revision, in 1981, made a serious and generally successful attempt to eliminate sex bias.

The SCII offers information about an individual's interests on three different levels. First, the test provides a general statement about the test-taker's interest patterns. These patterns suggest not only promising occupations but also characteristics of the most compatible work environments and personality traits affecting work. Second, the test reports how interested a person is in a specific work activity compared with other men and women. Finally, the occupational scales compare the test-taker with satisfied workers in some 90 different occupations. If you think you'd enjoy being a librarian, for example, you can compare yourself with other librarians and see how similar your likes and dislikes are. The occupational scales indicate how likely you are to be satisfied with the choice of a particular occupation.

Personality/vocational tests come in a variety of formats. Many are multiple choice; some require you to finish incomplete sentences; others are autobiographical questionnaires. No single test should ever be used as an absolute. Personality tests are more important for generating discussion and for providing data that can be used in making judgments.

In the Washington area, vocational guidance and testing are available from a variety of sources. The most comprehensive service is generally provided by private career counselors and career consultants. Their approaches and specialties vary greatly. Some primarily provide testing while others also offer long-term programs that include counseling, resume writing, preparing for the job interview, and developing a job marketing campaign. Fees usually range from $50 to several thousand dollars.

It's best to find a professional who specializes in the type of vocational help you need. You don't want to spend thousands of dollars on long-term counseling when you only need several sessions and tests. On the other hand, if you've had a history of employment problems or are feeling paralyzed in your job search, it is probably well to talk to a career counselor who is also qualified to conduct personal counseling.

Although the terms are often used synonymously, there is a difference between a career *counselor* and *consultant.* Most professionals use the title *counselor* if they have fulfilled educational and professional requirements to become a Licensed Professional Counselor. The practice of psychology also requires a license, and many psychologists provide career testing and counseling.

But a person can provide career services without a license. Professionals who aren't licensed often call themselves career *consultants.* This field attracts people from a wide variety of backgrounds, education, and levels of competency. That's why it's important to talk to people who have used the service you are considering. And check with the Better Business Bureau to make sure the service is not beset with complaints.

The lists of private sector, social service and governmental, and college career counseling resources that follow give you some idea of what counselors and consultants offer. Telephone these professionals to find out whether their services fit your needs. Because many career counseling and consulting firms are private, for-profit businesses with high overhead costs, they usually charge more for testing than local community colleges or social service agencies. A fuller discussion of services offered by career consultants is provided in Chapter 6.

What To Expect from a Career Counselor

What kind of help can you expect from a career counselor that you can't find on your own?

The first thing you'd probably notice is that a counselor really listens to you. They are trained to understand, not to judge. You may find yourself being more candid with a counselor after 30 minutes than you would be with a friend you've known for 30 years. The result of this type of interaction is, paradoxically, that you're likely to end up knowing yourself better.

While counselors are trained to understand and support you, they are not there simply to stroke your ego. Your mother or best friend might agree with your plan to change from sales to engineering. A counselor will point out that you've never managed to pass a course in higher mathematics.

A counselor will understand that career planning is an ongoing, lifelong process that manifests itself differently in the various stages of human development. It is a very different thing to hunt for a job at 21, 41, and 61.

Tests aren't the whole answer, but they can be a part of the answer. Counselors know how to interpret tests.

Career counselors aren't locked into outmoded job-search strategies. They can give you ideas on how to make more contacts, write a better resume, and interview with impact. They can spot where you're approach needs beefing up more readily than a non-professional.

For most people, a job search is a demanding, if not downright stressful, time. A counselor can provide both emotional support *and* expert advice.

Tips from career counselors

Psychologist Lewis Gordon warns against literal interpretations of tests. "I won't allow computer printouts of test results in my office because they're too often misleading. A test is a clinical instrument and should be individually interpreted by a qualified professional."

Psychologist Harold Haddle reminds job seekers that "career development is a process. What's best at one stage of your life may not be good for another. Your interests and needs change over time. You can't depend on ten-year-old test results to be valid."

Career counselor Bob Wilson says, "Good career counseling is not a labeling of a person, but involves a process of inspiring the discovery of your 'self.' This gives you the ability to see that certain occupations are not suitable expressions of that self and to be O.K. with that."

Career counselor John Ballew underscores the importance of job satisfaction in determining quality of life: "Since you spend so much time at work, you should invest a proportionate amount of time and effort to find the right work." ∎

14

CAREER COUNSELORS AND CONSULTANTS

Ability Potentials
3331 Duke St.
Alexandria, VA 22314
703-781-3719
Testing and 90-minute counseling session plus quarterly newsletter, $350.

Adult Family and Career Counseling Center
Prosperity Ave. and Little River Turnpike
3918 Prosperity Ave.
Fairfax, VA 20031
703-573-6623
Contact Patricia Morgan.
Offers a wide range of counseling services: networking, job search groups, career and life planning tailored to client needs. Fee variable. Job hunting, networking, and brainstorming groups.

BEMW Counseling and Training Associates
7984 D Old Georgetown Road
Bethesda, MD 20814
301-657-8922
Contact Irene N. Mendolsen.
Career transition counseling, outplacement testing, and assessment. Adult clients from college through retirement.

Borchard, David C.
4603 Governor Kent Court
Upper Marlboro, MD 20772
301-627-7741
Career assessments and retirement planning.

Career & Leadership Development Associates
1990 M Street, N.W.
Suite 800
Washington, DC 20036
703-671-0546
Contact Mac Saddoris.
Career counseling for all ages: new professionals, mid-managers, and retirees; offers professional development training for executives.

Career Changers & Company
Air Rights Center
7315 Wisconsin Ave., Suite 900 East
Bethesda, MD 20850
301-654-5155
Contact Karen Kaye.
Licensed job counseling, testing for career interests and abilities, programs for entry-level, mid-career, displaced workers, and corporate outplacement programs. $60/hr.

Career Counseling Consultation
4545 42nd St. N.W., Suite 304
Washington, DC 20016
202-966-7328
Contact Dr. Larney Gump.
Licensed vocational counseling, psychological testing, mid-career counseling.

How to Get a Job

Carr Careers
5070 Millwood Lane, N.W.
Washington, DC 20016
202-244-5232
Contact Ruth Carr.
Offers range of career counseling services.

Center for Personal Effectiveness
2025 I St. N.W., Suite 1112
Washington, DC 20005
202-223-2773
Assists with career decision-making, evaluation and transitions, work-related conflicts and stress. Hours by appointment. $85/hr.

Change & Growth Consulting
Woodbridge Counseling Center:
1334 G Street
Woodbridge, VA 22191
703-569-2029

Also:
Tysons Corner Area:
2136-A Gallows Road
Minchew Building
Dunn Loring, VA 22027
703-569-2029
Contact Barbara S. Woods.
Career testing, career/life planning counseling, and psychotherapy. Also emphasizes women's issues.

GSM Associates
1300 New York Ave., N.W.
Washington, DC 20005
202-408-0314
Contact Gloria Monick.
Comprehensive career counseling services: career evaluation and testing, self-marketing, job search strategies. Specializes in clients with transition issues. $75 per hour; $30 per test. Day and evening appointments.

Horizons Unlimited
1133 15th St. N.W., Suite 1200
Washington, DC 20005
202-296-7224

Also:
17501 McDade Court
Rockville, MD 20855
301-258-9338
Contact Marilyn Goldman.
Career testing and direction for students, mid-career, and pre-retirement; outplacement counseling.

Johnson O' Connor Research Foundation
201 Maryland Ave., N.E.
Washington, DC 20002
202-547-3922
Testing and discussion of results, $450.

Rockport Institute
2025 I St. N.W.
Washington, DC 20005
301-279-2383
Contact Nicholas Lore.
Career testing, assessment, and counseling. Range of fees.

Sansbury, Judith Lynch
8700 Ewing Drive
Bethesda, MD 20817
301-897-9238
Career counseling for various populations.

Schimel, Ruth
2424 Pennsylvania Ave., N.W., Suite 506
Washington, DC 20037
202-659-1772
Career and life planning consultation for individuals, dual-career couples; also offers collaborative groups and workshops. Flexible hours. $75/hr.

A Time for Every Purpose
3719 12th St. N.E.
Washington, DC 20017
202-526-4859
Contact Nedra Hartzell.
Career counseling for transitions, federal government employment and international careers.

Washington Assessment and Therapy Services (WATS)
3801 Connecticut Ave. N.W., Suite 203
Washington, DC 20008
202-364-8692
Contact Ronald Wynne.
Ability, interest, and personality testing and counseling. Services by doctoral level psychologists; insurance eligible. On red line of Metro.

Working From the Heart
1309 Merchant Lane
McLean, VA 22101
703-356-6136
703-827-0336
Contact Sonya Dyer or Jacqueline McMakin.
Wide range of career counseling services and workshops. Also offers Life Direction Lab.

SOCIAL SERVICE AND GOVERNMENT AGENCIES

Unlike professional employment agencies, career consultants, and executive search firms, social service and government agencies are not-for-profit. They offer a wide range of services, from counseling and vocational training to job placement and follow-up—and their services are usually free or for a nominal charge.

Arlington Community Action
1415 S. Queen St.
Arlington, VA 22206
703-979-2400

How to Get a Job

Hours: 9:00 a.m.-5:00 p.m., Monday-Friday
Assistance with job hunting through own resources or employment agencies.

Arlington Employment Center/Arlington County Department of Human Services

2050 N. 15th St.
Arlington, VA 22201
703-358-4820
Hours: Intake: 8:00 a.m.-8:45 a.m., Monday-Thursday; Office: 8:00 a.m.-5:00 p.m.
Designed for both job seekers and potential employers, this center offers a wide range of services, including counseling, job listings, and a career library. Free to county residents.

Careerscope

5485 Harper's Farm Road
Columbia, MD 21044
301-992-5042/301-596-1866
Hours: Office: 8:30 a.m.-1:00 p.m.; Groups, counseling in afternoons, evenings.
This non-profit center offers workshops and counseling for life/work planning. Includes skills identification, career research, stress management, and goal setting. Appointments available daytime and evenings, Monday through Saturday. Free orientations held weekly. Some fees after initial consultation.

Commission for Women

Counseling and Career Center
255 North Washington St.
Rockville, MD 20850
301-279-1800
Hours: 9:00 a.m.-5:00 p.m., Monday-Friday; 9:00 a.m.-9:00 p.m., Tuesday-Thursday.
Offers wide range of services. Some fees.

Employment Support Center

900 Massachusetts Ave. N.W., Suite 444
Washington, DC 20001
202-783-4747
Contact: Ellie Wegener
Hours: 9:30 a.m.-5:00 p.m.; evening appointments available; day/evening groups.
Non-profit organization offers a variety of services designed to promote the skills necessary to a successful job search. Free self-help support groups, job bank ($15/ 3 months), job consultations, monthly network meetings, employment-related seminars and workshops. Some fees. Groups throughout area.

Fairfax County Career Development Center for Women

12000 Government Center Pkwy, Suite 318
Fairfax, VA 22035
703-324-5730
Contact: Judy Sansbury
Hours: 8:30 a.m.-4:30 p.m., Monday-Friday
Services and information related to career development and employment. Assists women and men re-enter workplace, move ahead, seek career change, face job loss.

New Ventures Counseling Center

3501 Moylan Drive
Bowie, MD 20715

301-464-2622
Hours: vary.
Non-profit center serving primarily Prince George's County. Sliding scale fees.

Over 60 Employment Service
4700 Norwood Drive
Chevy Chase, MD 20815
301-652-8073
Hours: 9:00 a.m.-4:00 p.m.
Free service matching persons over 55 with jobs in all fields, vocations. Help with resumes.

People's Involvement
1100 First St., N.W.
Washington, DC 20001
202-797-3900
Hours: 9:00 a.m.-5:30 p.m.
Referrals for local job openings.

Washington Urban League
1375 Missouri Ave., N.W.
Washington, DC 20011
202-882-6555
An employment service center with extensive job bank, referral service, job counseling.

The Women's Center
133 Park St. N.E.
Vienna, VA 22180
703-281-2657
Hours: Monday-Thursday 9:00 a.m.-8:00 p.m.; Friday 9:00 a.m.-5:00 p.m.; Saturday 9:00 a.m.-4:00 p.m.
Legal, financial, psychological and professional services offered. Staffed by professionals in each discipline. Career mentoring and professional development offered. Sliding fees. Branches in Alexandria and Manassas.

Who's good?
Who's not?

A listing in this book does not constitute an endorsement of any consulting firm or vocational testing service. Before embarking on a lengthy or expansive series of tests, try to get the opinion of one or more people who have already used the service you're considering. You can also contact:

Better Business Bureau of Metropolitan Washington (202-393-8000)
District of Columbia Department of Consumer & Regulatory Affairs (202-727-7067)
Arlington County Citizens and Consumer Affairs (703-358-3260)
Montgomery County Consumer Affairs Office (301-217-7373) ∎

COLLEGES OFFERING VOCATIONAL TESTING AND GUIDANCE

Most colleges and universities permit only students, staff, and alumni to use their counseling and placement services. Some do, however, offer programs to the public at reduced fees. Below are a list of some of the area college counseling and career centers that offer community services. Please be sure to telephone first to determine when the facilities will be open to you.

American University
Career Center
Butler Pavilion, 5th floor
4400 Massachusetts Ave. N.W.
Washington, DC 20016
292-885-1800
Hours: Monday, Thursday, Friday: 9:00 a.m.-5:00 p.m.; Tuesday & Wednesday: 9:00 a.m.-8:00 p.m.
Career resource library, job listings, and periodicals open for public use.

George Mason University
Career Development Center
Student Union #1
4400 University Dr.
Fairfax, VA 22030-4444
703-993-2370
Hours: Monday-Friday: 8:30 a.m.- 5:00 p.m.; Tuesday: 8:30 a.m.-8:00 p.m.
Career library and job listings open for public use.

George Washington University
Counseling Center
718 21st St. N.W.
Washington, DC 20052
202-994-4860
Hours: Monday-Friday: 9:00 a.m.-5:00 p.m.
Contact Robert Wilson.
Vocational assessment and counseling for career development or career change; tests selected on individual basis. Testing and counseling fees variable to $350. Counseling only, $50 per hour.

Howard University
Counseling Center
C.B. Powell Bldg., Wing #1
6th and Bryant Sts. N.W.
Washington, DC 20059
202-806-6870
Hours: Monday, Wednesday, Thursday: 10:00 a.m.-2:30 p.m.
Vocational and therapy services open to community members; $30 initial visit; $75 per hour for each follow-up visit.

Northern Virginia Community College
Alexandria Campus
Career Counseling Service
3001 N. Beauregard St., Rm.232
Alexandria, VA 22311
703-845-6301
Hours: Monday-Thursday: 9:00 a.m.-7:30 p.m.; Friday: 9:00 a.m.-5:00 p.m.
Individual career counseling available by appointment.

Also:
Community Education Office
3001 N. Beauregard St., Rm. 366
703-845-6240
Hours: Monday-Thursday: 8:30 a.m.-7:45 p.m.; Friday: 8:30 a.m.-5:00 p.m.
Career assessment class, with testing, $53. Call for schedule.

University of the District of Columbia
Career Planning and Placement
4200 Connecticut Ave. N.W.
Building 38, Room 209
Washington, DC 20008
202-282-7557
Hours: Monday-Friday: 8:30 a.m.-5:00 p.m.
Research library, career counseling, and vocational testing open for public use.

University of Maryland, University College
Career Planning Services
University Blvd. at Adelphi Road
College Park, MD 20742-1624
301-985-7275
Hours: Monday-Friday: 8:30 a.m.-8:00 p.m.; Saturday: 8:00 a.m.-12:00 p.m.
Career resource center; career decision-making courses, $135 per credit; comput-
erized guidance and information by appointment; $90 for up to 5 sessions or $30
for one appointment; workshops, $25; individual counseling, $50 initial, $315 for
series, or $60 each follow-up session; and resume reviews, $60 per hour.

Advice for the Trailing Spouse

In corporate relocation jargon they are "trailing spouses," wives or hus-
bands who move with their spouses who have been transferred. Many may
have been uprooted from good jobs in their previous locations. Now,
they're forced to go job hunting again in a strange location.

"Often they react with anger and frustration, which only gets in the way
of their own job search or career development," says Colin Tipping, a
professional counselor and educator who now works in real estate and, as
president of International Relocation Bureau, Inc., conducts relocation
stress management workshops and offers spouse counseling services.

"The first thing a trailing spouse should do is deal with any anger and
frustration. Acknowledge it, accept it as OK, and express it as openly as
possible—if not to your spouse, then to a friend or professional counselor
who will listen and understand," advises Tipping. He then offers seven tips:

(1) Let go of attachments to the past, including a previous job or a
previous location, and take a good look at what the present has to offer.
Forgive your husband or wife for uprooting you and forget that you are a
trailing spouse. Claim back your power and take full responsibility for your
own life.

(2) View this move, and this new job search, as an opportunity to think
about your life, work, and priorities. Read Marsha Sinetar's book, *Do What
You Want and the Money Will Follow.*

(3) Evaluate your work history. Have you really done what you loved
to do? Did it make your heart sing? Or were you more attached to status,
power, control, image, or money?

(4) Think about what kind of work you really want to do and make a list of the possibilities. (Include getting more training, acquiring different skills, etc.)

(5) Be alive and open to the possibilities and opportunities around you.

(6) Visualize yourself doing what you love to do, set goals, and create plans that will lead to their achievement.

(7) Go for happiness.

Thinking of Starting Your Own Small Business?

Many basic questions about starting your own small company can be answered by the U.S. Small Business Administration. Free information can be obtained on a variety of topics, including loan programs, tax preparation, government contracts, and management problems.

Although simple questions can be answered by telephone, you'll learn more by making an appointment at one of the main offices to meet with staff members or volunteers from **SCORE** (Service Corps of Retired Executives). These helpful people are also stationed at local chambers of commerce throughout the metropolitan area. You may first want to attend a pre-business workshop. Following this, you will be matched up with a retired professional in your field who can share information that will help you get started in completing the next step: setting up a business plan.

An added bonus is the help you will receive from members of **ACE** (Active Corps of Executives), a volunteer group of working professionals; these folks are on hand to offer assistance.

These volunteers conduct seminars covering major topics of interest to new business owners.

Small Business Development Centers (SBDCs), located in several locations throughout the area, offer specialized workshops related to specific elements of running a business. They also provide counseling.

Veterans interested in starting a business can also call for specially designed programs and information.

Programs are scheduled regularly at the main offices; others are held at community colleges and elsewhere in the community. Ask for John B. Flanagan, a terrific help in answering your questions. Contact:

U.S. Small Business Administration/ SCORE Washington Office, 111 18th St. N.W., Washington, DC 20036, 202-634-1500

Writing a Resume That Works

Many people would rather get a root canal than come up with a resume. We think this aversion usually stems from confusion about the job objective. Once you know the sort of job you're looking for and why you're qualified to fill it, the resume sort of writes itself. In fact, we're convinced that the biggest benefit of writing your resume is that it forces you to answer those two questions clearly and succinctly. And once you're armed with answers to questions about your objective and qualifications, you'll be ready to knock 'em dead on the interview.

Keep in mind that *no one ever secured a job offer on the basis of a resume alone.* The way to land a good position is to succeed in the employment interview. *You have to convince a potential employer that you're the best person for the job. No piece of paper will do that for you.*

The resume also goes by the name of *curriculum vita* ("the course of one's life"), or *vita* ("life") for short. These terms are a little misleading, however. A resume cannot possibly tell the story of your life, especially since, as a rule, it shouldn't be more than two pages long. (Academic and scientific *vitae* are

23

the exceptions.) The French word *résumé* means "a summing up." In the American job market, a resume is a concise, written summary of your work experience, education, accomplishments, and personal background—the essentials an employer needs to evaluate your qualifications.

A resume is a simple marketing tool. Think of it as your personal ad. It will sometimes get you an interview. But it is often most effective when kept in reserve until after you've met an employer in person. Sending a follow-up letter after the interview, along with your resume, reminds the interviewer of that wonderful person he or she met last Thursday.

The Basics of a Good Resume

The resume is nothing for you to agonize over. But since almost every employer will ask you for one at some point in the hiring process, make sure that yours is a good one. Here are four guidelines to help you:

1. *Be sure it's up to date and comprehensive.* At a minimum it should include your name, address, and phone number; a complete summary of your work experience; and an education profile. (College grads need not include their high school backgrounds.)

2. *Keep the resume concise.* Most employers don't want to read more than two pages, and one page is preferable. Large companies are flooded with literally thousands of resumes every year. In many cases your resume will be scanned for 10-20 seconds, not read in detail. You must capture their attention quickly. Only then will you get a more careful reading. Describe your experience in short, pithy phrases. Avoid large blocks of copy. Your resume should read more like a chart than a chapter in a textbook. And it should look more like a chart than a short story.

There are no hard or fast rules about what to include besides your work experience or education. Statements about date of birth, marital status, and so on, are optional but are typically not included because they usually serve as screen-out devices. While the employer may want to know these things, they can be shared in a personal interview more effectively. Salary history and references should also be left out until the interview stage.

Remember, the resume is a sales tool and a very unique place to let an employer know of your unique skills and experiences. Anything unusually innovative or cost-effective that you've done should be described, briefly, on your resume as well as in an interview.

In general, your work experience should include the name, location, and dates of employment of every job you've held since leaving school, plus a summary of your responsibilities and, most important, your accomplishments on each job. If you have an extensive work history, you can present it chronologically. Begin with your present position and work backward to your first job. If you haven't had that many jobs, organize your resume to emphasize the skills you've acquired through experience.

3. *Keep your resume honest.* Never lie, exaggerate, embellish, or deceive. Tell the truth about your education, accomplishments, and work history. If a deliberate misrepresentation is discovered, you can be summarily dismissed. You needn't account for every single work day that elapsed between jobs, however. If you left one position on October 15 and began the next on January 2, you can minimize the gap by simply listing years worked instead of months.

4. *Your resume should have a professional look.* Whether you type it yourself or have it typed professionally, use a high-quality office typewriter

with a plastic ribbon (sometimes called a "carbon" ribbon). Do *not* use a household or office typewriter with a cloth ribbon. Does your resume look sharp enough to go out under your prospective employers' letterheads? If it doesn't, it's probably not sharp enough.

If your budget permits, consider having your resume typeset professionally or typed on a good-quality word processor. This being the computer age, you should have no trouble getting access to a computer at most university libraries. Many photocopying centers also rent out time on computers. Using a word processor with a laser printer gives you a choice of type faces, such as bold face, italics, and small caps. You can also request that the margins be justified (lined up evenly on the right and left sides, like the margins of a book).

Another advantage of typing your resume yourself on a word processor is that you can save it on a floppy disk. Then it will be very easy to edit your resume and tailor it for a particular company or position that you have in mind. Some job search experts suggest you submit custom resumes, specifically designed for each different company or job that you go after.

No matter what method you use to prepare your resume, be sure to *proofread* it before sending it to the printer. A misspelled word or typing error reflects badly on you, even if it's not your fault. Many people in personnel will automatically toss a resume that flaunts a blatant typo. Read every word out loud, letter for letter and comma for comma.

Get a friend to go over it for you. Then do it again yourself the next day. Backward.

Do *not* make copies of your resume on a photocopy machine unless it is a top-quality one. The resume you leave behind after an interview or send ahead to obtain an interview may be photocopied several times and copies of copies can be hard to read. You should also avoid such gimmicks as using colored paper (unless it's very light cream or light gray), or using a paper size other than 8 1/2" x 11". Professional photocopy centers will have a good choice of paper stocks with high rag content that are suitable for your resume.

Our purpose here is not to tell you how to write the ideal resume (there *is* no such thing) but rather to provide some general guidelines. The following books are full of all the how-to information you'll need to prepare an effective resume and are available from bookstores or your local library.

BOOKS ON RESUME WRITING AND COVER LETTERS

Beatty, Richard. *The Perfect Cover Letter.* New York: John Wiley and Sons, 1989.

Bostwick, Burdette. *Resume Writing.* New York: John Wiley and Sons, 1990.

Corwen, Leonard. *Your Resume: Key to a Better Job.* New York: Arco, 1988.

Coxford, Lola M. *Resume Writing Made Easy.* New York: Gorsuch, 1992.

Foxman, Loretta D., and Walter L. Polsky. *Resumes That Work: How to Sell Yourself On Paper.* New York: John Wiley and Sons, 1988.

Jackson, Tom. *The Perfect Resume.* New York: Anchor/Doubleday, 1990.

King, Julie Adair. *The Smart Woman's Guide to Resumes and Job Hunting.* Hawthorne, NJ: Career Press, 1991.

Krannich, Ronald L., and Caryl R. *Dynamite Resumes.* Manassas, VA: Impact, 1992.

Krannich, Ronald L. *High Impact Resumes and Letters.* Manassas, VA: Impact, 1992.

Lewis, Adele. *How to Write Better Resumes*. Woodbury, NY: Barron's Educational Series, 1989.

McDaniels, Carl. *Developing a Professional Resume and Vita*. Garrett Park, MD: Garrett Park Press, 1990.

Nadler, Burton Jay. *Liberal Arts Power: What It Is and How to Sell It on Your Resume*. Princeton, NJ: Peterson's Guides, 1989.

Parker, Yana. *The Resume Catalog*. Berkeley, CA: Ten Speed Press, 1988.

Williams, Frank. *200 Letters for Job Hunters*. Berkeley, CA: Ten Speed Press, 1990.

Wilson, Robert F., and Adele Lewis. *Better Resumes for Executives and Professionals*. New York: Barron's Educational Series, 1991.

Wood, Patricia B. *The 171 Reference Book*. Manassas, VA: Impact, 1991.

Yate, Martin J. *Cover Letters That Knock 'Em Dead*. Holbrook, MA: Bob Adams, 1992.

Should You Hire Someone Else to Write Your Resume?

In general, if you have reasonable writing skills, it's better to prepare your own resume than to ask someone else to do it. If you write your own job history, you'll be better prepared to talk about it in the interview. "Boiler plate" resumes also tend to look and sound alike. On the other hand, a professional resume writer can be objective about your background and serve as a sounding board on what you should and shouldn't include. You might also consider a professional if you have trouble writing in the condensed style that a good resume calls for.

Here is a list of Washington area firms that will assist you in preparing your resume. Remember that a listing in this book does not constitute an endorsement. Before engaging a professional writer, ask for a recommendation from someone whose judgment you trust—a personnel director, college placement officer, or a knowledgeable friend. Check with the Better Business Bureau and other consumer advocates listed in Chapter 2 to see if there have been any complaints made about the resume service you are considering.

How to choose a professional

Before engaging a professional to help you write your resume, run through the following checklist of questions.

What will it cost? Some firms charge a set fee. Others charge by the hour. Though many firms will not quote an exact price until they know the details of your situation, you should obtain minimum and maximum costs before you go ahead.

What does the price include? Does the fee cover only writing? Or does it include typesetting? Most firms will charge extra for printing.

What happens if you're not satisfied? Will the writer make changes you request? Will changes or corrections cost extra?

How do this writer's fees and experience stack up against others? It's wise to shop around before you buy writing services, just as you would when purchasing any other service. ■

PROFESSIONAL RESUME PREPARERS

Most of the firms listed below charge by the hour for their writing and editing services; they often have a two-hour minimum. These fees do not always include typesetting and/or copies of your resume, which could add significantly to the total cost. Usually it is possible to get an estimate of charges after an initial consultation. Do not hesitate to inquire about fees. A reputable firm will be very clear about all the charges.

Abilities Unlimited
5000 Seminary Road
Arlington, VA 22311
703-998-8738
Hours: 8:30 a.m.-5:00 p.m.; evening appointments can be arranged.
Resume critiques provided, $30 per hour.

All American Resumes
5881 Leesburg Pike, #302
Falls Church, VA 22041
703-578-4444
Hours: Monday-Friday: 9:00 a.m.-6:00 p.m.; Saturday: 10:00 a.m.-1:00 p.m.;
Wednesday and Thursday: evening appointments available.
Contact: Lewis Fields
Fees begin at $50 per hour. Entry, staff, mid- and senior-level resumes; also CEO and senior executive clients; military conversions, SF 171's and KSA's. Free consultation.

Alternative Business Systems
2000 L St. N.W., Suite 403
Washington, DC 20036
202-887-0771
Hours: Monday-Friday: 8:00 a.m.-6:00 p.m.
Contact: Geri Spieler
Fees: $45 per hour; typesetting, $40 page, partial pages prorated; changes, $10 each; Cover letters, $8.

Career Center
8730 Georgia Ave., Suite 390
Silver Spring, MD 20910
301-589-4778
Hours: Flexible; also Saturday and evening appointments.
Fees begin at $35. Free consultation; lifetime updating. Resumes, cover letters, military conversions, and SF 171's. 10 locations.

Career Changers & Company
Air Rights Center
7315 Wisconsin Ave., Suite 900 East
Bethesda, MD 20814
301-654-5155
Contact: Karen Kaye
Hours: 10:00 a.m.-7:00 p.m.
Fees: $75/hr., including word processing and storage. Writes and produces resumes, SF 171's, and cover letters.

How to Get a Job

Career Path Resume Service
1511 K St., N.W., Suite 1009
Washington, DC 20005
202-737-5947
Hours: Monday-Friday: 9:00 a.m.-5:00 p.m.; extended by appointment.
Contact: Steve Serebin or Bill Bassett
Fees: Resumes, $45-$500; SF 171's, $150-$700. Creates resumes, cover letters, correspondence, and SF 171's. Additional offices throughout Northern Virginia and Maryland.

Horizons Unlimited
1133 15th St. N.W.
Washington, DC 20005
202-296-7224
Hours: Evening and weekend appointments available.
Contact: Marilyn Goldman
Fees: $85 per hour. Resume writing, editing, and production. Cover letters and correspondence; SF 171's.

Resumes Plus
4802 Copley Lane, #268
Upper Marlboro, MD 20772
301-627-4590
Contact: Lee Waldrep
Fees: Negotiable. Resume critique, design, and production assistance.

How to get a lot of resume help for a little money

Many of the non-profit organizations listed in Chapter 6 conduct workshops on resume writing, often accompanied by the self-assessment process, which helps the job seeker write a well-thought-out document.

The **Arlington Employment Center** (2050 N. 15th St., Suite 117, Arlington, VA 22201, 703-358-4820) offers resume consultations and critique for only $30.

The **Women's Center of Northern Virginia** (133 Park St. N.E., Vienna, VA 22180, 703-281-2657) regularly offers resume-writing workshops at a nominal fee. Both centers have trained counselors and professionals whose skills are excellent. ■

What NOT To Do with Your Resume Once You Have It Printed

Do not change your resume except to correct an obvious error. Everyone to whom you show the resume will have some suggestion for improving it: "Why didn't you tell 'em that you had a scholarship?" or "Wouldn't this look better in italics?" The time to consider those kinds of questions is *before* you go to the typesetter. Obviously, if you have saved your resume on a floppy disk, it will be easier to revise. Even then, it's probably not worth the trouble to make a lot of nitpicky changes. Remember, there is no such thing as a perfect resume. Except typographically.

A second point to remember: do NOT send out a mass mailing. If you send letters to 700 company presidents, you can expect a response of from

1 to 2 percent—and 95 percent of the responses will be negative. The shotgun approach is expensive; it takes time and costs money for postage and printing. You'll get much better results if you are selective about where you send your resume. We'll discuss this at greater length in Chapter 5. The important thing is to concentrate on known hiring authorities in whom you are interested.

The power of verbs

Gary J. has been an engineer for firms all along the Beltway for 20 years. During those years he has changed jobs seven times, enhancing his career with each move. Gary realized early that using powerful, active verbs to describe his accomplishments made his resume stand out. Here are some sample verbs that job seekers in various career areas might use to help build a more effective resume.

Management
Controlled
Headed
Implemented

Methods and Controls
Restructured
Cataloged
Verified
Systematized

Public Relations/ Human Relations
Monitored
Handled
Sponsored
Integrated

Creative
Devised
Effected
Originated
Conceived

Advertising/ Promotion
Generated
Recruited
Tailored
Sparked

Communications
Facilitated
Edited
Consulted
Disseminated

Resourcefulness
Rectified
Pioneered
Achieved

Negotiations
Engineered
Mediated
Proposed
Negotiated

ELEMENTS OF A RESUME

NAME

| Address | City, State, Zip | Phone |

Job Objective: Vital piece of information. Many employers use as screening device or to signal job match; should grab attention and motivate employer to read further.

Employment: The more impressive your work history, the more prominently you should display it.

List employment in reverse chronological order, putting the most promotable facts—employer or job title—first.

Give functional description of job if work history is strong and supports job objective.

Skills:
- You may embed these in employment section.
- Put skills section first for career changers.
- Choose skills that are most relevant to job objective.
- Give short statements to support skills.
- Make support statements results oriented.
- Position most marketable skills first.

Education: List in reverse chronological order, putting the most promotable facts—school or degree—first. Mention any honors or achievements, such as high GPA or Dean's List.

Miscellaneous: Call this section anything applicable: Interests, Activities, Accomplishments, or Achievements.

Give only information that promotes your candidacy for the position for which you are applying.

References: Available upon request. (Don't waste space on names and addresses. List on a separate sheet.)

Remember: there are no concrete rules in resume preparation. Modify this guide, when necessary, to make the most favorable impression.

Choosing a Resume Format

There are a number of different methods for composing a quality resume. Every career counselor and resume compiler has his or her own favorite method and style. As the person being represented by the resume, *you* must choose the style and format that best suits and sells you. Many resume books will use different terms for the various styles. We will highlight the three most popular types.

1. *The chronological resume* is the traditional style, most often used in the workplace and job search; that does not mean it is the most effective. Positive aspects of the chronological resume include the traditionalist approach that employers may expect. It also can highlight past positions that you may wish your potential employer to notice. This resume is also very adaptable, with only the reverse chronological order of items as the essential ingredient.

2. *The functional resume* is most common among career changers, people reentering the job market after a lengthy absence, recent college graduates, and those wishing to highlight aspects of their experience not related directly to employment. This resume ideally focuses on the many skills one has used at his or her employment and the accomplishments one has achieved. It shows a potential employer that you can do and have done a good job. What it doesn't highlight is where you have done it.

3. *The combination resume* combines the best features of a functional resume and a chronological resume. This allows job seekers to highlight skills and accomplishments while still maintaining the somewhat traditional format of reverse chronological order of positions held and organizations worked for.

Here are some sample resumes to help you with your own. The books listed earlier in this chapter will supply many more examples than we have room for here.

31

SAMPLE CHRONOLOGICAL RESUME

GEORGE P. BURDELL
555 Maple Avenue
Bethesda, MD 20814
(301) 555-2436

OBJECTIVE

Position in technical management.

WORK EXPERIENCE

SAMPO CORPORATION   1986-1992

Manager, Marketing & Planning-(Taiwan)   1988-1992
- **Supervised** operations & staff of **new products development.**
- Instrumental in **making decisions** regarding **OEM new products** with clients such as: IBM, NCR, TI, Xerox, Quadram, etc.
- **Developed 4 new products:** Low-cost display monitor, oscilloscope, and two DEC-compatible terminals.
- Accomplishment: IPD **sales volume** in 1989: **$45,000,000; 50% increase** from 1987.

Manager, Mid-Atlantic Sales-(Rockville, MD)   1986-1988
- Generated **$3,000,000 in sales** of OEM display monitors to IBM(NC), NCR(SC), Quadram, Digital Control, & other local accounts.

EDWARDS ELECTRONICS   1978-1986

Sales Engineer-(Rockville, MD)   1985-1986
- Successfully collaborated with OEM engineers to **develop** monitors for computer & laser games such as Jungle King & Dragon's Lair.

Production Engineer-(Rockville, MD)   1983-1985
- Member of team credited with building **Maryland's first TV manufacturing plant.**
- **Involvement in this $7,000,000** project ranged from conceptualization to production of 600, 19" color sets daily.

Circuit Design Engineer-(Taiwan)   1978-1983
- Designed PIF, deflection & remote control circuit for color TV.

EDUCATION

George Washington University, Washington, DC:
MBA in marketing, 1986

Georgia Institute of Technology: **B.S.** in electrical engineering, 1978

REFERENCES

Furnished upon request

SAMPLE FUNCTIONAL RESUME

KATHY JONES
256 Sarasota Drive
Springfield, VA 22159
(703) 555-5902

OBJECTIVE: Seek position as an **administrative assistant,** utilizing my administrative, organizational, and computer skills.

SKILLS

Administrative
- Independently straightened out a major client's account for an advertising agency.
- Kept books and managed funds in excess of $80,000 for a non-profit corporation.
- Managed two rental properties.

Organizational
- Set up procedure for assigned experiments and procured equipment for a research laboratory.
- Planned course syllabi, assessed weaknesses of individual students to facilitate learning.

Computer
- Managed data input and generated monthly reports.
- Completed courses in FORTRAN and BASIC.

EMPLOYMENT

Computer Operator, Woolco, Arlington, VA	(1988-Present)
Trouble-shooter in accounting, Cargill, Wilson, and Acree, Washington, DC	(1986)
Instructor, Math Dept., Charlottesville, VA school system	(1982-85)

EDUCATION

M.S., Mathematics, University of Virginia	(1982)
B.A., Mathematics, University of Virginia	(1981)

REFERENCES

Furnished upon request.

SAMPLE COMBINATION RESUME

SUSAN SKINNER
122 Pine St.
Washington, DC 20006
(202) 555-0011

OBJECTIVE:	Software development position utilizing software and engineering skills.
EDUCATION:	**UNIVERSITY OF MARYLAND** GPA 3.7/4.0 M.S., Information and Computer Science 6/88 **WASHINGTON UNIVERSITY (ST. LOUIS)** A.B., Mathematics 5/83 GPA 3.5/4.0
QUALIFICATIONS:	▮ Designed and implemented multi-tasking operating system for the IBM-PC. ▮ Implemented compiler for Pascal-like language. ▮ Implemented simulation project using tasking in Ada. ▮ Designed electronic mail system using PSL/PSA specification language. ▮ Experienced in UNIX, MS-DOS, XENIX, CP/M operating systems. **Hardware:** ▮ IBM-PC (MS-DOS, Xenix), Pyramid 90x (UNIX), Cyber 990 (NOS), Data General MV/10000 (UNIX, AOS/VS).

WORK EXPERIENCE:

Neil Araki Programming Services—Rockville, MD   7/88-Present
> ▮ **UNIX Programmer**—Responsible for porting database applications to IBM-PC/AT system administration.

Strathmore Arts Center—Bethesda, MD   11/83-9/86
> ▮ **Computer Programmer**—Performed daily disk backup on Burroughs B-1955 machine. Executed database update programs and checks. User assistance.
> ▮ From 8/81 to 11/83, held full-time positions as **Box Manager** and **Accountant** for arts organizations in St. Louis and Washington, DC.

REFERENCES

Furnished upon request.

34

Writing a winning resume

Sioux Campbell, president of Blue Chip Enterprises, Inc., a career consulting firm, has helped thousands of anxious job searchers come up with the right resume. She begins her consultation with the assumption that there are generally more candidates than jobs. Accordingly, most employers look to screen rather than hire. This means a resume needs to stand out during a quick scan.

"Employers who consider a large number of candidates, typically review a resume in about 20 seconds," she says. "You've got to show them that you match their needs during this initial scan to attract more careful consideration."

She considers the job objective to be the thesis of the resume. Everything else is the argument that supports the thesis. Short-term memory is just that—short. But somehow, a good resume will impress whoever scans it with the candidate's strongest selling points. They stick in the reader's mind.

She recommends the following test. "Give your resume to several objective reviewers. Allow them 20 seconds. Then ask them what they picked up. Do they readily recall your strongest selling points? If they don't, your resume isn't as effective as it could be." ■

Always Include a Cover Letter

Never, never send your resume without a cover letter. Whether you are answering a want ad or following up an inquiry call or interview, you should always include a letter with your resume. If at all possible, the letter should be addressed to a specific person—the one who's doing the hiring—and not "To Whom It May Concern." You can generally track this information down with a few phone calls to the company in question.

A good cover letter, like a good resume, is brief—usually not more than three or four paragraphs. No paragraph should be longer than three or four sentences. If you've already spoken to the contact person by phone, remind him or her of your conversation in the first paragraph. If you and the person to whom you are writing know someone in common, the first paragraph is the place to mention it. You should also include a hard-hitting sentence about why you're well qualified for the job in question.

In the next paragraph or two, you should specify what you could contribute to the company in terms that indicate you've done your homework on the firm and the industry.

Finally, either request an interview or tell the reader that you will follow up with a phone call within a week to arrange a mutually convenient meeting.

Remember that the focus of your job search is to sell yourself as a match to fit an employer's needs. You should emphasize that you match the company's needs throughout all your communication—your resume, any phone calls, cover letters, and follow-up letters. Following are some sample cover letters to give you the idea.

SAMPLE COVER LETTER

5535 Spring Hill Lane
Chevy Chase, MD 20815
June 26, 1992
301-555-6886

Ms. Jacqueline Doe
Cahners Publishing Company
1333 H St. N.W.
Washington, DC 20004

Dear Ms. Doe:

As an honors graduate of Georgetown University with two years of copy editing and feature writing experience with the *Uptown Citizen,* I am confident that I would make a successful editorial assistant with Cahners.

Besides my strong editorial background, I offer considerable business experience. I have held summer jobs in an insurance company, a law firm, and a data processing company. My familiarity with word processing should prove particularly useful to Cahners now that you're about to become fully automated.

I would like to interview with you as soon as possible and would be happy to check in with your office about an appointment. If you prefer, your office can contact me between the hours of 11 a.m. and 3 p.m. at (301) 555-6886.

Sincerely,

Jesse Alban

SAMPLE COVER LETTER

May 15, 1992

2239 Forest Park Boulevard
1500 Rosewood
Alexandria, VA 22314

Mr. Ray Price
Post and Waters
1150 15th St. N.W.
Washington, DC 20071

Dear Mr. Price:

Your advertisement in the May 13 issue of *Accounting Today* for an experienced accountant seems perfect for someone with my background. My five years of experience in a small accounting firm in Philadelphia has prepared me to move on to a more challenging position in a large and prestigious firm like yours.

As you can see from my resume, my work experience includes not only basic accounting work but also some consulting with a few of our firm's bigger clients. This experience combined with an appetite for hard work, an enthusiastic style, and a desire to succeed makes me a strong candidate for your consideration.

I would appreciate the opportunity to discuss how my background could meet the needs of Post and Waters. I will call you within a week to try to arrange a convenient time to meet.

Sincerely,

Scott Harding
(703) 555-4414

SAMPLE COVER LETTER

December 2, 1992

228 S. Meadowlark Lane
Laurel, MD 20707

Dear Chris:

Just when everything seemed to be going so well at my job, the company gave us a Christmas present that nobody wanted—management announced that half the department will be laid off before the end of the year. Nobody knows yet just which heads are going to roll. But whether or not my name is on the list, I am definitely back in the job market.

I have already lined up a couple of interviews. But knowing how uncertain job hunting can be, I can use all the contacts I can get. You know my record—both from when we worked together at 3-Q and since then. But in case you've forgotten the details, I've enclosed my resume. I know that you often hear of job openings as you wend your way about Maryland and Virginia. I'd certainly appreciate your passing along any leads you think might be worthwhile.

My best to you and Sue for the holidays.

Cordially,

Richard Hobart
(301) 555-2468

**Eight ways to ruin
a cover letter**

1. Spell the name of the firm incorrectly.
2. Don't bother to find out the name of the hiring authority. Just send the letter to the president or chairman of the board.
3. If the firm is headed by a woman, be sure to begin your letter, "Dear Sir." Otherwise, just address it, "To Whom It May Concern."
4. Make sure the letter includes a couple of typos and sloppy erasures. Better yet, spill coffee on it first, then mail it.
5. Ramble on and on and on about your life and work experience.
6. Be sure to provide a phone number that has been disconnected, or one at which nobody is ever home.
7. Tell the firm you'll call to set up an appointment in a few days; then don't bother...OR tell them you'll wait to hear from them.
8. Call the firm at least three times the day after you mail the letter. Get very angry when they say they haven't heard of you. ■

Researching the Washington Job Market

We've said that the key to getting job offers is to convince employers that you match their needs. We'd add that the key to job satisfaction is finding a position whose responsibilities match your interests and abilities. This means you've got to know the job and the organization. Once you've figured out what kind of job you want, you need to find out as much as you can about which specific organizations might employ you. Your network of personal contacts can be an invaluable source of information about what jobs are available where. But networking can't do it all; at some point, you'll have to do some reading. This chapter fills you in on the directories, newspapers, and magazines you'll need in your search and notes the libraries where you can find them.

Libraries

Public Libraries are an invaluable source of career information. Most of the titles in this book can be found at the main branches or in college or university libraries that are open to the public. It is almost impossible, however, to "check-out" these publications. Most are reference books that do not circulate, although some of the career strategy and resume-preparation texts may be exceptions.

The most valuable resources in the library are the reference librarians. In some of the larger systems, there might be a career services librarian who is responsible for selecting the materials that you will use in your job search. A consultation with such a specialist can be extremely helpful, although in many libraries the business reference librarian may be the person most familiar with the materials available.

Always remember that the time a librarian can spend with you is limited. Learn how to find publications yourself, using the computerized or card catalog; save your more complicated questions for the times when the reference staff is not so busy.

Not just for Congress

Although the Library of Congress was established "for the purchase of such books as may be necessary for the use of Congress," it has become an invaluable resource for researchers in almost every field, including those seeking a job. Almost every source listed in this book, directories, professional publications, books on career strategies, etc., can be located there, even though the material may not be checked out. Although using the Library of Congress can be both confusing and time consuming, its resources and systems, once learned, might be useful in purposes other than job searching. You owe it to yourself to check it out: Library of Congress, 10 First St. S.E., Washington, DC, 202-707-5000. ■

The major public library systems with career or business information collections are listed below, along with the major college and university libraries. Remember that you do not have to be a resident or current student to use the non-circulating material. Be persistent. You may not always find what you need in one location; however, many of the materials a career consultant may charge you for using are available free from a library.

DISTRICT OF COLUMBIA LIBRARIES

Martin Luther King Memorial Library (Main Library)
901 G St. N.W.
Washington, DC 20001
202-727-1171

Chevy Chase Regional Library
Washington, DC 20015
202-727-1341

Georgetown Regional Library
3260 R St. N.W.
Washington, DC 20007
202-727-1353

How to Get a Job

Francis A. Gregory Regional
Alabama Ave. and 37th St. S.E.
Washington, DC 20020
202-727-1349

Woodridge Regional Library
Rhode Island Ave. and 18th St. S.E.
Washington, DC 20018
202-727-1401

NORTHERN VIRGINIA LIBRARIES

Alexandria City (Kate Waller Barrett) Library
717 Queen St.
Alexandria, VA 22314
703-838-4555

Arlington County Libraries
Central Library
1015 N. Quincy St.
Arlington, VA 22201
703-358-5990

Aurora Hills Branch/Arlington
735 18th St.
Arlington, VA 22202
703-358-5715

Columbia Pike Branch/Arlington
816 S. Walter Reed Drive
Arlington, VA 22204
703-358-5710

Fairfax County Libraries/Fairfax City Regional
3915 Chain Bridge Road
Fairfax, VA 22030
703-246-2741

Fairfax County Libraries/George Mason Regional
7001 Little River Turnpike
Annandale, VA 22003
703-256-3800

Fairfax County Libraries/Reston Regional
11925 Bowman Towne Drive
Reston, VA 22090
703-689-2700

Fairfax County Libraries/Sherwood Regional
2501 Sherwood Hall Lane
Alexandria, VA 22306
703-765-3645

Fairfax County Libraries/Tysons-Pimmit Regional
7584 Leesburg Pike
Falls Church, VA 22043
703-790-8088

Researching the job market

Getting the most out of a great resource

One of the best places for finding job-search information is the Central Library of the Arlington County Public Library System. There is an excellent business reference room, and Librarian Jane Larsen is terrific. She has organized a Career Section that houses many books on career development, job-hunting strategy, and profiles about different types of careers. Many job notices from nearby state and municipal personnel offices are posted, as well as announcements concerning career programs and workshops held in the area. The Reference staff is very helpful in locating pertinent company directories and other relevant publications. Be patient: this is an active and heavily used library, well worth a visit for job seekers. Computerized data base searches are available for a fee. ■

SUBURBAN MARYLAND LIBRARIES

MONTGOMERY COUNTY LIBRARIES

Bethesda Regional Library
7400 Arlington Road
Bethesda, MD 20814
301-986-4300

Gaithersburg Regional Library
18330 Montgomery Village Ave.
Gaithersburg, MD 20879
301-840-2515

Rockville Regional Library
99 Maryland Ave.
Rockville, MD 20850
301-217-3800

Silver Spring Library
8901 Colesville Road
Silver Spring, MD 20910
301-565-7689

Twinbrook Library
202 Meadow Hall Drive
Rockville, MD 20851
301-279-1980

Wheaton Regional Library
11701 Georgia Ave.
Wheaton, MD 20902
301-949-7710

White Oak Library
11701 New Hampshire Ave.

How to Get a Job

Silver Spring, MD 20904
301-622-2492

**Libraries with Job
Information
Centers**

Several of the Montgomery County libraries have Job Information Centers, which are collections of books, newspapers, magazines, and services to help with job searching and career decisions. The material is shelved separately and easy to locate. One of the most useful parts of the JIC is the material announcing local workshops related to career issues. These programs can be difficult to track down, and since they are frequently free or inexpensive, they shouldn't be overlooked. The JICs are located at the Bethesda, Gaithersburg, Silver Spring, and Twinbrook libraries. A special collection of business information, government documents, and legal references is now available at the Rockville library. ■

PRINCE GEORGE'S COUNTY LIBRARIES

Bowie Library
15210 Annapolis Road
Bowie, MD 20715
301-262-7000

Hyattsville Library
6530 Adelphi Road
Hyattsville, MD 20782
301-779-9330

College Park Library
4601 Calvert Road
College Park, MD 20740
301-927-1694

Beltsville Library
4319 Sellman Road
Beltsville, MD 20705
301-937-0294

Greenbelt Library
11 Crescent Road
Greenbelt, MD 20873
301-345-5800

COLLEGE AND UNIVERSITY LIBRARIES

Remember that the Career Services Departments at these and other schools listed in Chapter 2 have libraries devoted to this type of material.

American University Library
4400 Massachusetts Ave. N.W.
Washington, DC 20016
202-885-3220

Catholic University of America Library
620 Michigan Ave. N.E.
Washington,DC 20064
201-319-5070

George Mason University Library
4400 University Drive
Fairfax,VA 22030
703-323-2210

George Washington University Gelman Library
2130 H St. N.W.
Washington, DC 20052
202-994-6558

Georgetown University Library
37th & O St. N.W.
Washington, DC 20007
202-687-7452

Howard University Library
2400 6th St. N.W.
Washington, DC 20059
202-806-6100

University of Maryland Hornbake Library
College Park, MD 20742
301-405-9257

Directories

When you are beginning your research, whether of an entire industry or a specific company, there are four major sources of information with which you should be familiar. All four of these "gospels" are available at the public libraries or college libraries listed above.

Standard and Poor's Register of Corporations, Directors, and Executives (Standard and Poor's Publishing Co., 25 Broadway, New York, NY 10004) is billed as the "foremost guide to the business community and the executives who run it." This three-volume directory lists more than 45,000 corporations and 70,000 officers, directors, trustees, and other bigwigs.

Each business is assigned a four-digit number called a Standard Industrial Classification (S.I.C.) number, which tells you what product or service the company provides. Listings are indexed by geographic area and also by S.I.C. number, so it's easy to find all the companies in the Washington area that produce, say, industrial inorganic chemicals. You can also look up a *particular* company to verify its correct address and phone number, its chief officers (that is, the people you might want to contact for an interview), its products, and, in many cases, its annual sales and number of employees. If you have an appointment with the president of XYZ Corporation, you can consult *Standard and Poor's* to find out where he or she was born and went to college—information that's sure to come in handy in an employment interview. Supplements are published in April, July, and October.

The **Thomas Register of American Manufacturers** and **Thomas Register Catalog File** (Thomas Publishing Co., One Penn Plaza, New

How to Get a Job

York, NY 10119) is published annually. This 16-volume publication is another gold mine of information. Over 120,000 U.S. companies are included. You can look up a certain product or service and find out every company that provides it. (Since this is a national publication, you'll have to weed out companies that are not in the Washington area, but that's easy.) You can also look up a particular company to find out about branch offices, capital ratings, company officials, names, addresses, phone numbers, and more. The *Thomas Register* even contains five volumes of company catalogs. Before your appointment with XYZ Corporation, you can bone up on its product line with the *Thomas Register*.

Moody's Complete Corporate Index (Moody's Investor Service, 99 Church St., New York, NY 10007) gives you the equivalent of an encyclopedia entry on more than 20,000 corporations. This is the resource to use when you want really detailed information on a certain company. *Moody's* can tell you about a company's history—when it was founded, what name changes it has undergone, and so on. It provides a fairly lengthy description of a company's business and properties, what subsidiaries it owns, and lots of detailed financial information. Like the directories above, *Moody's* lists officers and directors of companies. It can also tell you the date of the annual meeting and the number of stockholders and employees.

The **Million Dollar Directory** (Dun & Bradstreet, Inc., Dun's Marketing Service, 3 Sylvan Way, Parsippany, NJ 07054) is a three-volume listing of approximately 120,000 U.S. businesses with a net worth of more than half a million dollars. Listings appear alphabetically, geographically, and by product classification and include key personnel. Professional and consulting organizations such as hospitals and engineering services, credit agencies, and financial institutions other than banks and trust companies are not generally included.

So much for the Big Four directories. The following list contains many additional directories and guides that may come in handy. Included below are many directories that may be useful in finding employment with federal and local governemnts. Most are available at the central or regional branch libraries throughout the area.

USEFUL DIRECTORIES

AdWeek Agency Directory
(Adweek New England, 100 Boylston St., Boston, MA 02116)
Lists ad agencies, public relations firms, media and media buying services, key personnel, major accounts. Annual.

The Almanac of American Employers: A Guide to America's 500 Most Successful Large Corporations
(Contemporary Books, Inc., 180 N. Michigan Ave., Chicago, IL 60601)
Alphabetical profiles of major corporations, including information about benefits, job turnover, and financial stability.

The Almanac of American Government Jobs and Careers
(Impact Publications, 9104-N Manassas Dr., Manassas Park, VA 22111, 703-361-7300)
Description of federal, state and local government employment, contact information, and job opportunities for hundreds of federal government agencies and employers.

The American Lobbyist's Directory
(Gale Research Company, 835 Penobscot Bldg., Detroit, MI 48226-4094)
Guide to U.S. lobbyists and their subjects of concern. Includes federal and state lobbyists and offices regulating their efforts. Indexed by name, represented organizations, and subject area.

America's Federal Jobs
(JIST Works, Inc., 720 North Park Ave., Indianapolis, IN 46202-3431, 317-264-3720)
Most like the *Federal Career Directory*; contains agency descriptions, employment process, tips for job hunters.

American Society for Training and Development, Washington DC Chapter-Membership Directory
(American Society for Training and Development, 4227 46th St., N.W., Washington, DC 20016, 202-362-1498)
Contact information for area members from human resource development profession. Also includes descriptions of area events, publications, calendar, etc.)

Association of Part Time Professionals Employer Directory
(APTP, 7700 Leesburg Pike, Suite 216, Falls Church, VA 22043, 703-734-7975)
List of employers who utilize part time professionals.

Billion Dollar Directory: America's Corporate Families
(Dun's Marketing Service, 3 Sylvan Way, Parsippany, NJ 07054)
Lists 2,600 U.S. parent companies and their 24,000 domestic subsidiaries. Organized alphabetically by name of parent company.

BNA's Directory of State Courts, Judges, and Clerks
(Bureau of National Affairs Books Distribution Center, 300 Raritan Center Parkway, Edison, NJ 08818, 201-225-1900)
Contact information and court number, district, and geographical area served, for over 13,000 state judges and court clerks in more than 2,100 state courts in the U.S. Bi-annual in summer.

The Book of States
(Council of State Governments, P.O. Box 11910 Iron Works Pike, Lexington, KY 40578)
Comprehensive information on structures, working methods, financing, and functional activities of state governments.

Braddock's Federal-State-Local Government Directory
(Braddock Communications, 909 N. Washington St., Suite 310, Alexandria, VA 22314, 703-549-6500)
Lists names, address, and phone numbers for 10,000 elected officials and key personnel at all levels of government. Bi-annual in summer.

Business Register
(Fairfax County Chamber of Commerce, 8391 Old Courthouse Road, Vienna, VA 22182)
Alphabetical membership list with company names, addresses, etc.

Capitol Jobs: An Insider's Guide to Finding a Job in Congress
(Tilden Press, 1526 Connecticut Ave. N.W., Washington, DC 20036, 202-332-1700)
Out-of-date, but still useful guide to Capitol Hill job-hunting strategy.

How to Get a Job

The Capitol Source
(National Journal, 1730 M St. N.W., Suite 1100, Washington, DC 20036, 202-857-1400)
Sections include government, corporate, professional, and media. Excellent guide has brief listings of major players in DC area. Twice a year. Essential.

The Career Guide: Dun's Employment Opportunities Directory
(Dun's Marketing Service, 3 Sylvan Way, Parsippany, NJ 07054)
Designed for those beginning a career: describes job prospects at hundreds of companies.

Charitable Organizations of the U. S.
(Gale Research Company, 835 Penobscot Bldg., Detroit, MI 48226-4094)
Comprehensive guide to largest, most active non-profit organizations. Profiles 800 organizations including contact information, administration and staff, history and purpose, activities and programs.

College Placement Annual
(College Placement Council, 62 Highland Ave., Bethlehem, PA 18017)
Directory of the occupational needs of over 1,200 corporations and government employers. Annual.

The Complete Guide to Public Employment
(Impact Publications, 9104-N Manassas Drive, Manassas Park, VA 22111, 703-361-7300)
Good guide for finding a federal job. Chapter on writing an effective federal application form. Includes federal, state and local government and non-governmental organizations.

Congressional Staff Directory
(Staff Directories, P.O. Box 62 Mt. Vernon, VA 22121, 703-739-0900)
Basic handbook on Congress. Bios of members and 3,200 top staff. Some information on congressional districts and staff composition. Essential for Hill job seekers. Twice a year.

Congressional Yellow Book
(Monitor Publishing, 1301 Pennsylvania Ave. N.W., Suite 1000, Washington, DC 20004, 202-347-7757)
Directory and pictures of members of Congress, including committees and key staff aides. Also, helpful facts about congressional districts.

Consultants and Consulting Organizations Directory
(Gale Research Company, 835 Penobscot Bldg., Detroit, MI 48226-4094)
Contains descriptions of 6,000 firms and individuals involved in consulting; indexed geographically. Annual supplement: *New Consultants*.

Contacts Influential (DC, Suburban Maryland/Northern Virginia)
(Contacts Influential, 1630 SW Morrison St., #100, Portland, OR 97205-1856, 1-800-451-2014)
Primarily a marketing tool. Brief information about companies of all sizes.

Corporate Technology Directory
(Corporate Technology Information Services, 12 Alfred St., Woburn, MA 01801)
Profiles of high-technology companies, including ownership, history, executives, and products. Indexed by company name, geography, technology, and product.

Corporate Yellow Book
(Monitor Publishing Company, 104 Fifth Ave., 2nd floor, New York, NY 10011)

Who's who at leading companies. Devoted to leading public manufacturers, service businesses, and utilities traded on U.S. stock exchange. Access to more than 39,000 executives and board members. Quarterly.

Covin's Washington Area Computer Job Guide
(Vandamere Press, P.O. Box 5243, Arlington, VA 22205)
Has two main sections: companies in the computer industry and companies with in-house data processing departments. Essential for job seekers in this field.

Data Sources: Hardware and Software Directory
(Ziff-Davis Publishing Company, 764 Gilman St., Berkeley, CA 94710)
Two-volume guide to most products, companies, services, and personnel in the nationwide computer industry.

Dictionary of Occupational Titles
(Bureau of Labor Statistics, 441 G St. N.W., Washington, DC 20212, 202-523-1221)
Information on job duties and requirements; describes almost every conceivable job. Updated 1991.

Directories in Print
(Gale Research Company, 835 Penobscot Bldg., Detroit, MI 48226-4094)
Contains detailed descriptions of all published directories: what they list, who uses them, and who publishes them.

Directory of Agencies
(National Association of Social Workers, 1425 H St. N.W., Washington, DC 20005)
Provides information on over 300 U.S. and international voluntary intergovernmental agencies involved in social work.

Directory of Business: Arlington County
(Economic Development Division, 2100 Clarendon Blvd., Suite 608, Arlington, VA 22201, 703-358-3520)
Lists businesses by industry category. Almost 8,000 firms included. Published every 2-3 years.

Directory of Business and Industry: Fairfax County, Virginia
(Fairfax County Economic Development Authority, 8300 Boone Blvd., Suite 450, Vienna, VA 22182, 703-790-0600)
Alphabetical arrangement of company listings with product index. Annual.

Directory of Construction Associations
(Professional Publications, 310 E. 44th St., New York, NY 10017)
Lists about 3,000 local, regional, and national professional associations, trade groups, government agencies, unions, and other information sources.

Directory of Executive Recruiters
(Kennedy Publications, Templeton Rd., Fitzwilliam, NH 03447, 603-585-2200)
Guide to placement services for executives. Profiles more than 2150 executive search firms nationwide; includes salary, industries and key contacts.

Directory of Foundations in the Greater Washington Area
(Community of Foundations of Greater Washington, 10002 Wisconsin Ave. N.W., Washington, DC 20007, 202-338-8993)
Lists public and private foundations and some corporations. Provides contact information, grant data and other details.

Directory of Maryland Municipal Officials
(Maryland Municipal League, 1212 West St., Annapolis, MD 21401, 301-268-5514)
Lists city and town officials. Annual.

Directory of Mental Health Resources
(Mental Health Association of Prince George's County, Inc., 96 Harry S. Truman Dr., Largo, MD 20772, 301-499-2107)
Guide to community service agencies for Prince George's, Charles, Calvert and St. Mary's counties.)

Directory of Women Entrepreneurs
(Wind River Publications, P.O. Box 450827, Northlake Branch, Atlanta, GA 30345, 404-496-5986)
3,200 women-owned businesses, companies with minority and women professional development programs, women's groups and organizations, and minority business assistance offices.

Dun's Directory of Service Companies
(Dun's Marketing Service, 3 Sylvan Way, Parsippany, NJ 07054)
Guide to public and private companies. Includes names and titles of key decision makers. Consists of headquarter and single location companies employing more than 50 people.

Dun's Regional Business Directory: Washington DC/Baltimore Area
(Dun's Marketing Service, 3 Sylvan Way, Parsippany, NJ 07054, 1-800-526-0651)
Covers public and private companies in metropolitan area, including Northern Virginia. Provides business rankings, key personnel, subsidiaries and divisions. Annual.

Electronic News Financial Fact Book and Directory
(Fairchild Publications, 7 W. 34th St., New York, NY 10001)
Background and financial information about leading companies in the electronics industry.

Encyclopedia of Associations
(Gale Research, 835 Penobscot Bldg., Detroit, MI 48226-4094)
14,000 local and national associations and professional clubs by categories. Indexed geographically.

Encyclopedia of Business Information Sources
(Gale Research, 835 Penobscot Bldg., Detroit, MI 48226-4094) Lists each industry's guides, handbooks, indexes, directories, yearbooks, data bases, associations, periodicals, and other statistical sources.

Engineering, Science & Computer Jobs
(Peterson's Guides, P.O. Box 2123, Princeton, NJ, 08543-2123)
Lists specific companies and government agencies within these industries.

The Enhanced Guide for Occupational Exploration
(JIST Works, Inc., 720 North Park Ave., Indianapolis, IN 46202-3431, 317-264-3720)
Provides job titles, descriptions and career assessment information for 2,500 jobs.

Everybody's Business
(Doubleday Currency, 666 Fifth Ave., New York, NY 10103)
Candid profiles of 400 American manufacturers of well-known, brand-name products.

Fairchild's Financial Manual of Retail Stores
(Fairchild Publications, 7 W. 34th St., New York, NY 10001)
Lists 500 publicly held companies in the U.S. and Canada that deal in retail trade.

Federal Career Directory
(U.S. Government Printing Office, Superintendent of Documents, Washington, DC 20402, 202-783-3238)
Comprehensive resource for information about federal jobs. Contains contact information for over 160 agencies, how and where to apply for employment, Office of Personnel Management overview, classification systems, and more.

Federal Jobs for College Graduates
(Prentice Hall, 15 Columbus Circle, New York, NY 10023, 800-922-0579)
Easy-to-read guide filled with job search tips and specific information on agencies, requirements and positions for entry-level job hunters.

Federal Personnel Office Directory
(Federal Reports, Inc., 1010 Vermont Ave. N.W., Washington, DC 20005, 202-393-3311)
Includes 1,500 federal hiring offices throughout the U.S., agency by agency, state by state. Each issue contains a section on how to apply for federal jobs and detailed information on special hiring programs.

Federal Regulatory Directory
(Congressional Quarterly, 1414 22nd St. N.W., Washington, DC 20036, 202-887-8500)
General section on regulatory process. Descriptions of agencies vary.

Federal Staff Directory
(Staff Directories, P.O. Box 62, Mt. Vernon, VA 22121, 703-739-0900)
Arranged by organization, with keyword and individual indexes to key staff in federal agencies. Over 30,000 executives listed; bios of 2,500. Twice a year.

Federal/State Executive Directory
(Carroll Publishing, 1058 Thomas Jefferson St. N.W., Washington, DC 20077-0007, 202-333-8620)
Provides information on both executive and legislative branches, including Cabinet departments, Congressional committee members and staff, areas of responsibility for legal and administrative assistants. Provides keyword indexes. Updated and published six times yearly.

Federal Yellow Book
(Monitor Publishing Company, 1301 Pennsylvania Ave. N.W., Washington, DC 20004, 202-347-7757)
Useful resource for researching particular offices. Used by many federal employees. Especially helpful at the beginning of a new Administration.

Finding a Federal Job Fast
(Impact Publications, 9104-N Manassas Dr., Manassas Park, VA 22111, 703-361-7300)
Secrets to finding jobs. Helpful in locating job vacancies, completing SF-171, marketing oneself, and getting hired.

Finding a Job in the Nonprofit Sector
(The Taft Group, 12300 Twinbrook Parkway, Suite 450, Rockville, MD 20852, 301-816-0210)
Overview of employment trends, job-hunting tips, and contact and employment-related information for 5,000 of largest non-profits in U.S.

How to Get a Job

Fortune Double 500 Directory
(Time, Inc., 229 West 28th St., New York, NY 10001)
Lists the 500 largest and the 500 second largest industrial corporations, as well as the largest banking, service, financial, and utilities firms in the U.S.

Franchise Opportunities Handbook
(U.S. Government Printing Office, Superintendent of Documents, Washington, DC 20402, 202-783-3238)
Lists over 1,200 franchise companies in the U.S. Includes information on their operation, size, history, capital needed and various forms of assistance available.

Gale Directory of Publications and Broadcast Media
(Gale Research, 835 Penobscot Bldg., Detroit, MI 48226-4094)
Lists national, local, and trade magazines, newspapers, and broadcasting stations by state. Annual.

Government Job Finder
(Planning Communications, 7215 Oak Ave., River Forest, IL 60305-1935)
Unbelievable source of information on how to locate job openings for federal, state, and local jobs. Arranged geographically and by type of resource.

Government Research Directory
(Gale Research, 835 Penobscot Bldg., Detroit, MI 48226-4094)
References 3,700 research facilities and programs in the U.S. government. Includes facilities owned/operated, contracted, test centers, research institutes, and related programs.

Great Careers
(Garrett Park Press, P.O. Box 190B, Garrett Park, MD 20896, 301-384-1889)
Comprehensive volume listing and describing hundreds of resources on wide variety of non-profit careers and organizations.

Guide to Special Issues and Indexes of Periodicals
(Special Libraries Association, 1700 18th St. N.W., Washington, DC 20009)
Alphabetical listing of consumer, trade, and technical periodicals.

Greater Washington Society of Association Executives-Membership Directory
(GWSAE, 1426 21st St. N.W., Suite 200, Washington D.C. 20036)
Contact information on 3600 member organizations in local chapters of professional associations. Annual.

HEATH Resource Directory
(HEATH Resource Center, One Dupont Circle, Suite 800, Washington, DC 20036-1193, 1-800-544-3284)
Excellent source of career and employment information for the hearing, mobility, and visually impaired; the learning disabled and others.

Hudson's Washington News Media Contacts Directory
(Hudson's Directories, 44 W. Market St., Rhinebeck, NY 12572)
Includes news services, wire services, newspapers, radio & TV news bureaus, magazines, etc. Annual.

International Advertising Association—Membership Directory
(IAA, 342 Madison Ave., Suite 2000, New York, NY 10173)
Covers 2,700 advertisers, agencies, media, etc. Arranged geographically and by function or service.

International Association for Personnel Women—Membership Roster
(IAPW, P.O. Box 969, Andover, MA 01810-0017)
Lists 1,500 members-at-large.

Internships and Job Opportunities in New York City and Washington, DC
(Grad Group, 86 Norwood Rd., West Hartford, CT 06117, 203-232-3100
Listings of local organizations with work and learning opportunities. Annual.

Job Hunter's Sourcebook: Where to Find Employment Leads and Other Job Search Resources
(Gale Research, 835 Penobscot Bldg., Detroit, MI 48226-4094)
Lists employment directories, manuals, and services for 155 types of professional occupation. Includes broad overview of sources of job hunting information.

Jobs '92
(Prentice Hall, 15 Columbus Circle, New York, NY 10023)
Good source of employers, professional associations, publications, and industry trends. Organized by state.

Jobs in Washington, DC
(Impact Publications, 9104-N Manassas Dr., Manassas Park, VA 22111, 703-361-7300)
Case stories from recent college graduates describing first year of employment in variety of settings and organizations around metropolitan Washington area. Includes types of jobs and contact information for employers.

Judicial Staff Directory
(Staff Directories, P. O. Box 62, Mt. Vernon, VA 22121, 703-739-0900)
Federal, circuit, district, bankruptcy, tax courts. Twice a year.

MacRae's State Industrial Directories: North Carolina, South Carolina & Virginia and Maryland, District of Columbia and Delaware.
(MacRae's Blue Books, 817 Broadway, New York, NY 10003)
Main section contains geographical listing of companies. Has alphabetical and industry indexes. Annual.

Manufacturer's Directory, Metropolitan Washington, DC
(Greater Washington Board of Trade, 1129 20th St. N.W., Washington, DC 20036, 202-857-5900)
Lists leading area manufacturing companies.

Maryland/DC Minority Supplier Development/Council Minority Business Directory
(Minority Business Directories, 9150-5B Rumsey Rd., Columbia, MD 21045, 301-997-7599)
Lists 500 businesses in DC and Columbia. Provides contact information and description of products and services.

Maryland High-Tech Directory
(Department of Economic and Employment Development, 217 Redwood St., 23rd floor, Baltimore, MD 21202, 1-800-OK-GREEN)
State info taken from their regular service for MD Office of Technology Development. Good company profiles. Includes high-growth list.

Maryland Industrial Directory
(Department of Economic and Employment Development, 217 Redwood St., 23rd floor, Baltimore, MD 21202, 1-800-OK-GREEN)

How to Get a Job

Formerly Maryland Manufacturers Directory. Alphabetical, geographical, and industry listing. Annual.

Membership Directory Greater Washington Board of Trade
(Greater Washington Board of Trade, 1129 20th St. N.W., Washington, DC 20036, 202-857-5900)
Alphabetical list of members, with industry index.

Metropolitan Washington Telecommunications Directory for the Deaf
(President's Committee for People with Disabilities, 814 Thayer Ave., Suite 303, Silver Spring, MD 20910)

The Minority Career Book
(Bob Adams, Inc., 260 Center St., Holbrook, MA 02343)
Guide to career planning and job search, office politics, and cultural diversity. Includes sample resumes and cover letters.

Montgomery County Business Directory
(Information Publications, Inc., 1680 E. Gude Dr., Rockville, MD 20850, 301-309-8868)
Information on nearly 10,000 county businesses. Provides addresses, phone numbers, industry, and size of business.

Municipal/County Executive Directory
(Carroll Publishing, 1058 Thomas Jefferson St. N.W., Washington, DC 20077-0007, 202-333-8620)
More than 65,000 entries describing all U.S. municipalities. Lists 32,000 elected, appointed, and career officials and provides information about larger municipalities (over 15,000 population).

The Municipal Yearbook
(International City Management Association, 1120 G St. N.W., Washington, DC 20005)
Helpful information on local government questions and issues. Includes statistics about composition of municipal revenue structures. Contains 10 separate directories of more than 70,000 employees and municipal officials.

Municipal Yellow Book
(Monitor Publishing, 104 Fifth Ave., New York, NY 10011, 212-627-4140)
Lists contact information for 20,000 key elected and administrative officials of leading cities, counties, and municipal jurisdictions. Also includes outline of municipal and county departments, agencies, and subdivisions. Semiannual.

National Organizations of State Government Officials Directory
(The Council of State Governments, P.O. Box 11910, Iron Works Pike, Lexington, KY 40578-9989, 800-800-1910)
Lists more than 140 organizations associated with state government. Includes addresses, phone numbers, membership requirements, programs, publications, and organizational structures.

National Trade and Professional Associations
(Columbia Books, 1212 New York Ave. N.W., Suite 300, Washington, DC 20005)
Lists most associations and labor unions in the U.S. and Canada. Indexed geographically and by key words.

Newsletters in Print
(Gale Research, 835 Penobscot Bldg., Detroit, MI 48226-4094)
Reference guide to newsletters, financial services, and association bulletins.

Occupational Outlook Handbook
(Bureau of Labor Statistics, 441 G St. N.W., Washington, DC 20212, 202-523-1221)
Describes in clear language what people do in their jobs, the training and education required, earnings, working conditions, and employment outlook. Annual.

O'Dwyers Directory of Public Relations Firms
(J.R. O' Dwyer & Company, 271 Madison Ave., New York, NY 10016)
Describes almost 1,000 public relations firms, their key personnel, local offices, and accounts. Indexed geographically.

The Paralegal's Guide to U.S. Government Jobs
(Federal Reports, 1010 Vermont Ave. N.W., Suite 408, Washington, DC 20005, 202-393-3311)
General information on hiring procedures, standards, and forms. Contains directory of federal agencies that hire the most paralegals.

Political Resource Directory
(Political Resources, Inc., P.O.Box 363, Rye, NY 10580)
Compilation of political professional organizations providing services and products to and for the political community. Covers U.S. and abroad.

Public Interest Groups in Washington, DC
(Common Cause, 2030 M St. N.W., Washington, DC 20036)
Partial listings of groups working on variety of issues in the area. Lists names, addresses, and descriptions of organizations.

Reference Book of Corporate Management
(Dun's Marketing Service, 3 Sylvan Way, Parsippany, NJ 07054)
National directory of 2,400 companies with at least $20 million in sales; includes biographies of key personnel and directors, with past jobs noted.

Regional Directory of Minority and Women Owned Business Firms
(Business Research Services, 2 East 22nd St., Suite 202, Lombard, IL 60148)
Eastern Volume; 22,500 organizations listed. Includes contact information, minority group, number of employees, description of products and services, and references.

Regional, State and Local Organizations
(Gale Research, 835 Penobscot Bldg., Detroit, MI 48226-4094)
5 regional volumes. 47,000 listings including professional associations, social welfare and public affairs organizations, resources and referral centers.

Resource Directory for Greater Washington Entrepreneurs
(Greater Washington Board of Trade, Business Development Bureau, 1129 20th St. N.W., Washington, DC 20036, 202-857-5950)
Identifies about 110 venture capital firms and funds plus non-financial resources in the metropolitan area.

Standard Directory of Advertising Agencies
(Reed Reference Publishers, 121 Chanlonn Rd., New Providence, NJ 07974, 1-800-521-8110)
The Red Book of 4,000 advertising agencies and their 60,000 accounts. Published quarterly.

Standard Periodical Directory
(Oxbridge Communications, 150 5th Ave., New York, NY 10011)

How to Get a Job

Profiles magazines by interest categories. Descriptions include circulation and staff names. Indexed by subject.

State Elected Officials and the Legislatures
(The Council of State Governments, P.O. Box 11910, Iron Works Pike, Lexington, KY 40578-9989, 800-800-1910)
Contact information for members of state legislative bodies and elected officials with statewide jurisdiction. Bi-annual in March.

State Executive Directory
(Carroll Publishing, 1058 Thomas Jefferson St. N.W., Washington, DC 20077-0007, 202-333-8620)
Lists officers, committee heads, legislators, managers of boards and authorities, and department heads. More than 92,000 listings. Annual.

State Government Research Directory
(Gale Research, Detroit, MI)
Detailed information on 850 state research units. Includes keyword, agency, and subject indexes.

State Legislative Leadership, Committees, and Staff
(The Council of State Governments, Iron Works Pike, P.O. Box 11910, Lexington, KY 40578-9989, 800-800-1910)
Names, addresses, and phone numbers of state legislative leaders, committee and chairpersons, principal legislative staff officers, and staff members. Includes organizational patterns. Bi-annual in June.

State Yellow Book
(Monitor Publishing, 104 Fifth Ave., New York, NY 10011, 212-627-4140)
Specific information on executive and legislative branches for every state. Also includes counties in each state.

Storming Washington: An Insider's Guide to National Government
(American Political Science Association, 1527 New Hampshire Ave. N.W., Washington, DC 20036, 202-483-2512)
Helpful guide to planning for and getting government internships. Includes contact information about local organizations and descriptions of participating college and university internship programs.

Travel Industry Personnel Directory
(Capital Cities Media, Inc., 7 West 34th St., New York, NY 10001, 212-630-3880)
More than 20,000 listings, including sales and executive personnel, hotel representatives, tourist information offices, travel trades associations, government agencies.

United Black Fund, Inc., of Greater Washington, Directory of Member Agencies
(United Black Fund, 1012 14th St. N.W., Suite 300, Washington, DC, 20005, 202-783-9300)
Useful guide to community services. Updated yearly.

U.S. Government Manual
(U.S. Government Printing Office, Superintendent of Documents, Washington, DC, 20402-9325, 202-783-3238)
The official handbook of the federal government. Provides comprehensive information about all branches of the government and independent quasi-agencies, international organizations, and committees.

Virginia Business
(Media General Business Communications, Inc., 411 East Franklin St., Suite 105, Richmond, VA 23219, 804-649-6999)
Special issues include annual "50 Largest Private Companies," and "50 Largest Public Companies."

Virginia Business Resource Directory
(Virginia Employment Commission, Employment Information Services Division, 703 Main St., P.O. Box 1358, Richmond, VA 23211, 804-786-7496)
Describes state and local agencies and programs which provide services to or regulate Virginia businesses. Includes lists of business associations and chambers of commerce, and financing sources.

Virginia Industrial Directory
(Virginia Chamber of Commerce, 9 S. 5th St., Richmond, VA, 23219, 804-644-1607)
Alphabetical, geographical, and industry listing of firms. Employment size categories included. Annual.

Virginia Municipal League Directory
(Virginia Municipal League, 13 E. Franklin St., P.O. Box 12164, Richmond, VA 23241, 804-649-8471)
Lists elected officials and department heads for all municipalities and counties, planning district commissions, regional planning agencies, some state and federal offices, and statewide government professional organizations.

Virginia Review Directory of State and Local Government Officials
(County Publications, P.O. Box 860, Chester, VA 23831, 804-748-6351)
Very complete directory of state and local government. Annual in spring.

Ward's Business Directory of U.S. Private and Public Companies
(Gale Research, 835 Penobscot Bldg., Detroit, MI 48226-4094) Guide to more than 107,000 companies. Offers 20 items of information per listing. Includes very small companies to very large. Organized by state and product line.

Washington Business. The Post 200
(Washington Post, 1150 15th St. N.W., Washington, DC 20071)
April issue of weekly business section. Detailed profiles of largest publicly held DC area firms. Contains list of area's top private firms.

Washington Business Journal. Book of Lists
(Washington Business Journal, 2000 N. 14th St, Arlington, VA 22201, 703-875-2200)
Compilation of rankings that have appeared in weekly newspaper. Very useful for many of the area's top service firms.

Washington '92
(Columbia Books, 1212 New York Ave. N.W., Suite 330, Washington, DC 20005, 202-898-0662)
Includes the government, corporations, public interest groups, associations, media, etc. Excellent descriptions of the organizations, with names and addresses. Annual.

Washington Information Directory
(Congressional Quarterly, 1414 22nd St. N.W., Washington, DC 20037, 202-887-8500)
Good source for official Washington. Includes departments, agencies, Congress. Key staff names and addresses. Annual.

How to Get a Job

Washington Post Travel Directory
(Washington Post, Travel Advertising, 1150 15th St. N.W., Washington, DC 20071, 202-334-7753)
Guide to metropolitan area travel industry. Provides description and contact information on hundreds of companies, including airlines, transportation agencies, tour companies. Also offers calendar of special travel sections printed in the *Post*. Annual.

Washington Representatives
(Columbia Books, 1212 New York Ave. N.W., Suite 330, Washington, DC 20005, 202-898-0662)
Basically a directory of registered lobbyists and government relations representatives. Listed by individual and by organization. Annual.

The Washington Technology Almanac
(Washington Technology, 1953 Gallows Road, Vienna, VA 22182, 703-848-2800)
Profiles of local technical companies; includes fast-50 and top 25 area employers. 250-plus companies.

Where to Start
(Cornell University Career Center, Peterson's Guides, P.O.Box 2123, Princeton, NJ 08543-2123)
Excellent bibliography of books and periodicals on wide range of careers. Includes numerous sources of job hunting and job openings.

Who's Who in Alexandria Business
(Alexandria Chamber of Commerce, 801 N. Fairfax St., Suite 403, Alexandria, VA 22314, 703-549-1000)
Overview of Alexandria, its officials and chamber committees and members. Organized by business classification.

Who's Who in Congress
(Congressional Quarterly, 1414 22nd St. N.W., Washington, DC 20037, 202-887-8500)
Pocket guide to congressional leadership. Contains staff profiles, committee assignments, explanation of congressional bell system, and much more.

Writer's Market
(Writer's Digest Books, F & W Publications, 1507 Dana Ave., Cincinnati, OH 45207)
Lists over 400 publishers including editorial needs, pay rates, and submission requirements. Also includes information on how literary agents work and buyers of freelance material. Annual.
(Also publish *Songwriter's Market*).

Yearbook of International Organizations
(K.G. Saur Verlag GmbH & Comp. KG, Heilmanstrasse 17, Postfach 711009, W-8000, Munich, Germany)
More than 26,650 worldwide organizations indexed by name, address, and description.

Newspapers

Answering want ads is one of several tasks to be done in any job search, and generally among the least productive. According to *Forbes* magazine, only about 10 percent of professional and technical people find their jobs through want ads. Like any other long shot, however, answering want ads sometimes pays off. Be sure to check not only the classified listings but also the larger display ads that appear in the Sunday business sections of the major papers. These ads are usually for upper-level jobs.

Help-wanted listings generally come in two varieties: open advertisements and blind ads. An open ad is one in which the company identifies itself and lists an address. Your best bet is *not* to send a resume to a company that prints an open ad. Instead, you should try to identify the hiring authority (see Chapter 5) and pull every string you can think of to arrange an interview directly.

The personnel department is in business to screen out applicants. Of the several hundred resumes that an open ad in a major newspaper is likely to attract, the personnel department will probably forward only a handful to the people who are actually doing the hiring. It's better for you to go to those people directly than to try to reach them by sending a piece of paper (your resume) to the personnel department.

Blind ads are run by companies that do not identify themselves because they do not want to acknowledge receipt of resumes. Since you don't know who the companies are, your only option in response to a blind ad is to send a resume. This is among the longest of long shots and usually pays off only if your qualifications are exactly suited to the position that's being advertised. Just remember that if you depend solely on ad responses, you're essentially conducting a passive search, waiting for the mail to arrive or the phone to ring. Passive searchers usually are unemployed a long time.

Newspaper business sections are useful not only for their want ads but also as sources of local business news and news about personnel changes. Learn to read between the lines. If an article announces that Big Bucks, Inc., has just acquired a new vice-president, chances are that he or she will be looking for staffers. If the new veep came to Big Bucks from another local company, obviously that company may have at least one vacancy, and possibly several.

MAJOR NEWSPAPER RESOURCES

Washington Post
1150 15th St. N.W.
Washington, DC 20071
202-334-6000
Extensive classified section in Sunday's edition. "Washington Business" is a feature of Monday's edition; it contains news of local companies, executive changes, and a business calendar.

Washington Times
3600 New York Ave. N.E.
Washington, DC 20002
202-636-3000
While attempting to be a competitor to the *Post,* the *Times* simply can not match its classified section.

New York Times
229 W. 43rd St.
New York, NY 10036
212-556-1234
The huge Sunday classified section has some DC jobs listed, as well as the Business section. However, it is difficult to get the complete Sunday edition in DC; you must have a special subscription.

How to Get a Job

Wall Street Journal
200 Liberty St.
New York, NY 10281
212-416-2000
Easily available in DC; classifieds do carry Washington positions.

National Business Employment Weekly
Box 300
Princeton, NJ 08543
609-520-4000
Reprints the want ads from the *Wall Street Journal* for that week.
Good career advice.

OTHER DAILY NEWSPAPERS

Alexandria Journal
Arlington Journal
Fairfax Journal
Montgomery Journal
Prince George's Journal

Journal Newspapers
6883 Commercial Drive
Springfield, VA 22159
703-750-2000
All are free, weekly community newspapers with local news and information.

Northern Virginia Sun
2710-C Prosperity Ave.
Fairfax, VA 22031
703-204-2800

SUBURBAN AND COMMUNITY NEWSPAPERS

There are many outstanding community newspapers in the Washington metropolitan area. Most carry want ads and all feature stories and items about local
businesses and business people that will give you more input for your job search.

Alexandria Gazette-Packet
717 N. St. Asaph St.
Alexandria, VA 22314
703-549-0004
Weekly community newspaper.

Arlington Courier
P.O. Box 580
McLean, VA 22101
703-356-3320
Weekly community newspaper.

Beltsville News
4903 Prince George's Ave.
Beltsville, MD 20705
301-937-6834
Weekly community newspaper.

Current
5125 MacArthur Blvd., Suite 10
Washington, DC 20016
202-244-7223
Weekly community newspapers for Northwest DC, Georgetown, and Rock Creek areas.

Bowie-Blade News
Box 770
Bowie, MD 20715
301-262-3700
Weekly community newspaper.

Capitol Spotlight Newspaper
529 14th St. N.W.
Washington, DC 20045
202-628-0700
Weekly newspaper directed toward black community.

Catholic Standard
5001 Eastern Ave.
Hyattsville, MD 20782
301-853-4599
Weekly religious newspaper.

Chronicle Express
2 Professional Drive
Gaithersburg, MD 20879
301-258-7434
Weekly newspaper covering Montgomery, Prince George's, and Frederick counties.

City Paper
724 9th St. N.W.
Washington, DC 20001
202-628-6528
Weekly community newspaper.

El Pregonero
5001 Eastern Ave.
Hyattsville, MD 20017
202-853-4504
Weekly Spanish newspaper; includes regional and national news and classified ads.

Fairfax Connection
12040 South Lake Drive
Reston, VA 22091
703-648-9100
Weekly community newspaper. Also publishes for: Burke, Reston, Herndon, Fairfax West, Centerview, McLean/Great Falls, Vienna/Oakton/Tysons, Springfield, Manassas areas.

Gaithersburg Gazette
18705 N. Frederick Road
Gaithersburg, MD 20879
301-948-3120

Weekly community newspaper. Also publishes for: Germantown, Bethesda, Rockville, Chevy Chase, Potomac areas.

Georgetowner
P.O. Box 3528
Washington, DC 20007
202-338-4833
Regional newspaper. Twice monthly.

Greenbelt News Review
15 Park Way
Greenbelt, MD 20768
301-441-2662
Weekly community newspaper.

Herndon Times
1760 Reston Parkway, No. 411
Reston, VA 22090
703-437-5400
Weekly community newspaper.

Laurel Leader
615 Main St.
Laurel, MD 20707
301-725-2000
Weekly suburban community newspaper.

McLean Providence Journal
6819 Elm St.
McLean, VA 22101
703-356-3320
Weekly community newspaper for McLean. Also publishes for Great Falls area.

Montgomery County Sentinel
Box 1272
Rockville, MD 20850
301-948-4630
Weekly community newspaper.

Northwest Current
5428 MacArthur Blvd
Washington, DC 20016
202-244-7223
Bi-weekly community newspaper.

Potomac Almanac
9910 River Road
Potomac, MD 20854
301-983-3350
Weekly community newspaper with classified ads for Potomac, Rockville, Gaithersburg.

Prince George's Sentinel
Box 207
Hyattsville, MD 20781
301-306-9500
Weekly community newspaper covering county news; includes legal ads and notices and classified ads.

Reston Times
1760 Reston Parkway, Suite 101
Reston, VA 22090
703-437-5400
Weekly community newspaper.

Rockville Gazette
18705 N. Frederick Road
Gaithersburg, MD 20879
301-948-3120
Weekly community newspaper.

Silver Spring Record
7676 Fenton St.
Silver Spring, MD 20910
301-589-6400
Weekly newspaper covering Silver Spring and Wheaton areas.

Springfield Connection
12040 South Lake Drive
Reston, VA 22091
703-648-9100
Weekly community newspaper.

Takoma Voice
6926 Willow St. N.W.
Washington, DC 20012
202-882-5271
Monthly newspaper including Hyattsville, Takoma Park, Langley Park, DC, and
Silver Spring areas. Includes news, features, classified ads.

Vienna Times
1760 Reston Parkway, Suite 101
Reston, VA 22090
703-437-5400
Weekly community newspaper.

Uptown Citizen
4101 River Road N.W.
Washington, DC 20016
202-966-2266
Bi-weekly community newspaper.

Washington Afro-American
2002 11th St. N.W.
Washington, DC 20001
202-332-0080
Special interest newspaper; published twice weekly.

Washington Blade
724 9th St. N.W., 8th floor
Washington, DC 20001
202-347-2038
Gay and lesbian community and national newspaper; published weekly.

Washington Jewish Week
12300 Twinbrook Pkwy.
Rockville, MD 20852

How to Get a Job

301-230-2222
Weekly special interest newspaper.

Washington Journal
1113 National Press Building
Washington, DC 20045
202-628-0404
Weekly German language newspaper, covering local and international news.

National Business Magazines

Business Week
1221 Avenue of the Americas
New York, NY 10020
212-997-1221
Weekly.

Forbes
60 5th Ave.
New York, NY 10011
212-620-2200
Bi-weekly.

Fortune
1271 Avenue of the Americas
New York, NY 10020
212-586-1212
Published 26 times a year.

Money
1271 Avenue of the Americas
New York, NY 10020
212-522-1212
Monthly.

Newsweek
444 Madison Ave.
New York, NY 10022
212-350-4000
Weekly. Includes business coverage.

Time Magazine
1271 Avenue of the Americas
New York, NY 10022
212-586-1212
Weekly. Includes business coverage.

U.S. News & World Report
2400 N St. N.W.
Washington, D.C. 20037-1196
202-955-2000
Weekly. Provides domestic and international news and information.

Venture
521 5th Ave.
New York, NY 10075

212-682-7373
Monthly.

Working Woman
342 Madison Ave.
New York, NY 10173
212-309-9800
Monthly. Good career advice articles.

Local Business Magazines

All of the above national magazines are available at libraries and news-stands. The following are specific to the Washington scene and contain news more applicable to that area.

Washington Business Journal
2000 N. 14th St.
Arlington, VA 22201
703-875-2200
Weekly metropolitan business newspaper.

Montgomery County Business Journal
7676 Fenton St.
Silver Spring, MD 20910
301-589-6400
Weekly county-wide business newspaper. Includes listings of newly incorporated businesses.

Nation's Business
1615 H St. N.W.
Washington, DC 20062
202-463-5663
Monthly magazine for small to medium-sized business owners and managers. Includes congressional articles. Published by U.S. Chamber of Commerce.

Regardie's
1010 Wisconsin Ave. N.W., Suite 600
Washington, DC 20007
202-342-0410
Monthly business magazine covering DC metropolitan area.

Job-Hunt Related Publications and Services

The following newspapers, magazines, and services are designed solely to offer job listings and job-related information and advice. **Additional sources specifically pertaining to government jobs are listed in Chapter 11.**

AAR/EEO Affirmative Action Register
8356 Olive Blvd.
St. Louis, MO 63132
314-991-1335
"The only national EEO recruitment publication directed to females, minorities, veterans, and the handicapped." Monthly magazine consists totally of job listings.

How to Get a Job

Careers and the disABLED
Equal Opportunity Publications
44 Broadway
Greenlawn, NY 11740
516-261-9080
3 issues/year, $10 annual subscription. Over 60 display ads for entry-level positions with employers who certify that they are equal opportunity employers. Readers submit resume for referral to employers for free.

CEO Job Opportunities Update
2011 I St. N.W., Suite 600
Washington, DC 20006
202-331-3828
Twice monthly publication listing chief-executive and senior-staff openings at foundations, professional societies, trade associations and other non-profits. Seven issues for $90.

Community Jobs
1516 P St., N.W.
Washington, DC 20036
202-667-0661
Monthly nationwide listings of jobs with community organizations and advocacy groups.

Contract Engineer Weekly
CE Publications, Inc.
P.O. Box 97000
Kirkland, WA 98083
206-823-2222
Weekly magazine of job opportunities for contract engineers.

Federal Career Opportunities
(Federal Research Service, P.O. Box 1059, Vienna, VA 22033, 703-281-0200)
Bi-weekly listing of job openings.

Federal Jobs Digest
P.O. Box 594
Millwood, NY 10546
Elaborate listing of job opportunities with the federal government.

International Employment Hotline
P.O. Box 6170
McLean, VA 22106
703-573-1628
Monthly listing of overseas jobs. Provides a resume service for subscribers.

Job Opportunities Bulletin
TransCentury Corporation
1724 Kalorama Road, N.W.
Washington, DC 20009
202-328-4400
Bimonthly, $25 annual subscription. Lists job/vacancy announcements and "Jobseekers" ads in international development, primarily for work in Third World countries. About 25 to 35 job ads, including a moderate number of government positions, appear in the typical issue. Typical positions include accountants, agriculturalists, administrators, medical personnel, teachers, refugee affairs engineers, project managers, forestry, and environment.

Job Placement Exchange
4-Sights Network
16625 Grand River
Detroit, MI 48227
313-272-3900
Free. Part of national computer system for the blind or visually impaired; requires use of computer modem. Once resume is added, people are matched with jobs or specialized training. Also offers Occupational Information Library for the Blind. A database directory describing over 500 relevant jobs, including educational requirements, technical devices needed to accomplish each job listed, and employers likely to hire.

JOBS
The Alder Group
8601 Georgia Ave., Suite 400
Silver Spring, MD 20910
301-587-1111.
Bi-weekly employment newspaper distributed free in area newsboxes.

Legal Employment Newsletter
P.O. Box 36601
Grosse Point, MI 48236
Newsletter lists open legal positions, as well as career opportunities in the public-private sector.

National and Federal Legal Employment Report
Federal Reports
1010 Vermont Ave. N.W.
Washington, DC 20005
202-393-3311
Monthly in-depth listings of attorney and law-related jobs in federal government and with other public and private employers throughout the U.S.

Opportunities in Non-Profit Organizations
ACCESS: Networking in the Public Interest
67 Winthrop St.
Cambridge, MA 02138
617-495-2178
Monthly listings of non-profit jobs around the country, organized by type of non-profit.

Opportunities in Public Affairs
The Brubach Corporation
1100 Connecticut Ave. N.W., Suite 700
Washington, DC 20036
202-861-5885
Bi-weekly listings of jobs on Capitol Hill, in government affairs, legislative and public policy, public relations, marketing, and media. Includes internships and volunteer opportunities. Eight weeks for $29.

Positions Openings List
Greater Washington Society of Association Executives
1426 21st St. N.W., #200
Washington, DC 20036
202-429-9370
Bi-weekly publication of jobs in associations. $40/non-members, $20/members for 3-month subscription.

How to Get a Job

The Search Bulletin
"Career Opportunities for Executives and Professionals"
The Beacon Group
8300 Boone Boulevard, Suite 500
Vienna, VA 22181
703-848-9220
Listing of jobs with corporations, salaries above $50K and $100K. For 6 bi-weekly issues, $97.

Job Hotlines

Here's a way to find out about job openings by "letting your fingers do the walking." Just dial any one of the numerous telephone job banks and listen to the taped recordings that describe available positions and how to apply. **The federal government joblines are listed in the "Government" section in Chapter 11.**

If you have trouble getting through, it could be that: 1)the number has been changed or disconnected; 2)it "rings" but is actually "busy"; or 3)the message is being changed. Hang in there. If all else fails, call the personnel office for job information.

Although some of these job hotlines are sponsored by particular professional associations (see Chapter 5), many listings are available at no charge other than what you might spend for a telephone call. Area job information lines include:

Local Government:

Alexandria City, VA	703-838-4422
Arlington County, VA	703-538-3363
Fairfax City, VA	703-385-7860
Fairfax County, VA	703-246-4600
Montgomery County, MD	301-217-2240
Prince George's County, MD	301-952-3408

Universities:

American	202-885-2639
Catholic	202-319-5263
George Mason	703-993-8799
Georgetown	202-687-2521
Howard	202-806-7712
Maryland	301-405-5677

Miscellaneous:

Amtrak	202-906-3866
C&P Telephone	202-347-7070
Fairfax Nursing Center	703-385-0013
Giant Food	301-881-5782
Group Health Association	202-364-2080
Metro	703-538-3350
Metro Library Council	202-962-3712
Maryland Capital Parks and Planning Commission	301-927-5101
Natl. Assn. Security Dealers	301-590-0781

Smithsonian	202-287-3102
Virginia Library Association	703-519-8027
Washington Gas & Light	202-750-5814
Women in Communications	1-800-765-9424

Trade and Special Interest Magazines

Every industry or service business has its trade press—that is, editors, reporters, and photographers whose job it is to cover an industry or trade. You should become familiar with the magazines of the industries or professions that interest you, especially if you're in the interviewing stage of your job search. They tell you what's happening in the field and who's doing what. Your prospective employers are reading the industry trade magazines; you should be too.

Trade magazines are published for a specific business or professional audience; they are usually expensive and available by subscription only. For those not to be found at the library, call up the magazine's editorial or sales office and ask if you can come over to look at the latest issue.

The following magazines have editorial offices in the Washington area, reporting area news about the people and businesses in their industry. Many carry local want ads and personnel changes. For a complete listing of the trade press, consult the *Standard Periodical Directory* at the library.

TRADE AND SPECIAL INTEREST MAGAZINES

Adult Education Quarterly
1112 16th St. N.W., Suite 420
Washington, DC 20036
202-463-6333
Quarterly journal of theory and research in adult and continuing education.

Advertising Age
529 14th St.
National Press Building, Suite 814
Washington, DC 20045
202-662-7200
Weekly magazine covering national and international news and trends in advertising and marketing industries.

Aging
U.S. Government Printing Office
Superintendent of Documents
Washington, DC 20402
202-783-3238
Quarterly magazine sharing information about programs and activities in geriatric field.

Air & Space
370 L'Enfant Promenade S.W.
10th floor
Washington, DC 20024-2518
202-287-3733
Aviation and aerospace magazine, six times yearly.

Air Force
1501 Lee Highway

Arlington, VA 22209-1198
703-247-5822
Monthly magazine for management personnel of USAF, government agencies and aerospace industry.

American Banker
1325 G St. N.W., Suite 900
Washington DC 20005
202-347-5529
Daily tabloid covering government policies on financial services. Provides profiles of people involved in regulative and legislative activities.

American Horticulturist
P.O. Box 0105
Mt. Vernon, VA 22121-0105
703-768-5700
Monthly magazine of horticulture and gardening.

American Metal Market
1333 H St. N.W., Suite 570
Washington DC 20005
202-682-3200
Daily newspaper covering government affairs, markets, mergers, environmental issues and trends for all metal industries.

American Psychologist
750 First St. N.E.
Washington DC 20002
202-336-5500
Monthly journal of American Psychological Association. Includes empirical, theoretical and practical articles.

American Rehabilitation
U.S. Government Printing Office
Superintendent of Documents
Washington, DC 20402
202-783-3238
Quarterly magazine on rehabilitation of the handicapped.

American Scholar
1811 Q St. N.W.
Washington, DC 20009
202-265-3808
Quarterly journal containing articles and essays on intellectual, artistic, literary, and scientific subjects.

American Shipper
National Press Building, Room 1269
Washington, DC 20045
202-347-1678
Monthly magazine covering maritime trade and ocean shipping news.

American Teacher
555 New Jersey Ave. N.W.
Washington, DC 20001-2079
202-879-4400
Newspaper focusing on issues of education and the labor union, eight times yearly.

Architecture
1735 New York Ave. N.W.
Washington, DC 20006
202-828-0993
Monthly magazine for architects, interior designers, engineers, and architecture students.

Armed Forces Journal International
2000 L St. N.W., Suite 520
Washington, DC 20036
202-296-0450
Monthly magazine concerning the armed services, national security, and defense.

Association Management
1575 I St. N.W.
Washington, DC 20005
202-626-2722
Monthly national business magazine for executives who manage associations. Includes Executive Search and Position Wanted sections.

Association Trends
4948 St. Elmo Ave., Suite 306
Bethesda, MD 20814
301-652-8666
Weekly newspaper for staff professionals of volunteer organizations including trade associations and professional societies. Classified ads for full-time positions.

Automotive News
814 National Press Building
Washington, DC 20045
202-662-7200

Aviation Week & Space Technology
1120 Vermont Ave. N.W., Suite 1222
Washington, DC 20005
202-833-6000
Weekly general news magazine for aerospace industry. Includes governmental affairs, programs, and analysis.

Barron's
6630 Tansey Drive
Falls Church, VA 22042
703-534-4231
Weekly business magazine focusing on market trends, views, and advice related to finance and investments.

Broadcasting Magazine
1705 DeSales St. N.W.
Washington, DC 20036-4480
202-659-2340
Weekly magazine covering radio, television, cable, and satellite industries.

Brookings Review
1775 Massachusetts Ave. N.W.
Washington, DC 20036
202-797-6243
Quarterly magazine presenting research and policy proposals on economic, foreign policy, and governmental affairs.

How to Get a Job

Cable World
2000 L St. N.W., Suite 702
Washington, DC 20036
202-331-3710
Weekly magazine on all facets of industry, including technical, management, advertising, and programming.

Cablevision
1333 H St. N.W., Suite #570
Washington, DC 20005
202-682-3222
Bi-weekly magazine offering business trends and politics affecting cable industry.

Career Development Quarterly
5999 Stevenson Ave.
Alexandria, VA 22304
703-823-9000
Quarterly journal for career counselors and career education professionals in schools, colleges, private practice, government agencies, personnel departments in business and industry, and employment counselors.

Carousel
7815 Old Georgetown Rd.
Bethesda, MD 20814-2415
301-654-8664
Tabloid newspaper containing articles about writing and literary activities, six times yearly.

Changing Times
1729 H St. N.W.
Washington, DC 20006
202-887-6400
Monthly personal business magazine featuring new and existing products and services, including information on investments, insurance, taxes, education, health care, and career and retirement planning.

Chronicle of Higher Education
1255 23rd St. N.W.
Washington, DC 20037
202-828-3500
Weekly magazine of higher education. Includes large classified section.

Common Cause
2030 M St. N.W.
Washington, DC 20036
202-833-1200
Magazine of people, power, and politics in Washington. Published six times yearly.

Communications Daily
2115 Ward Court N.W.
Washington, DC 20037
202-872-9200
Daily newsletter covering business developments, regulations, and trends.

Communications Week
1222 National Press Building
Washington, DC 20045

202-737-6229
Weekly magazine of news and market information.

Congressional Digest
3231 P St. N.W.
Washington, DC 20007
202-333-7332
Magazine covers issues in Congress from all sides, 10 times yearly.

Corrections Today
8025 Laurel Lakes Ct.
Laurel, MD 20707
301-206-5100
Covers corrections, law enforcement, and rehabilitation, seven times yearly.

Credit
1101 14th St. N.W.
Washington, DC 20005
202-289-0400
A financial services magazine, six times yearly.

Daily Bond Buyer
1325 G St. N.W., Suite 900
Washington, DC 20005
202-393-1270
Financial newspaper on municipal market, major dealers, tax questions, government regulations on bonds and legislation; five days weekly.

Daily News Record
1333 H St. N.W., Suite 570
Washington, DC 20005
202-682-3200
Daily newspaper of news on fashion merchandising industry, including import/exports.

Defenders
1244 19th St. N.W.
Washington, DC 20036
202-659-9510
Wildlife and conservation magazine, published six times yearly.

Defense News
6883 Commercial Drive
Springfield, VA 22159
703-750-2000
Weekly defense industry journal.

Editor & Publisher
National Press Building, Suite 1128
Washington, DC 20045
202-662-7234
Weekly newspaper about technology, advertising, business, newspeople, government regulations, and legislation.

Educational Researcher
1230 17th St. N.W.
Washington, DC 20036-3078

How to Get a Job

202-223-9485
Journal of educational research, nine times yearly.

Education Week
4301 Connecticut Ave. N.W.
Washington, DC 20008
202-686-0800
News magazine on educational happenings, K-12, 40 times yearly. Includes job listings.

Engineering Times
1420 King St.
Alexandria, VA 22314
703-684-2875
Monthly magazine covering technology news and professional issues for engineering audience.

Environment
4000 Albemarle St. N.W.
Washington, DC 20016
202-362-6445
Trade magazine covering environmental problems and solutions, ten times yearly.

Exceptional Children
1920 Association Drive
Reston, VA 22091
703-620-3660
A special education journal, six times yearly.

Far Eastern Economic Review
1025 Connecticut Ave. N.W., Suite 800
Washington, DC 20036
202-862-9286
Weekly magazine of political and economic news on Northeast Asia. Covers business links, trade policy, and diplomatic stories.

Federal Computer Week
3110 Fairview Park Drive, Suite 1040
Falls Church, VA 22042
703-876-5100
Magazine on technological developments, new products and research, classifieds. 37 times yearly.

Federal Register
U.S. Government Printing Office
Superintendent of Documents
Washington, DC 20402
202-783-3238
Provides information on regulations and legal notices issued by federal agencies, five days weekly.

Federal Times
6883 Commercial Drive
Springfield, VA 22159
703-750-2000
Weekly magazine on federal bureaucracy and technology in government.

Financial Services Report
7811 Montrose Rd.
Potomac, MD 20854
301-340-2100
Bi-weekly newsletter for banks and financial institutions.

Forbes
600 National Press Building
Washington, DC 20045
202-628-2344
Bi-weekly business magazine, including company portraits, trends.

Foreign Policy
2400 N St. N.W.
Washington, DC 20037
202-862-7940
Quarterly journal on U.S. policy.

Foreign Service Journal
2101 E St. N.W.
Washington, DC 20037
202-338-4045
Monthly publication for professionals in foreign affairs.

Foreign Trade
6849 Old Dominion Drive
McLean, VA 22101-3705
703-448-1338
Magazine covering international business, six times yearly.

Fortune
1050 Connecticut Ave. N.W.
Washington, DC 20036
202-861-4041
Bi-weekly news magazine about business: current affairs, trends, company profiles, index.

Foundation News
1828 L St. N.W.
Washington, DC 20036
202-466-6512
Magazine for professionals in non-profit organizations and foundations, six times yearly. Job ads for professional positions.

The Futurist
4916 St. Elmo Ave.
Bethesda, MD 20814-6089
301-656-8274
Magazine exploring social and technological changes, six times yearly.

The Gerontologist
1275 K St. N.W., Suite 350
Washington, DC 20005-4006
202-842-1275
Journal presenting new concepts, clinical ideas, and applied research in gerontology. Includes book and audio-visual reviews. Six times yearly.

How to Get a Job

Government Computer News
8601 Georgia Ave., Suite 300
Silver Spring, MD 20910
301-650-2000
Bi-weekly magazine for federal and state government technical and management executives; covers computers, communication news, trends, applications, and products related to government operations.

Government Executive
1730 M St. N.W., Suite 1100
Washington, DC 20036
202-862-0600
Monthly magazine for government executives.

Health and Social Work
7981 Eastern Ave.
Silver Spring, MD 20910
301-565-0333
Quarterly magazine on social work practices in the health field.

Health Education
1900 Association Drive
Reston, VA 22091
703-476-3400
Journal on health education topics, six times yearly.

Historic Preservation
1785 Massachusetts Ave. N.W.
Washington, DC 20036
202-786-0503
Magazine on architectural preservation, six times yearly.

Hospital Topics
4000 Albemarle St. N.W.
Washington, DC 20016
202-842-1275
202-362-6445
Magazine presenting articles for hospital administrators, department heads, and professionals in variety of health-related fields. Six times yearly.

Industry Week
1350 Connecticut Ave. N.W., Suite 902
Washington, DC 20036
202-223-6650
Bi-weekly magazine, including stories about people, government, and profiles in manufacturing industry.

Information Times
555 New Jersey Ave. N.W.
Suite 800
Washington, DC 20001
202-639-8262
Tabloid serving the electronic and print information industry, six times yearly.

International Economy
1133 Connecticut Ave. N.W., Suite 901
Washington, DC 20036
202-861-0791

Magazine with articles on macro-economic issues, international finance, book reviews, and research findings, six times yearly.

Kiplinger Washington Letter
1729 H St.
Washington, DC 20006
202-887-6400
Weekly general interest magazine, including economics, politics, small business issues, projections and trends for the area.

Legal Times
1730 M St. N.W., Suite 802
Washington, DC 20036
202-457-0686
Weekly legal newspaper, covering law, lobbying, and politics in Washington.

Lodging
1201 New York Ave. N.W.
Washington, DC 20005
202-289-3100
Directed toward management staff of hotels and motels.

Management World
American Management Society
1101 14th St. N.W., No. 1100
Washington, DC 20005-5601
Magazine covering management trends and procedures for lower- and mid-managers, six times yearly.

Mobile Products News
7811 Montrose Rd.
Silver Spring, MD 20854
301-340-2100
Monthly magazine covering the mobile communications products industry.

Modern Maturity
601 E St., N.W.
Washington, DC 20049
202-434-2277
Bi-monthly magazine of general interest to those over 55 years old. Some career-related articles.

Monthly Labor Review
U.S. Government Printing Office
Superintendent of Documents
Washington, DC 20402
202-783-3238
Monthly publication reporting on labor issues.

Museum News
1225 I St. N.W.
Suite 200
Washington, DC 20005
202-289-1818
For museum employees and trustees, six times yearly.

National Defense
2101 Wilson Blvd., Suite 400

Arlington, VA 22201-3061
703-522-1820
Magazine on North American defense industrial base, 11 times yearly.

National Geographic
17th & M St. N.W.
Washington, DC 20036
202-857-7000
Monthly magazine featuring articles on geography, culture, natural history, and the environment.

National Law Journal
927 National Press Building
Washington, DC 20045
202-662-8930
Weekly newspaper for lawyers, including legal and public policy news.

National Parks
1015 31st St. N.W.
Washington, DC 20007
202-944-8565
Magazine on conservation, outdoor activities, and travel. Published six times yearly.

National Review
1291 National Press Building
Washington, DC 20045
202-662-8850
Conservative political journal published twice monthly. A few classifieds.

NEA Today
1201 16th St. N.W.
Washington, DC 20036
202-822-7200
Educational magazine, eight times yearly.

New Republic
1220 19th St. N.W., Suite 600
Washington, DC 20036
202-331-7494
Weekly magazine featuring current events, commentaries and reviews.

Occupational Outlook Quarterly
U.S. Government Printing Office
Superintendent of Documents
Washington, DC 20402
202-783-3238
Quarterly magazine providing occupational and employment information.

Oil Daily
1401 New York Ave. N.W., Suite 500
Washington, DC 20005
202-662-0700
Daily petroleum and energy industry magazine.

Parks and Recreation Magazine
3101 Park Center Drive, 12th floor
Alexandria, VA 22302

703-820-4940
Monthly magazine focusing on research, technical advances, professional development for executives, public officials and community leaders who manage public and private park and recreational facilities.

Personnel Management
1231 25th St. N.W.
Washington, DC 20037
Magazine on personnel management issues, twice weekly.

Policy Review
214 Massachusetts Ave. N.E.
Washington, DC 20002
202-546-4400
Quarterly magazine presenting conservative view of news and policy trends, including domestic, social, and foreign policy.

Preservation News
1785 Massachusetts Ave. N.W.
Washington, DC 20036
202-673-4000
Monthly newspaper featuring historical preservation and architecture.

The Professional Geographer
Association of American Geographers
1710 16th St. N.W.
Washington, DC 20009
202-234-1450
Quarterly geographical magazine.

Public Administration Review
American Society for Public Administration
1120 G St. N.W., Suite 500
Washington, DC 20005
202-393-7878
Public administration journal, six times yearly.

The Public Interest
1112 16th St. N.W.
Suite 530
Washington, DC 20036
202-785-8555
Quarterly magazine focusing on sociology, politics, economics, and domestic policy.

Public Relations Quarterly
3415 Lowell St. N.W.
Washington, DC 22016-5024
202-537-0302

Publishers Weekly
716 S. Wayne St
Arlington, VA 22204
703-521-4187
Weekly magazine on news, trends, and government actions affecting book publishing industry.

How to Get a Job

Restaurateur
7926 Jones Branch Drive, Suite 530
McLean, VA 22102-3390
703-356-1315
Monthly magazine focusing on needs of metro area restaurateurs.

Satellite News
7811 Montrose Road
Potomac, MD 20854
301-340-2100
Weekly magazine for the communications and satellite industries.

Science
1333 H St. N.W.
Washington, DC 20005
202-326-6501
Weekly magazine focused on science, scientific research, and public policy.

Sea Technology
1117 N. 19th St.
Arlington, VA 22209
703-524-3136
Monthly magazine on oceanography, including new products, research and
development, trends. Bi-weekly newsletter includes marketplace section.

Space Times
6352 Rolling Rd., No. 102
Springfield, VA 22152-2816
703-866-0020
Magazine of American Astronautical Society, six times yearly.

Special Libraries
1700 18th St. N.W.
Washington, DC 20009
202-234-4700
Quarterly journal of Special Libraries Association. Includes papers on administration, organization, and operation of special libraries, research reports, and
professional development articles.

Variety
1483 Chain Bridge Road, Suite 202
McLean, VA 22101
703-448-0510
Weekly show business and entertainment magazine. Includes relevant legislative
actions.

Voluntary Action Leadership
1111 N. 19th St., Suite 500
Arlington, VA 22209
703-276-0542
Quarterly magazine on volunteer programs.

Washington Area Realtor
10400 Connecticut Ave., Suite 510
Kensington, MD 20895
301-949-4781
Monthly trade magazine for realtors in the area.

Waste Age
1730 Rhode Island Ave. N.W., Suite 1000
Washington, DC 20036
202-861-0708
Monthly magazine providing news on solid and hazardous waste and pollution control.

Local Feature Magazines and Newspapers

The following periodicals do not necessarily cover business news but can be valuable sources of information about the Washington area itself, information you need to be a well-informed Washingtonian.

Capitol Sports Focus
4733 Bethesda Ave.
Bethesda, MD 20814
301-657-1580
Monthly tabloid of articles on new products, events, personal profiles, and classifieds.

Hill Rag
224 7 St. S.E., Suite 300
Washington, DC 20003
202-543-8300
Bi-weekly community newspaper with articles on quality of schools, crime, real estate, dining, etc.

Intermission
6205 Redwood Lane
Alexandria, VA 22310
703-971-7530
Monthly news magazine for the performing arts.

InTowner
1627 17th St. N.W.
2nd floor
Washington, DC 20009
202-234-1717
Community paper for residents of downtown neighborhoods.

Leaves Magazine
4701 Sangamore Road
Bethesda, MD 20816
301-229-4000
Magazine providing news about Northwest DC and Montgomery County. A real estate publication, six times yearly.

Mid-Atlantic Country
6401 Golden Triangle Dr., Suite 120
Greenbelt, MD 20770-3225
301-220-2300
Monthly magazine offering information on leisure, resort, retirement, country inns, etc., for mid-Atlantic region.

New Dominion Magazine
210 Reinekers Lane
Alexandria, VA 22314

703-683-7336
Magazine for and about Northern Virginia, six times yearly.

Northern Virginia Sun
135 Park St. N.E.
Vienna, VA 22180
703-204-2800
Community newspaper with classifieds for Arlington, Falls Church, Fairfax City, twice weekly.

Roll Call
900 2nd St. N.E.
Washington, DC 20002
202-289-4900
Congressional newspaper, twice weekly.

Washington Monthly
1611 Connecticut Ave. N.W.
Washington, DC 20009
202-462-0128
Journal of politics and government, ten times yearly.

Washington Quarterly
1800 K St. N.W.
Washington, DC 20006
202-887-0200
Quarterly journal covering various aspects of foreign policy.

Washingtonian
1828 L St. N.W.
Washington, DC 20036
202-296-3600
Monthly metropolitan interest magazine. Watch for special job hunters' issues.

Developing a Strategy:
The ABCs of Networking

Success doesn't just happen. Neither does a successful job search. It's the result of careful planning. Before you rush out to set up your first interview, it's important to come up with a plan. We believe a plan isn't a plan unless it's on paper. Your plan should include researching the job market and how to systematically contact potential employers.

This chapter and Chapter 7 will cover specific techniques and tools that you'll find useful in your search. But before we get to them, a few words are in order about your overall approach.

It's Going To Take Some Time

Looking for a new job is no easy task. It's as difficult and time-consuming for a bright young woman with a brand-new MBA as it is for a fifty-year-old executive with years of front-line experience. Every once in a while someone lucks out. One of Tom's clients established a record by finding a new position in four days. But most people should plan on two to six months of full-time job hunting before they find a position they'll really be happy with.

According to *Forbes* magazine, the older you are and the more you earn, the longer it will take to find what you're looking for—in fact, up to six months for people over 40 earning more than $40,000. People under 40 in the $20,000-$40,000 bracket average two to four months.

Your line of work will also affect the length of your search. Usually, the easier it is to demonstrate tangible bottom-line results, the faster you can line up a job. Lawyers, public relations people, and advertising executives are harder to place than accountants and sales people, according to one top personnel specialist.

Be Good to Yourself

Whether or not you're currently employed, it's important to nurture your ego when you're looking for a new job. Rejection rears its ugly head more often in a job search than at most other times, and self-doubt can be deadly.

Make sure you get regular exercise during your job search to relieve stress. You'll sleep better, feel better, and perhaps even lose a few pounds.

Take care of your diet and watch what you drink. Many people who start to feel sorry for themselves tend to overindulge in food or alcohol. Valium and other such drugs are not as helpful as sharing your progress with your family or a couple of close friends.

Beef up your wardrobe so that you look and feel good during your employment interviews. There's no need to buy an expensive new suit, especially if you're on an austerity budget, but a new shirt, blouse, tie, pair of shoes, or hairstyle may be in order.

Maintain a positive outlook. Unemployment is not the end of the world; few people complete a career without losing a job at least once. Keep a sense of humor, too. Every job search has its funny moments. It's OK to joke about your situation and share your sense of humor with your friends and family.

Life goes on despite your job search. Your spouse and kids still need your attention. Try not to take out your anxieties, frustrations, and fears on those close to you. At the very time you need support and affirmation, your friends may prefer to stay at arm's length. You can relieve their embarrassment by being straightforward about your situation and by telling them how they can help you.

Put Yourself on a Schedule

Looking for work is a job in itself. Establish a schedule for your job search and stick to it. You may not be able to control when you land a job or even when you line up a good interview. But you CAN control how you spend each day. If you work hard and systematically, you'll be less likely to give in to self-doubt and depression. You'll also get a good job that much quicker.

If you're unemployed, work full time at getting a new job—from 8:30 a.m. to 5:30 p.m. five days a week, and from 9:00 a.m. to 12:00 noon on Saturdays. During a job search, there is a temptation to use "extra" time for recreation or to catch up on household tasks. Arranging two or three exploratory interviews will prove a lot more useful to you than washing the car or cleaning out the garage. You can do such tasks at night or on Sundays, just as you would if you were working. Besides, you ARE working—working hard and systematically to get the best job you can possibly get as quickly as you can get it.

Don't take a vacation during your search. Do it after you accept an offer and before you begin a new job. You might be tempted to "sort things out on the beach." But taking a vacation when you're unemployed isn't as restful as it sounds. You'll spend most of your time worrying about what will happen when the trip is over.

Even if you're currently employed, you should go about your job search seriously and systematically. Establish regular hours, give yourself deadlines, be persistent. If you're scheduling interviews, try to arrange several for one day so that you don't have to take too much time away from your job. You might also arrange interviews for your lunch hour. You can make phone calls during lunch or on your break time. You'd also be surprised at how many people you can reach before and after regular working hours, especially in Washington since people work both earlier and later than other cities.

Tax deductible job-hunting expenses

A certified public accountant offers the following tips on deducting job-hunting expenses on the income tax form. To qualify for certain deductions, you must hunt for a job in the same field you just left, or in the field that currently employs you. For example, someone who has worked as a public school teacher could not be compensated for the cost of getting a real estate license and seeking a broker's job.

If you are unemployed or want to switch jobs, expenses can be deducted on the Income Tax Statement of Employee Business Expenses or itemized on Schedule A of Form 1040. Expenses you can deduct include preparing, printing, and mailing resumes; vocational guidance counseling and testing; and the standard government reimbursement for miles driven to and from job interviews. Telephone, postage, and newspaper expenses are also deductible. While seeking work out of town, additional deductions are allowed for transportation, food, and lodging. ■

Watch Your Expenses

Spend what you have to spend for basic needs such as food, transportation, and housing. But watch major expenditures that could be delayed or not made at all. The kids will still need new shoes, but a $200 dinner party at a fancy place could just as well be changed to sandwiches and beer at home.

Keep track of all expenses that you incur in your job search, such as telephone and printing bills, postage, newspapers, parking, transportation, tolls, and meals purchased during the course of interviewing. These may all be tax deductible.

Networking Is the Key to a Successful Job Search

The basic tasks of a job search are fairly simple. Once you've figured out what kind of work you want to do, you need to know which companies might have such jobs and then make contact with the hiring authority. These tasks are also known as researching the job market and generating leads and interviews. Networking, or developing your personal contacts, is a great technique for finding out about the market and industrial trends and is unsurpassed as a way to generate leads and interviews.

Networking is nothing more than asking the people you already know to help you find out about the job market and meet the people who are actually doing the hiring. Each adult you know has access to at least 300 people you do not know. Of course, a lot of them will not be able to do much in the way of helping you find a job. But if you start with, say, 20 or 30 people, and each of them tells you about 3 other people who may be able to help you, you've built a network of 60 to 90 contacts.

Mark S. Granovetter, a Harvard sociologist, reported to *Forbes* magazine that "informal contacts" account for almost 75 percent of all successful job searches. Agencies find about 9 percent of new jobs for professional and technical people, and ads yield another 10 percent or so.

How To Start

To begin the networking process, draw up a list of all the possible contacts who can help you gain access to someone who can hire you for the job you want. Naturally, the first sources, the ones at the top of your list, will be people you know personally: friends, colleagues, former clients, relatives, acquaintances, customers, and club and church members. Just about everyone you know, whether or not he or she is employed, can generate contacts for you.

Don't forget to talk with your banker, lawyer, insurance agent, dentist, and other people who provide you with services. It is the nature of their businesses to know a lot of people who might help you in your search. Leave no stone unturned in your search for contacts. Go through your Christmas card list, alumni club list, and any other list you can think of.

On the average, it may take 10 to 15 contacts to generate 1 formal interview. It may take 5 or 10 of these formal interviews to generate 1 solid offer. And it may take 5 offers before you uncover the exact job situation you've been seeking. You may have to talk to as many as 250 people before you get the job you want. The maximum may be several hundred more.

Don't balk at talking to friends, acquaintances, and neighbors about your job search. In reality, you're asking for advice, not charity. Most of the people you'll contact will be willing to help you, if only you tell them *how.*

Here's an example of a networking letter

March 1, 1992
Marcia Trammel
Box 7457
University of Maryland
College Park, MD 20707

Mr. Tom Jones, Vice-President
Public Relations
Dynamic Enterprises
5610 Rockville Pike
Rockville, MD 20852

Dear Mr. Jones:

Dr. Smith of the Communications Department here at the University suggested that I contact you for information about public relations work at the corporate level.

I'm a communications major who will be graduating in three months. I've been on the Dean's List every quarter but two, all while I was putting myself through school. I completed an internship this past summer with a small public relations firm in Bethesda. I'm eager to learn more about public relations work and opportunities in Washington.

I will call you next week to see if you can fit me into your busy schedule. Dr. Smith sends her warmest regards.

Sincerely,

Marcia Trammel
(301) 555-9876

The Exploratory Interview

If I introduce you to my friend George at a major Washington bank, he will get together with you as a favor to me. When you have your meeting with him, you will make a presentation about what you've done in your work, what you want to do, and you will ask for his advice, ideas, and opinions. That is an exploratory interview. As is true of any employment interview, you must make a successful sales presentation to get what you want. You must convince George that you are a winner and that you deserve his help in your search.

The help the interviewer provides is usually in the form of suggestions to meet new people or contact certain companies. I introduced you to George. Following your successful meeting, he introduces you to Tom, Dick, and Mary. Each of them provides additional leads. In this way, you spend most of your time interviewing, not staying at home waiting for the phone to ring or the mail to arrive.

A job doesn't have to be vacant in order for you to have a successful meeting with a hiring authority. If you convince an employer that you would make a good addition to his or her staff, the employer might create a job for you where none existed before. In this way, networking taps the "hidden job market." And it's the "hidden job market" where most of the good jobs are. Besides, if you make a good impression and stay in touch, one of your contacts might have a hot lead for you two weeks from now.

To make the most of the networking technique, continually brush up on your interviewing skills (we've provided a refresher course in Chapter 7). Remember, even when you're talking with an old friend, you are still conducting an exploratory interview. Don't treat it as casual conversation.

Another term for this initial get-together is the "informational interview." This meeting can get you more than additional contacts and news about who's hiring. View it as an opportunity to find out more about the field you're researching. Every time you learn something new, that bit of information becomes grist for formal interviews later on.

Ask each contact to take a look at your resume. Even though they don't have a job to offer you, they might next month. They also may be able to comment on any gaps in your qualifications. Encourage such frankness. Once you know what your shortcomings are, you'll be in a better position to handle tough questions during formal interviews. You also may be able to rectify professional gaps through study or volunteer work.

Developing Professional Contacts

Friends and acquaintances are the obvious first choice when you're drawing up a list of contacts. But don't forget professional and trade organizations, clubs, and societies—they are valuable sources of contacts, leads, and information. In certain cases, it isn't necessary for you to belong in order to attend a meeting or an annual or monthly lunch, dinner, or cocktail party. Many such groups also publish newsletters, another valuable source of information on the job market and industry trends. Some professional associations offer placement services to members, in which case it may be worth your while to join officially. At the end of this chapter, we've provided a list of selected organizations that might prove useful for networking purposes.

If you're utterly new to Washington and don't as yet know a soul, your job will naturally be tougher. But it's not impossible. It just means you have to hustle that much harder. Here are some first steps you should take. Start attending the meetings of any professional society or civic organization of which you've been a member in the past. Find a church, temple, or religious organization that you're comfortable with and start attending. Join a special interest group. It could be anything from The Sierra Club to Parents Without Partners.

If you're just out of college, work through your alumni association to find out who else in Washington attended your alma mater. If you were in a fraternity or sorority, use those connections. If you're not a member of any of the groups mentioned above, now's the time to join.

Once you've taken the trouble to show up at a meeting, be friendly. Introduce yourself. Tell people you talk to what your situation is, but don't be pushy. You've come because you're interested in this organization and what it stands for. Volunteer to serve on a committee. You'll get to know a smaller number of people much better, and they'll see you as a responsible, generous person, a person they'll want to help. Do a bang-up job on your committee and they'll want to help all the more.

Executive network-ing

The higher your rung on the corporate ladder, the greater the chances that networking with executives outside your own field will pay off. If you're looking for a top spot in electronics, don't pass up a chance to discuss your credentials and employment needs with the recruiting executive of, say, an advertising firm. He or she just might have the hidden connection that could land you a great job.

One hiring exec from a large corporation reports: "I network with recruiters from more industries than most people would think, both industries that are related to ours and those that are not. It helps to find out what talent is available. If one of my contacts has someone in a file they don't need and I do, they're happy to tell me about that person. And I work the same way." ■

Keeping Yourself Organized

The most difficult part of any job search is getting started. A pocket calendar or engagement diary that divides each work day into hourly segments will make your job much easier. As you start meeting the people who are in a position to hire you, notice that they invariably rely on just such a planner. Do you really want to appear less professional than your interviewers?

You should keep a personal log of calls and contacts. You may want to develop a format that's different from the one shown here. Fine. The point is to keep a written record of every person you contact in your job search and the results of each contact.

Your log (it can be a notebook from the dime store) will help keep you from getting confused and losing track of the details of your search. If you call someone who's out of town until Tuesday, say, your log can flag this call so it won't fall between the cracks. It may also come in handy for future job searches.

Your log's "disposition" column can act as a reminder of additional sources of help you'll want to investigate. You'll also have a means of timing the correspondence that should follow any interview.

Date	Name & Title	Company	Phone	Disposition
2/10	Chas. Junior, V.P. Sales	Top Parts	(703) 277-5500	Interview 2/15
2/10	E. Franklin Sales Manager	Frameco	466-0303	Out of town until 2/17
2/10	L. Duffy Dir. Marketing	Vassar Inc.	826-6112	Out of office. Call in aft.

2/10	P. Lamm Sls. Dir.	Golfco Ent.	(301) 386-9100	Busy to 2/28 Call then.
2/10	E. Waixel VP Mktg. & Sales	Half'n'Half Foods	(703) 338-1055	Call after 2

If you're unemployed and job hunting full time, schedule yourself for three exploratory interviews a day for the first week. Each of these meetings should result in at least three subsequent leads. Leave the second week open for the appointments you generated during the first. Maintain this pattern as you go along in your search.

We can't emphasize too strongly how important it is that you put yourself on a job-searching schedule, whether or not you're currently employed. A schedule shouldn't function as a straightjacket, but it ought to serve as a way of organizing your efforts for greatest efficiency. Much of your job-hunting time will be devoted to developing your network of contacts. But you should also set aside a certain portion of each week for doing your homework on companies that interest you (see Chapter 4) and for pursuing other means of contacting employers (we'll get to these in a minute).

As you go through your contacts and begin to research the job market, you'll begin to identify certain employers in which you're interested. Keep a list of them. For each one that looks particularly promising, begin a file that contains articles about the company, its annual report, product brochures, personnel policy, and the like. Every so often, check your "potential employer" list against your log to make sure that you're contacting the companies that interest you most.

Go for the Hiring Authority

The object of your job search is to convince the person who has the power to hire you that you ought to be working for him or her. The person you want to talk to is not necessarily the president of the company. It's the person who heads the department that could use your expertise. If you're a salesperson, you probably want to talk with the vice-president of sales or marketing. If you're in data processing, the vice-president of operations is the person you need to see.

How do you find the hiring authority? If you're lucky, someone you know personally will tell you whom to see and introduce you. Otherwise, you'll have to do some homework. Some of the directories listed in Chapter 4 will name department heads for major companies in the Washington area. If you can not otherwise find out who heads the exact department that interests you, call the company and ask the operator. (It's a good idea to do this anyway since directories go out of date as soon as a department head leaves a job.)

Use an introduction wherever possible when first approaching a company—that's what networking is all about, anyway. For those companies that you must approach "cold," use the phone to arrange a meeting with the hiring authority beforehand. Don't assume you can drop in and see a busy executive without an appointment. And don't assume you can get to the hiring authority through the personnel department. If at all possible, you don't want to fill out any personnel forms until you have had a serious interview. The same goes for sending resumes (see Chapter 3). In general, resumes are better left behind, *after* an interview, than sent ahead to generate a meeting.

Telephone Tactics

Cold calls are difficult for most job seekers. Frequently, a receptionist or secretary, sometimes both, stands in your way to the hiring authority you want to reach. One way around this is to call about a half-hour after closing. There's a good chance that the secretary will be off to happy hour, and the boss will still be finishing up the XYZ project report. Only now there will be no one to run interference for him or her.

Generally, you're going to have to go through a support staffer, so the first rule is to treat her (more likely than not it will be a woman) courteously and accord her the same professional respect you'd like to be accorded yourself. She is not a girl. She is not "just a secretary." Often, part of her job is to keep unsolicited job hunters out of her boss's hair. You want her to be your ally, not your adversary. If possible, sell her on what a wonderfully qualified person you are and how it is to her boss's advantage to have you aboard.

Don't leave your name and expect a return call. Instead, ask when there's a convenient time you might call back. Or allow yourself to be put on hold. You can read job-search literature or compose cover letters while you wait. Be sure and keep your target's name and title and the purpose of your call in a log before you, however. You don't want to be at a loss for words when you're finally put through.

Other Tactics for Contacting Employers

Direct contact with the hiring authority—either through a third-party introduction (networking) or by calling for an appointment directly—is far and away the most effective job-hunting method. Your strategy and schedule should reflect that fact, and most of your energy should be devoted to direct contact. It's human nature, however, not to put all your eggs in one basket. You may want to explore other methods of contacting potential employers, but they should take up no more than a quarter of your job-hunting time.

Calling or writing to personnel offices may occasionally be productive, especially when you know that a company is looking for someone with your particular skills. But personnel people, by the nature of their responsibility, tend to screen out rather than welcome newcomers to the company fold. You're always better off going directly to the hiring authority.

Consider the case of a company that runs an ad in *The Wall Street Journal*. The ad may bring as many as 600 responses. The head of personnel asks one of the secretaries to separate the resumes into three piles according to age: "under 30," "over 30," and "I don't know." The personnel chief automatically eliminates two of the three stacks. He or she then flips through the third and eliminates all but, say, eight resumes. The personnel specialist will call the eight applicants, screen them over the phone, and invite three for a preliminary interview. Of those three, two will be sent to the hiring authority for interviews. That means that 598 applicants never even got a chance to make their case.

Statistically, fewer than one out of four job hunters succeed by going to personnel departments, responding to ads (either open or blind, as described in Chapter 4), or using various employment services. Some do find meaningful work this way, however. We repeat, if you decide to use a method other than networking or direct contact, don't spend more than 25 percent of your job- hunting time on it.

BOOKS ON JOB-HUNTING STRATEGY

As you might expect, many books have been written on job-hunting strategy and techniques. Here is a list of selected resources.

Baber, Anne and Waymon, Lynne. *Great Connections.* Manassas, VA: Impact Publications, 1992.

Bastress, Fran. *The Relocating Spouse's Guide to Employment.* Manassas, VA: Impact Publications, 1989.

Bolles, Richard N. *The Three Boxes of Life and How to Get Out of Them.* Berkeley, CA: Ten Speed Press, 1983.

Bolles, Richard N. *What Color Is Your Parachute?* Berkeley, CA: Ten Speed Press, 1993. Annual updates.

Camden, Thomas M. *The Job Hunter's Final Exam.* Chicago: Surrey Books, 1990.

Cohen, Steve, and Paulo de Oliveira. *Getting to the Right Job.* New York: Workman Publishing, 1987.

Dublin, Judith A., and Melanie R. Keveles. *Fired For Success.* New York: Warner Books, 1990.

Figler, Howard. *The Complete Job Search Handbook.* New York: H. Holt & Co., 1988.

Fowler, Julianne. *How to Get the Job You Want in Tough Times.* Los Angeles: Lowell House, 1991.

Gerberg, Robert Jameson. *The Professional Job Changing System.* New York: Performance Dynamics, Inc., 1986.

Haldane, Bernard. *Career Satisfaction and Success: A Guide to Job Freedom.* New York: Amacom, 1982.

Half, Robert. *How to Get a Better Job in This Crazy World.* New York: Crown, 1990.

Henderson, David G. *JOB SEARCH: Marketing Your Military Experience in the 1990's.* Manassas, VA: Impact Publications, 1990.

Krannich, Ronald, and Caryl, R. *Network Your Way to Job & Career Success: Your Complete Guide to Creating New Opportunities.* Manassas, VA: Impact Publications, 1989.

Lee, W. Dean. *Beyond the Uniform.* Manassas, VA: Impact Publications, 1991.

Leeds, Dorothy. *Marketing Yourself: The Ultimate Job Seeker's Guide.* New York: Harper Collins, 1991.

Mayer, Jeffrey J. *Find the Job You've Always Wanted in Half the Time With Half the Effort.* Chicago: Contemporary Books, 1992.

Moore, David J. *Job Search for the Technical Professional.* New York: Wiley, 1991.

Morin, William J., and James C. Cabrera. *Parting Company: How to Survive the Loss of a Job and Find Another Successfully.* San Diego: Harcourt Brace Jovanovich, 1991.

O'Brien, John A. *Job Search Organizer.* Washington, DC: Miranda Associates, 1990.

Parker, Linda Bates. *Career Portfolio.* Cincinnati, Ohio: The University of Cincinnati, 1990.

Riehle, Kathleen A. *What Smart People Do When Losing Their Jobs.* New York: Wiley, 1991.

SELECTED WASHINGTON AREA PROFESSIONAL ORGA-NIZATIONS, TRADE GROUPS, NETWORKS, CLUBS, AND SOCIETIES

The following organizations provide a variety of membership services. They are ready-made for networking, forming relationships, and gathering inside information. We have noted specifically their employment-related activities. You should contact the groups directly that best suit your career game plan and ask for details about their programs and other services.

Also see the special federal and local sections on "Professional Organi-zations for Networking in Government," which you will find in Chapter 11.

You might also want to check the "Professional Organizations" entries arranged by industry category in Chapter 12, where large associations headquartered in Washington are listed.

Advertising Club of Metropolitan Washington
7200 Wisconsin Ave., #200
Bethesda, MD 20814
301-656-2582
Contact: Laurie Dunlap
Association for advertising, financial, and printing professionals. Monthly newsletter includes classifieds. Frequent seminars and outings for networking.

Alexandria Bar Association
520 King St.
Alexandria, VA 22314
703-548-1106
Contact: J. Max Weintraub
Association for attorneys and law students. Publishes a newsletter that has classified ads.

American Bar Association. Washington Office
1800 M St. N.W.
Washington, DC 20036
202-331-2200
Contact: Sharon Greene
Association for attorneys, law students, legal administrators, and law librarians. *ABA Journal* has classified section with employment listings.

American Federation of Television & Radio Artists
5480 Wisconsin Ave.
Bethesda, MD 20815
301-657-2560
Contact: Courtney Caro
Association of performers. Bi-monthly publication on changes, trends, and events. Maintains hotline: 301-654-7483

American Institute of Architects. Northern Virginia Chapter
205 S. Patrick St.
Alexandria, VA 22314
703-549-9747
Contact: Debbie Miller, Executive Director
Publishes newsletter with openings. Job referral service. Fax resume to 703-549-9783.

How to Get a Job

American Institute of Architects. Washington Chapter
1777 Church St. N.W.
Washington, DC 20009
202-667-1798
Contact: G. Martin Moeller, Jr., Intern AIA, Executive Director.
Association for architects and professionals in related fields.
Keeps book of resumes in office. Maintains job openings file.

American Institute of Certified Public Accountants. Washington Office
1455 Pennsylvania Ave. N.W.
Washington, DC 20004
202-737-6600
Association of professional accountants. Publishes monthly journal and professional development brochures.

American Marketing Association. Metropolitan Washington Chapter
5327 28th St., N.W.
Washington, DC 20015-1329
202-363-1671
Contact: Arlene Farber-Sirkin, President
A diverse group of marketing professionals. Monthly publication includes classified ads. Maintains job bank for members. Meetings throughout the year.

American Society of Civil Engineers. Washington Office
1015 15th St. N.W.
Washington, DC 20005
202-789-2200
Contact: Michael Good, National Capital Section
Professional society for civil engineers. New York office publishes journal with some job listings. Local clearinghouse of jobs for members only: 301-983-9777

American Society for Training and Development
4227 46th St. N.W.
Washington, DC 20016
202-362-1498
Contact: Michele Porzel
Professional group for human resources, career development, and training professionals. Publishes membership directory, monthly newsletter, and holds monthly meetings, training seminars, and interest groups throughout the year. Provides position referral service and maintains internship clearinghouse.

American Society of Mechanical Engineers. Washington Office
1825 K St. N.W.
Washington, DC 20006
202-785-3756
Professional society for mechanical engineers. For publications, call: 1-800-843-2763

Apartment and Office Building Association of Metro Washington
1050 17th St. N.W., 300
Washington, DC 20036
202-296-3390
Contact: Peggy Jeffers, Executive Director
Group of apartment and building owners and managers. Bi-monthly news magazine and legislative reports. Monthly networking luncheons offered.

Arlington County Bar Association
1400 N. Courthouse Road
Arlington, VA 22201
703-358-3390
Contact: Robert Goulder
Association for attorneys. Office keeps informal book with listings of jobs, offices to rent, etc. Newsletter does have classified section.

Art Directors Club of Metropolitan Washington
407 Thayer Ave.
Silver Spring, MD 20910
301-608-2196
Contact: Chris Culotta
Monthly newsletter has ads.

Arts Club of Washington
2017 I St. N.W.
Washington, DC 20006
202-732-1039
Contact: Jane Case Williams
Group for variety of artists to exhibit and view work.

Association for Educators and Rehabilitators of the Blind and Visually Impaired
206 North Washington St., Suite 320
Alexandria, VA 22314
703-548-1884
Organization for professionals affiliated with rehabilitation. Provides information on careers in rehabilitation and publishes excellent booklet on career choice.

Bar Association of the District of Columbia
1819 H St. N.W., 12th floor
Washington, DC 20006
202-223-6600
Contact: Allison Lawanson
Association for attorneys. Monthly newsletter and professional development brochures. Quarterly meetings and variety of social events, luncheons, and retreats.

Internships can lead to permanent relationships

Internships abound in Washington. Every congressional office, executive department or agency, trade association, public interest group, media organization, or one-person lobbying office has at least one intern. Most often these are not paid positions, although some offer small stipends. However, many offer something worth its weight in unpaid hours: exposure.

It is not unusual for an internship to turn into a full-time job offer, particularly after graduation. Even when this doesn't happen, the contacts interns make can be invaluable. Throughout this book, almost everyone interviewed emphasized the same thing: get to know people and get your name and work known in your field. Informal working relationships often produce formal job situations.

How to Get a Job

Here are two good directories of internships available: *Complete Guide to Washington Internships* (Brooklyn, NY: JMP Enterprises, 1990); and *1992 Internships* (Cincinnati, OH: Writer's Digest Books, annual). ■

Bar Association of Montgomery County
27 W. Jefferson St.
Rockville, MD 20850
301-424-3454
Contact: Janet VanPelt
Association for attorneys. Newsletter has some classifieds. Monthly meetings, committees, frequent social events.

Chemical Society of Washington
1155 16th St. N.W.
Washington, DC 20036
202-638-3864
Contact: Norma Riddick
Society for chemists, chemical engineers, and technicians. Monthly newsletter excluding summers. Dinner meetings monthly between October-May. Maintains employer clearinghouse and referral system.

DC Dietic Association
1250 I St. N.W., Suite 700
Washington, DC 20005
202-289-4215
Contact: Clara Schneider
Has Employment Exchange information.

Dental Society of Northern Virginia
4330-N Evergreen Lane
Annandale, VA 22003
703-642-5298
Contact: Ellen Flanagan
Professional society for licensed dentists. Informal card file kept in office. Newsletter has ads. Continuing education meetings five to six times yearly.

Dental Society of the District of Columbia
502 C St. N.E.
Washington, DC 20002
202-547-7613
Monthly newsletter has classifieds. Resume file kept in office.

Direct Marketing Association of Washington
655 15th St. N.W.
Washington, DC 20005
202-347-6245
Contact: Wendy Walker
Publishes "Job Exchange" in monthly newsletter for both employers and job seekers.

District of Columbia Bar
1707 L St. N.W., 6th floor
Washington, DC 20036
202-331-3883
Contact: Yvonne Inniss

96

Professional association for attorneys. Informal file of job announcements kept in office.

District of Columbia Hospital Association
1250 I St. N.W., Suite 700
Washington, DC 20005
202-682-1581
Contact: Joan Lewis
Association for health care professionals. Publishes *Directions*, newsletter for members.

District of Columbia Institute of CPA's
1666 K St. N.W., Suite 907
Washington, DC 20006
202-659-9183
Contact: May Downs
Association for professional accountants. Newsletter has small classified section.

District of Columbia Life Underwriters Association
1922 F St. N.W.
Washington, DC 20006
202-463-6100
Contact: Jeff Hamblem, Membership Director
Association for underwriters. Publishes bi-monthly newsletter for members. Meetings held six times a year.

District of Columbia Nurses' Association
5100 Wisconsin Ave.N.W., Suite 306
Washington, DC 20016
202-244-2705
Publishes *Capital Nurse*, which includes job openings. Annual meetings.

Fairfax Bar Association
4110 Chain Bridge Road, Suite 303
Fairfax, VA 22030
703-246-2740
Contact: Amy Ford
Association for attorneys. Monthly newsletter. Frequent social events.

Federal Bar Association
1815 H St. N.W., Suite 408
Washington, DC 20006
202-638-0252
Contact: Sam Friedman
Lawyers "Job Bulletin Board" has both employers and job seekers listed. Local chapters have regular meetings.

Federal Communications Bar Association
P.O. Box 34434
Bethesda, MD 20817
301-299-7299
Contact: Timothy Sabin, Executive Director
Association for attorneys and technicians who practice before FCC. Also has non-attorney members. Monthly newsletter, luncheons, and educational programs.

Federal Energy Bar Association
1900 M St. N.W., Suite 620
Washington, DC 20036

How to Get a Job

202-223-5625
Contact: Lorna Wilson
Association for energy practitioners. Two meetings yearly. Other meetings held on special topics throughout year.

Funeral Directors Association of Washington
2222 Wisconsin Ave. N.W.
Washington, DC 20007
202-333-6680
Monthly meetings.

Greater Washington Food Wholesalers Association
1008 Pennsylvania Ave. S.E.
Washington, DC 20003
202-544-2200
Contact: Paul Pascal
Monthly meetings.

Greater Washington Society of Association Executives
1426 21st St. N.W., Suite 200
Washington, DC 20036
202-429-9370
Contact: Laurie Kailo
Association for managers of professional associations. Career counseling for fee. Reference information on area associations. Position openings list subscription available. Monthly brown bag lunches.

Hotel Association of Washington
1201 New York Ave. N.W., Suite 601
Washington, DC 20005
202-289-3141
Contact: Robin Floyd
Professional association for general managers of hotels. Monthly meetings except July and August. Variety of social events.
Employment chairperson sends out job announcements to members.

Meetings are for meeting people

Laid off during a real estate slump, one enterprising 42-year-old escrow officer decided she would keep her finances flourishing by doing something she enjoyed—gardening. After a few phone calls to friends and former business associates, her newly formed Landscape Redecorating Service was in full bloom.

At the same time, she attended every possible escrow association meeting, dinner, and other professional event. "I set a goal," she recalls, "to contact at least three escrow company owners at each meeting, to let them know I was looking and available. Then I'd drop them a note to give them my phone number in case they wanted to get in touch right away."

About four months after her first dinner meeting, an officer from one of the larger title companies called her for an interview. "He couldn't get me working on that desk fast enough," she remembers. "The $15 I'd spent on that ticket was the best investment I ever made." ◼

Medical Society of the District of Columbia
1707 L St. N.W., Suite 400
Washington, DC 20036
202-466-1800
Association for physicians. Monthly newsletter includes classifieds. Annual meetings. Committee meetings monthly.

Montgomery County Association of Realtors
1355 Piccard Drive
Rockville, MD 20850
301-590-2000
Contact: Colleen Medd
Association of real estate professionals. Monthly newsletter. Monthly committee meetings. Variety of events.

Montgomery County Medical Society
15855 S. Crabbs Branch Way
Rockville, MD 20855
301-921-4300
Contact: Claire Sherwin
Professional society for physicians. Office will accept applications for office support services and refer them to doctors. Topical magazine with classifieds, ten times yearly. Seven general membership meetings, variety of committee meetings yearly.

Mortgage Bankers Association of Metropolitan Washington
P.O. Box 22050
Alexandria, VA 22304
703-461-9000
Association for mortgage bankers. Eight meetings yearly. Committees. Variety of social events.

National Association of Women Business Owners. Capital Area Chapter
1377 K St. N.W., Suite 153
Washington, DC 20005
301-608-3490
Hosts monthly small business breakfasts and other events.

National Bar Association
1225 11th St. N.W.
Washington, DC 20001
202-842-3900
Contact: Iris Edgecomb
Group of minority attorneys. Informal employment book kept in office.

National Capital Area Paralegal Association
Box 19124
Washington, DC 20036
202-659-0243
Extensive services for members: job bank, job-hunting handbook, list of Washington area employers of paralegals. Annual job-hunting workshop.

National Press Club
529 14th St. N.W., 13th floor

How to Get a Job

Washington, DC 20045
202-662-7500
Contact: Julia Schoo
Private club for professional journalists. "Weekly Record" has job listings.
Bulletin board of resumes and jobs.

Northern Virginia Association of Realtors
8411 Arlington Blvd.
Fairfax, VA 22031
703-207-3200
Contact: Lewis Zietz
Association of real estate professionals. Monthly magazine. Annual meeting.
Committee meetings throughout year.

Northern Virginia Building Industry Association
12600 Fair Lakes Circle, Suite 260
Fairfax, VA 22033
703-968-7352
Contact: Heidi Gray
Association for builders and sub-contractors. Regional and chapter meetings
several times yearly.

Printing Industry of Metropolitan Washington
7 West Tower
1333 H St. N.W.
Washington, DC 20005
202-682-3001
Contact: Carol Cornelius
Association for professionals in printing-related fields.

Public Relations Society of America. National Capitol Chapter
11130 Main St.
Fairfax, VA 22030
703-691-9212
Association for public relations professionals from entry level to senior positions.
Contact office for employment person's name. Does maintain job referral service.
Call hotline: 703-385-2949.

Purchasing Management Association of Washington
1350 New York Ave. N.W., Suite 615
Washington, DC 20005
202-393-1780
Contact: Linda Lauritzen
Association for managers in purchasing positions. Maintains resume bank.

Restaurant Association of Metropolitan Washington
7926 Jones Branch Drive, Suite 530
McLean, VA 22102
703-356-1315
Contact: Gus Ladas
Association for professionals in restaurant industry. Monthly magazine. Job
openings available on tape: 703-356-2709. Monthly seminars for networking.

Suburban Maryland Building Industry Association
1400 Mercantile Lane, Suite 250
Landover, MD 20785
301-925-9490

Travel Industry Association of America
1133 21st St. N.W., Suite 800
Washington, DC 20036
202-293-1433
Contact: Judith Olagues, Membership and Development
Diverse association of professionals including hotels, airlines, attractions, tour companies, chambers of commerce, visitors and convention bureaus. Monthly newsletter with industry trends, staff changes, association business. Annual meetings and marketplace.

Trial Lawyers Association of Metropolitan Washington
1818 N St. N.W.
Washington, DC 20036
202-659-3532
Contact: Mary Gizzo
Organization for attorneys, paralegals, law clerks, and law students. Quarterly newsletter includes classifieds. Informal job referrals through office. Monthly dinner meetings.

Washington DC Association of Realtors
777 14th St. N.W., Suite 200
Washington, DC 20005
202-628-4494
Contact: Amy Baxter
Group of area real estate professionals. Monthly newsletter and monthly meetings and educational/training programs.

Washington Independent Writers
733 15th St. N.W., Suite 220
Washington, DC 20005
202-347-4973
Maintains job line and job listings for members. Call 202-347-4067.

Washington Press Club Foundation
1061 National Press Building
Washington, DC 20045
202-393-0613

Washington Psychiatric Society
1400 K St. N.W., Suite 202
Washington, DC 20005
202-682-6270
Contact: Rosemary Polley
Society for psychiatrists. Newsletter lists job openings and real estate for rent. Monthly council, continuing education, and committee meetings.

Washington Retail Liquor Dealers Association
5010 Wisconsin Ave. N.W.
Washington, DC 20016
202-362-2511
Contact: Jean Goldberg
Association for Class A dealers only. Monthly newsletter and meetings. Informal job referrals through office.

Washington Teachers Union
1030 15th St. N.W., Suite 865
Washington, DC 20005
202-682-2472

How to Get a Job

Contact: Elaina Dobsen
Union for educators. Resume referral, job listings, and job hotline.

White House Correspondents Association
1067 National Press Building
Washington, DC 20045
202-737-2934
Contact: Penny Dixon: 301-871-6200
Group for journalists assigned to White House or who work with organizations covering White House news. Annual dinner meeting held in May.

Women Executives in State Government
122 C St. N.W., Suite 840
Washington, DC 20001-2109
202-628-9374
Contact: Jane Ribadeneyra
Association for women managers. Bi-monthly newsletter. Job bank. Annual meeting. Quarterly board and regional meetings.

Women in Government Relations
1325 Massachusetts Ave. N.W., Suite 510
Washington, DC 20005-4131
202-347-5432
Professional association for professionals in government. Bi-monthly newsletter. Monthly mailings to members for events. Job bank for members. Annual meeting.

Women's Bar Association of the District of Columbia
1819 H St. N.W., Suite 1250
Washington, DC 20006
202-785-1540
Contact: Linne Frey
Association for women attorneys or law students working for government or private firms. Newsletter nine times a year. Members may use "Job Notebooks" with recent listings kept in office.

Turning volunteer work into a job

After spending many years working as a volunteer for various organizations, Marion Simon's daughters advised her to "stop giving it away." She decided to look for paid employment. But because she had never held a paid job, Marion was not sure how to begin her job search.

"As a woman in my middle years, I wondered where in the world I would go," says Marion. "I had a good education and a great deal of volunteer experience. I had planned and orchestrated large benefits and had done an inordinate amount of fund raising over the years. I also had done community work in the inner city.

"Then I happened to mention my job search to the president of a hospital where I had done a great deal of volunteer work," says Marion. "He asked me not to take a job until I had talked to him. Later, he hired me as his special assistant, with the charge to 'humanize the hospital.' Over a period of time, I developed a patient representative department.

"When I began the job 11 years ago, I was a one-person operation. As time went on, I added staff. I currently supervise a staff of 9, plus about 25 volunteers. The job of patient representative is now a full-fledged profession. Many women in the field began as volunteers. They knew a lot about the hospital where they were volunteering and thus made the transition into a paid position easily."

We asked Marion what advice she has for volunteers who want to move into the paid work force. "Go to the career counseling departments of some of the small colleges. Ask them to review your background and tell you what kinds of jobs you may be qualified for. If they suggest that you need additional training, get it. But before you go back to school, investigate the kinds of jobs available in your chosen field. Think about how you can use your volunteer experience in a paid position. Take what you've done and build from it."

In job search lingo, Marion analyzed her volunteer work and identified her *functional* skills. If you can sell Girl Scout cookies, you can sell other products and services. If you coordinated fund raising for the church building fund, you can coordinate projects for a salary. You just have to convince the hiring authority that your skills are transferrable. ■

Using Professional Employment Services

Finding a good job is a hard job. So your first impulse may be to turn that job over to professional employment services. After all, don't the pros have all the job listings? Unfortunately, they don't.

Yes, it's smart to use every available resource to generate leads and interviews. But professional employment services vary from agencies that specialize in temporary clerical help to executive recruiters who deal primarily with top-management types. Employment agencies, career consultants, and executive recruitment firms differ greatly in the kinds of services they offer and in how—and by whom—they get paid. You can save yourself a lot of time, effort, and possibly money if you're familiar with the different kinds of professional employment services. One handbook that might prove useful is the *National Directory of Certified Counselors* (National Board for Certified Counselors, 3 D Harris Way, Greensboro,NC 27403).

Employment Agencies

Employment agencies act as intermediaries in the job market between buyers (companies with jobs open) and sellers (people who want jobs). Agencies are paid for placing people. The fee may be paid by the company, but in some cases it is paid by the worker. Agencies that specialize in restaurant and domestic help, for example, often charge the worker a fee. Usually the placement fee amounts to a certain percentage of the worker's annual salary.

Employment agencies seldom place a candidate in a job that pays more than $30,000 a year. Most employment agencies concentrate on support jobs. Supervisory openings may be listed, too, but employment agencies usually don't handle middle or upper-management positions. In the computer field, for example, computer operators, programmers, and perhaps systems analysts could find work through an agency. But directors of data processing or MIS (management information systems) would go to an executive search firm or would job hunt on their own.

A company that's looking for a secretary gains certain advantages by going to a reputable agency. It doesn't have to advertise or screen the hundreds of resumes that would probably pour in from even a small want ad in the Sunday *Washington Post*. A good employment agency will send over only qualified applicants for interviews. Referrals are made quickly, and there is no cost to the company until it hires the secretary. For many companies, it's worth it to pay an agency fee to avoid the hassle of prescreening dozens, if not hundreds, of applicants.

The advantage to the agency of a successful placement (besides the fee) is repeat business. After two or three referrals work out well, an employment agency can generally count on receiving future listings of company vacancies.

The value to the job seeker of using an employment agency depends on a number of factors, including the quality of the agency, the kind of work you're looking for, how much experience you have, and how broad your network of personal and business contacts is.

In general, an agency's loyalty will be to its source of income. Agencies are more interested in finding you a job than in finding you job satisfaction. Agencies are likely to pressure you to accept a job you don't really want, just so they can collect their fee. With few exceptions, an agency probably can't do much more for you than you could do for yourself in an imaginative and energetic job search. (Of course, there's the rub—conducting an imaginative and energetic job search.) If a company has to pay a fee to hire you, you're at a disadvantage compared with applicants who are "free." Giving an employment agency your resume could be a serious mistake if you're trying to conduct a confidential job search.

On the other hand, a good agency can help its candidates develop a strategy and prepare for employment interviews. This training can be most valuable to people who are inexperienced in job-hunting techniques. (Of course, you can probably learn job-search strategy and skills more inexpensively by reading the books in our bibliography or attending an adult education class at one of the local colleges.) Agency pros should know the market, screen well, and provide sound advice. A secretary who tries to investigate the Washington market on his or her own will very likely take longer to get the "right" job than someone who uses a quality agency.

How to Get a Job

Dealing with employment agencies

"After deciding to use an employment agency," according to one career counselor, "the job hunter needs to have a clear idea of what he or she is looking for. A reputable agency will not want to antagonize either their clients (the employers) or the prospective employee. Occasionally, however, an employee is scheduled for an inappropriate interview, resulting in some embarrassment for both the interviewer and the interviewee. Sometimes this is the agency's fault, but many times the person looking for a job does not express his or her interests clearly."

Some advice for people using employment agencies: make sure that the agency knows exactly what you are looking for in your career, such as job description, location, and salary. Also, listen carefully to job and company descriptions when deciding on who to interview with. The job hunter should be able to sift out interviews that sound inappropriate and to accept those that match their demands. ■

Historically, certain employment agencies engage in practices that can only be called questionable at best, and the field as a whole is trying to polish up a somewhat tarnished image. There are, of course, a number of reputable, highly professional employment agencies. But as in any profession, there are also crooks. It's still a practice in some agencies to advertise non-existent openings to attract applicants for other, less desirable positions.

So much for the pros and cons of employment agencies. If you decide to try one, be sure it's a reputable firm. Ask people in your field to recommend a quality agency, and consult the Better Business Bureau and other resources listed in Chapter 2 to see if there have been any complaints about the agency you're considering. Most important, *be sure to read the contract thoroughly, including all the fine print, before you sign it.* If you have any questions, or if there's something you don't understand, don't be afraid to ask. It's your right. Make sure you know who is responsible for paying the fee and what the fee is. Remember that *in some cases, an agency's application form is also the contract.*

When you go to an employment agency, treat it the same way you'd treat a job interview. Don't misrepresent yourself, but try to make them think of you as highly marketable. If the agency sees you as very difficult to place, they won't consider you a cost-effective client. If you've paid up-front money, too bad. Even if you haven't, you may have just wasted time that could be better spent conducting your own effective job search.

Here, then, is a selective listing of Washington area employment agencies, including their areas of specialty.

EMPLOYMENT AGENCIES

ADIA Personnel Services
1140 19th St. N.W., Plaza Level
Washington, DC 20006
202-857-0800
Office support staff.

Accountants on Call
8000 Towers Crescent Dr.
Vienna, VA 22182
703-525-6100
Variety of accounting positions.

Celebrity Medical Personnel
1110 Fidler Lane, Suite 900
Silver Spring, MD 20752
301-587-1808
Receptionists, technicians, physician assistants, physicians, and medical consultants.

Arthur Diamond
1140 Connecticut Ave. N.W., Suite 508
Washington, DC 20036
202-466-4200
Real estate, associations, office support.

Doyle Personnel
1800 K St. N.W., Suite 622
Washington, DC 20006
202-296-2885
General, secretarial.

Executive Recruiters
7315 Wisconsin Ave., Suite 333 East
Bethesda, MD 20814
301-469-3100
Retail, technical.

Georgetown Employment Service
1660 L St. N.W., Suite 301
Washington, DC 20036
202-333-7797
Legal, general.

Marsha Levey
1015 18th St. N.W., Suite 700
Washington, DC 20036
202-659-0877
Legal support and law firm management staff.

NRI Group
1899 L St. N.W., Suite 301
Washington, DC 20036
202-466-3370
Secretarial.

How to Get a Job

Prince George's Employment Service
7050 Chesapeake Rd., Suite 201
Hyattsville, MD
301-731-9600
Full service agency. Professional and support staff. Includes aviation.

A. Fran Shields Associates
1800 Diagonal Road, Suite 600
Alexandria, VA 22314
703-684-9090
Office staff

Snelling Personnel
1612 K St. N.W., Suite 308
Washington, DC 20006
202-223-3540
General, legal

TempWorld
1050 17 St. N.W., Suite 750
Washington, DC 20036
202-466-7884
General, paralegal.

Career Consultants

If you open the employment section of the Sunday *Washington Post* or the *Wall Street Journal,* you'll see several ads for career consultants (also known as career counselors or private outplacement consultants). The ads are generally directed to "executives" earning yearly salaries of anywhere between $20,000 and $300,000. Some ads suggest that the consultants have access to jobs that are not listed elsewhere. Others claim, "We do all the work." Most have branch offices throughout the country.

Career consultants vary greatly in the kind and quality of services they provide. Some may offer a single service, such as vocational testing or preparing resumes. Others coach every aspect of the job search and stay with you until you accept an offer. The fees vary just as broadly and range from $100 to several thousand dollars. *You,* not your potential employer, pay the fee.

There are many reputable consulting firms in Washington. But, as is true of employment agencies, some career consultants have been unethical.

A qualified career consultant can be a real asset to your job search. But *no consultant can get you a job.* Only you can do that. You are the one who will participate in the interview, and you are the one who must convince an employer to hire you. A consultant can help you focus on an objective, develop a resume, research the job market, decide on a strategy, and/or train you in interviewing techniques. But you can't send a consultant to interview in your place. It just doesn't work that way.

Don't retain a career consultant if you think that the fee will buy you a job. The only reason you should consider a consultant is that you've exhausted all the other resources we've suggested here and still feel you need expert and personalized help with one or more aspects of the job search. The key to choosing a career consultant is knowing what you need and verifying that the consultant can provide it.

Check references. A reputable firm will gladly provide them. Check the Better Business Bureau and other resources listed in this book. Has anyone lodged a complaint against the firm you're considering? Before you sign anything, ask to meet the consultant who will actually provide the services you want. What are his or her credentials? How long has the consultant been practicing? Who are the firm's corporate clients?

Read the contract carefully before you sign it. Does the contract put the consultant's promises in writing? Has the consultant told you about providing services that are not specified in the contract? What does the firm promise? What do you have to promise? Are all fees and costs spelled out? What provisions are made for refunds? For how long a time can you use the firm's or consultant's services?

Be sure to do some comparison shopping before you select a consultant. A list of Washington area firms you might want to investigate is given in Chapter 2.

Executive Search Firms

An executive search firm is one that is paid by a company to locate a person with specific qualifications that meet a precisely defined employment need. Most reputable executive search firms belong to an organization called the Association of Executive Recruiting Consultants (AERC). The association publishes a code of ethics for its membership.

A search firm never works on a contingency basis. Only employment agencies do that. The usual fee for a search assignment is 30 percent of the first year's salary of the person to be hired, plus out-of-pocket expenses, which are billed on a monthly basis. During hard times, most companies forgo retaining search firms because it's so expensive.

It's difficult to get an appointment to see a search specialist. Executive search consultants have only their time to sell. If a specialist spends time with you, he or she can't bill that time to a client. If you can use your personal contacts to meet a search professional, however, by all means do so. Executive specialists know the market and can be very helpful in providing advice and leads.

Search firms receive dozens of unsolicited resumes every day. They seldom acknowledge receipt. They keep only a few for future search needs or business development. They really can't afford to file and store them all. Sending your resume to every search firm in Washington will be useful only if one firm coincidentally has a search assignment to find someone with *exactly* your background and qualifications. It's a long shot, similar to answering blind want ads.

If you're middle or upper management

"Almost any busy business professional can benefit from a management search firm," says Joe MacWiggins, Corporate Vice-President for New Business Development with MSI International, a multi-national personnel services company.

"Corporate human resource departments are faced with growing responsibilities in taking care of the people already employed by their companies. Many have little time left over to recruit and hire professionals," says

MacWiggins. "A management search firm can go straight to the company's top decision makers, the people who have the final say in who gets the job. It's a very time-efficient method."

The management search divisions of MSI International specialize in locating experienced middle and upper managers for Fortune 1,000 companies and other growing businesses.

"A management search firm is not for someone who is changing careers," MacWiggins emphasizes. "Unlike employment agencies, where the emphasis is on 'what do you *want* to do?' we look for people with established skills in a given field.

"Males, females, and minorities are equally valuable to the industry. We look for growth-oriented people who are ready to move up, who have good people skills and good communications skills, as well as proven accomplishments and high-level references. If you've got all that going for you," he concludes, "then we'll be able to assist you in making a job change in a relatively short period of time." ■

The following is a selected list of executive search firms in the Washington area.

EXECUTIVE SEARCH FIRMS

Robert Celery Associates
1155 Connecticut Ave. N.W., Suite 500
Washington, DC 20036
202-331-0090

Heidrick & Struggles
2000 K St. N.W., Suite 610
Washington, DC 20006
202-466-5410
All fields. Senior vice-president and vice-presidents.

Interface Group/Boyden Ltd.
1025 Thomas Jefferson St. N.W., Suite 410E
Washington, DC 20007
202-342-7200
Senior-level management of various fields.

JDG Associates
1700 Research Blvd., Suite 103
Rockville, MD 20850
301-340-2210
High-tech firms, computer scientists, engineers, finance, and accounting.

Korn / Ferry International
900 19th St. N.W., Suite 200
Washington, DC 20006
202-822-9444
Executives at $75k, 10-15 years experience.

Management Recruiters
1660 L St. N.W. Suite 606
Washington, DC 20036
202-785-3000
Environmental and civil engineering, insurance, marketing.

Susan C. Miller Associates
1090 Vermont Ave. N.W., Suite 800
Washington, DC 20005
202-408-6880
Mostly law field.

Russell Reynolds Associates
1850 K St. N.W., Suite 365
Washington, DC 20006
202-628-2150
All fields.

Savoy Partners, Ltd.
1899 L St. N.W., Suite 1001
Washington, DC 20036
202-887-0666
All fields. Senior executives, $90k and up.

Source EDP
1667 K St. N.W., Suite 950
Washington, DC 20006
202-293-9255
Finance, accounting.

Also:
7918 Jones Branch Rd., Suite 540
McLean, VA 22102
703-790-5610
Computer, engineering.

Help for vets

The work of the Vietnam Veterans of America in establishing memorials is well known. But many people do not realize that this group has also established over 100 outreach centers nationwide. The main objective of these centers is to help men and women veterans adjust to civilian life.

The centers offer a variety of services. Primarily, they offer psychological counseling to veterans experiencing readjustment challenges. They solicit job listings from both the public and private sectors and help with resumes and SF 171 forms. Veterans who need additional help are referred to appropriate counseling groups, health agencies, and other organizations.

The **Veterans Outreach Center**, 801 Pennsylvania Ave. S.E., Washington, DC, 202-745-8400, is open weekdays, 8:30-4:30, and appointments are suggested but not necessary. ■

How To Succeed In an Interview

If you've read straight through this book, you already know that networking (see Chapter 5) is one of the most important and useful job-hunting techniques around. Networking is nothing more or less than using personal contacts to research the job market and to generate both exploratory and formal job interviews.

Networking and interviewing go hand in hand; all the contacts in the world won't do you any good if you don't handle yourself well in an interview. No two interviews are ever identical, except that you always have the same goal in mind: to convince the person to whom you're talking that he or she should help you find a job or hire you personally. An interview is also an exchange of information. But you should never treat it as you would a casual conversation, even if the "interviewer" is an old friend.

Preparing for the Interview: The 5-Minute Resume

Whether you're talking to the housewife next door about her brother-in-law who knows someone you want to meet, or going through a final, formal interview with a multi-national corporation, you are essentially making a sales presentation—in this case, selling yourself. Your goal is to convince the interviewer that you have the ability, experience, personality, maturity, and other characteristics required to do a good job and to enlist the interviewer's help in getting you that job.

In an informal interview you'll be talking first to friends and acquaintances. Most of the people you'll be talking to will *want* to help you. But they need to know who you are, what you've done, what you want to do, and, most important, how they can help you.

To prepare for any interview, first perfect what we like to call the five-minute resume. Start by giving a rough description, not too detailed, of what you're doing now (or did on your last job) so that when you're telling your story the listener isn't distracted by wondering how it's going to end.

Then go all the way back to the beginning—not of your career but of your life. Talk about where you were born, where you grew up, what your folks did, whether or not they're still living, what your brothers and sisters do, and so on. Then trace your educational background briefly, and, finally, outline your work history from your first job to your latest.

"What!" say many of our clients. "Drag my PARENTS into this? Talk about my crazy BROTHER and the neighborhood where we grew up?"

Yes, indeed. You want to draw the listener into your story, to make him or her interested enough in you to work for you in your search. You want the interviewer to know not only who you are and what you have achieved but also what you are capable of. You also want to establish things in common with the listener. The more you have in common, the harder your listener will work for you. Co-author Tom Camden, we are not ashamed to admit, is a master of the five-minute resume. Here's how he would begin a presentation to someone like the neighbor down the street:

"Would it be all right with you if I gave you a broad-brush review of my background? Let you know what I've done, what I'd like to do? That'll give us some time to talk about how I should go about this job search. Maybe I could pick your brain a little about how you can help me. OK?

"Currently, I'm president of Camden Associates, a national career outplacement firm.

"Originally, I'm from the southwest side of Chicago. I'm 54 years old, married, with five grown children.

"My father was a security guard at IIT Research Institute; my mother is retired. She used to work for Walgreens—made aspirins, vitamins, and pills. I'm the oldest of four children. My brother John does the traffic 'copter reports for a Chicago radio station. My sister Connie is a consultant for an industrial relations firm.

"I went to parochial schools. When I was 14, I left home and went into a monastery. I stayed there until I was 19. Then I went to Loyola University, studied psychology, got my degree in '59. I was also commissioned in the infantry.

"I started my graduate work in Gestalt psychology. In 1960 Kennedy called up troops for the Berlin crisis. That included me, so I spent a year on active duty. Following that, I came back and continued my graduate work in industrial relations..."

Tom took exactly a minute and a half to make this part of his presentation, and he's already given his neighbor several areas in which they may have something in common. He's volunteered enough information not only to get the neighbor interested in his story but to let the neighbor form judgments about him.

People don't like to play God, says Tom. Yet it's a fact of life that we constantly form judgments about each other. In an interview—even an exploratory, informal one—you may as well provide enough information to be judged on who you *are* and not on what someone has to guess about your background. What does it mean to be the oldest of four kids? What can you deduce from Tom's middle-class background?

The typical personnel professional will tell you that the number of brothers and sisters you have has nothing to do with getting a job. Technically, that's true. The law says that an employer can't ask you how old you are, your marital status, and similar questions. Yet anyone who's considering hiring you will want to know those things about you.

The typical applicant begins a presentation with something like, "I graduated from school in June, nineteen-whatever, and went to work for so-and-so." Our task in this book is to teach you how *not* to be typical. Our experience has convinced us that the way to get a job offer is to be *different* from the rest of the applicants. You shouldn't eliminate the first 20 years of your life when someone asks you about your background! That's the period that shaped your basic values and personality.

Neither should you spend *too* much time on your personal history. A minute or two is just about right. That gives you from three to eight minutes to narrate your work history. Most exploratory interviews, and many initial employment interviews, are limited to half an hour. If you can give an oral resume in five to ten minutes, you have roughly twenty minutes left to find out what *you* want to know (more on that shortly).

The five-minute resume revisited

Psychologist and career expert Gayle Roberts has her own slant on the five-minute resume. She believes that "while nothing works every time, you should try to emphasize those aspects of your personal history that have a bearing on your current qualifications for the job your seeking.

"For example, I am one of those rare creatures who always liked school. I got along fine with the teachers. I even liked studying and taking tests. I liked to learn, and I still do. That's part of why I choose to work in an academic setting. I think it's helpful to mention my long history as a book worm any time I'm applying for a position that requires research, writing, or critical thinking skills. I don't think I'd mention it if I were going for a sales position.

"I personally wouldn't recommend saying too much about your past unless you can connect it to the present in a way that makes you look like a better job candidate. Everybody has a number of revealing personal anecdotes. The trick is to pick the right ones." ■

A word about your work history. If you've done the exercises in Chapter 2, or written your own resume, you ought to be able to rattle off every job you've had, from the first to the latest, pretty easily. In the oral resume you want especially to *emphasize your successes and accomplishments* in each job. This will take some practice. We are not accustomed to talking about ourselves positively. From childhood we're conditioned that it's not nice to brag. Well, we are here to tell you that if you *don't* do it in the interview, you *won't* get the offer.

If you're a recent college graduate and don't yet have an impressive employment history, you can emphasize your successes and accomplishments in class and extracurricular activities. Also, you want to particularly emphasize achievements in areas pertinent to the field you hope to enter. You want to highlight those skills that qualify you to fill the position you're seeking. Analyze yourself in terms of your functional skills, such as administrative, writing, analytical. Then talk about those functional skills that match the duties of the job you're going for.

We repeat: *the interview is a sales presentation.* It's the heart of your job search, your effort to market yourself. In an exploratory interview, the listener will be asking, "Should I help this person?" In a formal interview, the employer will be asking, "Should I hire this person?" In either case, the answer will be "yes" only if you make a successful presentation, if you convince the interviewer that you're worth the effort.

So, the first step in preparing for any interview, formal or informal, is to *practice your five-minute resume.* Go through it out loud enough times so that you're comfortable delivering it. Then work with a tape recorder and critique yourself. Try it out on a couple of friends.

When you're preparing for a formal employment interview, *do your homework* on the company. This advice is merely common sense. But it's surprising how many candidates will ask an interviewer, "What does this company do?" Don't be one of them. Before you go in for an employment interview, find out everything you can about the company—its history, organization, products and services, and growth expectations. Get hold of the company's annual report, catalogs, and brochures. Consult your networking contacts, and use the resources suggested in Chapter 4.

How to stand out in a crowd

A senior employment relations representative for one of the nation's largest employers headquartered in the Washington area offers the following tip for standing out in a crowd of interviewees.

"Almost everybody will show up well dressed, with a neatly-typed resume and as professional a manner as he or she can muster. You have to show an employer that you're someone special. Try bringing a *backup book* with you to every interview, one that contains examples of your work. If you're a secretary, bring some samples of your snazziest typing. If you're a research chemist, perhaps you've published something that you can show or maybe articles have appeared about your work or you can bring along a product that utilizes your research. It all depends on what you do for a living, of course, but use your imagination." ■

Steps to a Successful Interview

Before the Interview

■ Self-assessment: identify strengths, goals, skills, etc.
■ Research the company.
■ Rehearse what you plan to say. Practice answers to common questions.
■ Prepare questions to ask employer.

During the Interview

■ Make sure you arrive a few minutes early.
■ Greet the interviewer by his/her last name; offer a firm handshake and a warm smile.
■ Be aware of non-verbal communication. Wait to sit until you are offered a chair. Sit up straight, look alert, speak clearly and forcefully but stay relaxed. Make good eye contact, avoid nervous mannerisms, and try to be a good listener as well as a good talker. Smile.
■ Follow the interviewer's lead, but try to get the interviewer to describe the position and duties to you fairly early in the interview so that you can then relate your background and skills in context.
■ Be specific, concrete, and detailed in your answers. The more information you volunteer, the better the employer gets to know you.
■ Offer examples of your work that document your best qualities.
■ Answer questions as truthfully and as frankly as you can. Do not appear to be "glossing over" anything. On the other hand, stick to the point and do not over-answer questions. The interviewer may steer the interview into ticklish political or social questions. Answer honestly, trying not to say more than is necessary.

Closing the Interview

■ Don't be discouraged if no definite offer is made or specific salary is discussed.
■ If you get the impression that the interview is not going well and that you have already been rejected, do not let your discouragement show. Once in a while, an interviewer who is genuinely interested in you may seem to discourage you to test your reaction.
■ A typical interviewer comment toward the close of an interview is to ask if you have any questions. Prepare several questions ahead of time, and ask those that weren't covered during the interview.

How to Get a Job

■ At the conclusion of your interview, ask when a hiring decision will be made. Also, thank your interviewer for his or her time and express your interest in the position.

After the Interview

■ Take notes on what you feel you could improve upon for your next interview.

■ If you are interested in the position, type a brief thank-you letter to the interviewer, indicating your interest.

■ If offered the position, one to two weeks is a reasonable amount of time to make a decision. All employment offers deserve a written reply whether or not you accept them.

How to dress

A young friend of ours who wanted to break into investment banking finally landed her first big interview with Charles Schwab & Co. It was fairly easy for her to do her homework on a company of that size. Two days before the interview, however, it suddenly dawned on her that she had no idea how to dress. How did she solve her problem?

"It was pretty easy, actually, and fun, too," says Susan. "All I did was go and hang around outside the office for 15 minutes at lunchtime to see what everyone else was wearing."

However, we recommend that even if the office attire is casual, one should still dress professionally. One career counselor recommends that one should "always dress one step above the attire of those in the office where you are interviewing." ■

What Interviewers are Looking For

■ **General Personality**: Ambition, poise, sincerity, trustworthiness, articulateness, analytical ability, initiative, interest in the organization. (General intelligence is assumed.) Different organizations look for different kinds of people—personalities, style, appearance, abilities, and technical skills. Always check the job specifications. Don't waste time talking about a job you can't do or for which you don't have the minimum qualifications.

■ **Personal Appearance**: A neat, attractive appearance makes a good impression and demonstrates professionalism.

■ **Work Experience**: Again, this varies from job to job, so check job specifications. If you've had work experience, be able to articulate the importance of what you did in terms of the job for which you are interviewing and in terms of your own growth or learning. Even if the work experience is unrelated to your field, employers look upon knowledge of the work environment as an asset.

■ **Verbal Communication Skills**: The ability to express yourself articulately is very important to most interviewers. This includes the ability to listen effectively, verbalize thoughts clearly, and express yourself confidently.

■ **Skills:** The interviewer will evaluate your skills for the job, such as organization, analysis, and research. It is important to emphasize the skills which you feel the employer is seeking and to give specific examples of how you developed them. This is the main reason why it is important to engage in self-assessment prior to the interview.

■ **Goals/Motivation:** Employers will assess your ability to articulate your short-term and long-term goals. You should seem ambitious, yet realistic about the training and qualifications needed to advance. You should demonstrate interest in the functional area or industry and a desire to succeed and work hard.

■ **Knowledge of the Interviewer's Organization and Industry:** At a minimum, you really are expected to have done some homework on the organization. Don't waste interview time asking questions you could have found answers for in printed material. Know the firm's position and character relative to others in the same industry. General awareness of media coverage of an organization and its industry is usually expected.

Office decor reveals personality

"You can tell a lot about a company by carefully scrutinizing the office environment during a job interview," says Evan Sullivan. He made a careful study of the decor, layout, and orderliness of several offices the last time he went job hunting.

"Each office has a distinct personality," he says. During his survey he found that a boss's office with soft, comfortable furniture often indicated that the supervisor was easy-going—the type who didn't mind if people lingered to chat. Firmer, more utilitarian chairs could be a tip-off that the person in charge was a no-nonsense type.

Evan used the office decor to determine how he would handle himself in an interview. In an office lined with sports trophies, he inevitably mentioned his football experience. When he noticed during one interview that a manager had a cluttered desk and briefcase, he stressed his organizational skills.

"Use your powers of observation and gut feelings to your advantage in an interview," Sullivan says. We agree wholeheartedly. ■

Handling the Interview

In an exploratory, or informal, interview most of the people you'll talk with will want to help you. But they need to know how. After you've outlined your personal and work history, ask your contact how he or she thinks your experience fits into today's market. What companies should you visit? Specifically, what people should you talk with?

When someone gives you advice or a recommendation to call someone else, do it! Few things can be more irritating than to provide free counsel to someone who then ignores it. If your contact suggests that you call Helen Smith, call her!

In a formal employment interview, there are several typical questions you can expect to encounter, though not necessarily in this order:

> Tell me about yourself. (This is your cue for the five-minute resume.)
>
> Why do you want to change jobs?
>
> What kind of job are you looking for now?
>
> What are your long-range objectives?
>
> What are your salary requirements?
>
> When could you be available to start here?
>
> Tell me about your present organization.
>
> What kind of manager are you?
>
> How would you describe yourself?
>
> What are your strengths and weaknesses?

(In the course of his career, Tom Camden has posed this question to untold numbers of applicants. "They'll list two or three strengths," he says, "and then can't wait to tell me about their weaknesses." Don't be one of those people! Accentuate the positive. Remember, this is a competitive interview.)

> Describe your present boss.
>
> To whom can I talk about your performance?
>
> Are you open to relocation?
>
> How long have you been looking for a new job?
>
> Why are you interested in this company? (This is your golden opportunity to show the interviewer that you've done your homework on the organization.)

Practice your answers to these questions *before* you go in for the interview. It's probably best not to memorize a verbatim answer, but you should have a clear idea of how you'll respond to all the standard questions. Anticipate other questions you might be asked, and develop answers for them. In general, keep your responses positive. Never volunteer a negative about yourself, another company, or a former employer. Even if you hate your present boss, describe your areas of disagreement in a calm, professional manner. You are selling *yourself,* not downgrading others. It makes you appear whiny and petty if you simply complain about the tyrant you work for.

Show interest in the company you're interviewing. Be enthusiastic about the prospect of working for them. You can probably remember how demoralizing it was to be interviewed by someone who seemed disinterested, even bored by your presence. Well, interviewers have feelings too.

Even if you're not particularly interested in the company, always conduct the interview as if you were dead set on getting the job.

The interviewer will apply your responses to the questions he or she *really* wants answered:

Does the applicant have the ability to do the job?

Can he or she manage people?

How does he or she relate to people?

What kind of person is this? A leader? A follower?

What strengths does he or she have that we need?

Why the number of job changes so far?

Where is he or she weak?

How did the applicant contribute to present and past employers?

What are his or her ambitions? Are they realistic?

Is he or she too soft or too tough on subordinates?

What is this person's standard of values?

Does he or she have growth potential?

Is there a health problem anywhere?

What is the nature of the "chemistry" between us?

What will the department manager think of this applicant as opposed to the others?

Should this person get an offer?

The interview should not be a one-sided affair, however. Questions that you should ask the interviewer are equally important in this exchange of information. For example, you have to know about the job, the organization, and the people in your future employment situation. It's necessary to use your judgment to determine how and when to ask questions in an interview. But without the answers, it will be next to impossible for you to make a sound decision if you receive an offer. Some of the questions you want answered are:

What are the job's responsibilities?

What is the organization's recent history? Its current objectives? Its market position? Where are its other offices/branches located? What distribution systems does it use?

To whom will I report? What's his or her background?

What are the communication channels in the organization?

Why is the job available?

Where will this job lead?

What are the toughest problems I'll have to solve in order to be successful on this particular job?

How much autonomy will I have to get the job done?

How much supervision will I receive to get the job done?

What kind of resources are available for this position? (office support, budget, etc.)

What opportunities are there for training and professional development?

What about travel requirements?

Where is the job located?

Are there any housing, school, or community problems that will develop as a result of this job?

What is the salary range? (Do not raise the question of explicit salary at this point.)

What is the detailed benefit picture?

What is the company's relocation policy?

When will an offer decision be made?

What references will be required?

When would I have to start?

What is the personality of the organization?

Do the job and organization fit my plan for what I want to do now?

What's the next step?

During the interview, you should focus first on selling yourself. Next, try to find out as much as you can about the job and the organization. As for salary, remember that the company is looking for what you can do for them, not how they can help you. During a first interview all you really need to know is the salary range. Once the employer shows more interest in you or makes you an outright offer, you can negotiate salary and benefits.

Sow's ear to silk purse

We asked a very successful corporate executive how he would handle an interview in which he was asked to name his main weakness. "You have to turn tough questions like that one around to your advantage," he replied. "I think I'd tell the employer that my biggest problem is that I'm a workaholic." ■

Career guides

Some companies administer standardized tests to see if applicants are qualified for certain kinds of work, such as secretarial, data processing, and the like. Many of the libraries listed in Chapter 4 have an impressive number of workbooks to help you prepare for the most common tests. These include study guides for elevator operators, computer programmers, women in the armed forces, law and court stenographers, laboratory aides, supervisory engineers, even mortuary caretakers! Reviews for state board exams for nurses and certified public accountants are also available.

Following the Interview

Many job seekers experience a kind of euphoria after a good interview. Under the impression that a job offer is imminent, a candidate may discontinue the search. This is a serious mistake. The decision may take weeks, or may not be made at all. On the average, about six weeks elapse between the time a person makes initial contact with a company and receives a final answer. If you let up on the search, you will prolong it. Maintain a constant sense of urgency. Get on with the next interview. Your search isn't over until an offer is accepted and you actually begin the new job. Besides, the next organization you interview with might have an even better job.

Always follow up an interview with correspondence. The purpose of the letter is to supplement the sales presentation you made. Thank the interviewer for his or her time and hospitality. Express interest in the position (ask for the order). Then mention up to three additional points to sell yourself further. Or reiterate your primary selling point. Highlight how your specific experience or knowledge is directly applicable to the organization's immediate needs. If you forgot to mention something important in the interview, say it now. If possible, try to comment on something the interviewer said. Use that comment to show how your interests and skills perfectly match what they're looking for. Try to establish a date by which a decision will be made.

If you think you could benefit from professional counseling in interviewing skills, consider the resources suggested in Chapter 2. You might also find it helpful to refer to some of the following books:

BOOKS ABOUT INTERVIEWING

Allen, Jeffrey. *How to Turn an Interview Into a Job.* New York: Simon & Schuster, 1988.

Biegelein, J.I. *Make Your Job Interview a Success.* New York: Arco, 1987.

Bloch, Deborah. *How to Have a Winning Job Interview.* Lincolnwood, Illinois: VGM Career Horizons, 1992.

Danna, Jo. *Winning the Job Interview Game: Tips for the High-Tech Era.* Briarwood, NY: Palamino Press, 1986.

Fear, Richard. *The Evaluation Interview.* New York: McGraw-Hill, 1990.

French, Albert L. *How to Locate Jobs and Land Interviews.* Hawthorne, NJ: Career Press, 1991.

Fry, Ron. *101 Great Answers to the Toughest Interview Questions.* Hawthorne, NJ: Career Press, 1991.

Jackson, Tom. *Guerrilla Tactics in the New Job Market.* New York: Bantam Books, 1991.

Kohlmann, James D. *Make Them Choose You: The Executive Selection Process.* Englewood Cliffs, NJ: Prentice Hall, 1987.

Krannich, Caryl Rae, & Ronald L. *Interview for Success.* Manassas, VA: Impact Publications, 1992.

Marcus, John J. *The Complete Job Interview Handbook.* New York: Harper & Row, 1988.

Medley, H. Anthony. *Sweaty Palms: The Neglected Art of Being Interviewed.* Berkeley, CA: Ten Speed Press, 1991.

Stoodley, Martha. *Information Interviewing: What It Is and How To Use It In Your Career.* Garrett Park, MD: Garrett Park Press, 1990

Yate, Martin John. *Knock 'em Dead: With Great Answers to Tough Interview Questions.* Boston: Bob Adams, 1990.

How to get the most from your references

Don't give a prospective employer a list of your references until they ask for one. Always brief your references before you supply an interviewer with their names and numbers. Tell the references what company you're interviewing with and what the job is. Give them some background on the organization and the responsibilities you'll be asked to handle. Provide them with a copy of your resume to refresh their memory on what an outstanding candidate you are. Your references will then be in a position to help sell your abilities. Finally, don't abuse your references. If you give their names too often, they may lose enthusiasm for your cause. ■

What To Do If Money Gets Tight

Any job search takes time. One particularly pessimistic career counselor we know suggests you plan to spend about two weeks of search time for every thousand dollars you want to earn per year. (Pity the poor soul who wants to make $60,000!) A more optimistic estimate for a job search is around three months, provided the search is conducted full-time. Of course, the field you want to enter, your qualifications, and your income requirements all have a big influence on how long things will take. (Not to mention how well you follow good job-hunting advice!)

If you already have a full-time job, it will take you longer to find a new one. But at least you will be receiving a paycheck while you're looking. This chapter is intended for those who are unemployed and facing the prospect of little or no income during the search.

When the financial squeeze is on, the first thing to do is make a thorough review of your liquid assets and short-term liabilities. Ask yourself how much cash you can expect to receive during the next three months from the following sources, plus any others you might come up with:

How to Get a Job

Savings

Securities

Silver and gold

Insurance loan possibilities

Second mortgage possibilities

Unemployment compensation

Severance pay

Accrued vacation pay

Personal loan sources (relatives, friends)

Sale of personal property (car, boat, stamp collections, etc.)

Then you should consider exactly what bills absolutely must be paid. Don't worry about your total outstanding debt. Many creditors can be stalled or might be willing to make arrangements to forgo principal as long as interest payments are made. Talk to each of your creditors to see if something can be worked out.

The final step is easy—if sometimes painful. You compare the amount of money you have on hand or expect to receive with the amount you know you'll have to spend. The difference tells you exactly what kind of financial shape you're in.

The old adage has it that it's better to be unemployed than underemployed. If you can afford it, it's wise not to take a part-time or temporary job. The more time you spend looking for a good full-time position, the sooner you're likely to succeed. But if the cupboard looks pretty bare, it may be necessary to supplement your income any way legally possible in order to eat during the search.

Try to find part-time or temporary work that leaves you as free as possible to interview during the day. For this reason, many people choose to drive a cab at night or work in a bar or restaurant during the evenings. This kind of job gives you the advantage of flexible hours, but the pay is not always desirable. Commissioned sales positions abound in almost every industry. But if your personality isn't suited to sales work, don't pursue it. You'll find it very frustrating.

Good advice from a bartender

One of our friends, a successful freelance illustrator, spent several years tending bar part-time in various popular Washington saloons to support his drawing habit.

"The best places to look for part-time work," he says, "are those where you're already known. Bar owners will rarely hire a bartender who walks in off the street or fresh out of Famous Bartending School's two-week course. That's because it's very easy for bartenders to steal. An owner wants to know someone, to have a sense of a person's character, before he hires a bartender.

"So if you're looking for part-time work— and this goes for waiters and waitresses, too— spend some time in the place for a couple of weeks. Get to know the people who work there and the regular customers, and become one of the regulars yourself. Learn how the place operates. Every bar or restaurant has its own way of doing things, from handling special orders to taking care of rowdy customers. The more you know about a place, the easier it is to step in when somebody calls in sick or quits." ■

It's best if you can locate part-time work in your chosen field. The pay is usually more attractive, and you can continue to develop your network of contacts. Many professionals can freelance. An administrative assistant, for example, might be able to find part-time work at a law firm. An accountant might be able to do taxes on a part-time basis and still gain access to new referrals.

Another option for those of you with an entrepreneurial flair is to sell your services on a contractual basis to employers when you interview with them. Say you're a computer programmer. A company might not have enough computer work to justify hiring someone to fill a full-time position. So you suggest they hire you on a temporary basis until the project is complete. Or one day a week because that's all the time it will take. Or on an as needed basis. The advantage to a company is that they don't have to pay you any benefits (except those you're able to negotiate for). The advantage to you is income in your chosen field.

People with technical skills can work themselves into becoming full-time freelancers in just this way. They might even talk an employer OUT of hiring them full time and negotiate contract work in order to maintain the freedom of their self-employed status.

Here are some additional sources to consider when the money is really tight and you need part-time or temporary work.

SELECTED SOURCES FOR PART-TIME AND TEMPORARY WORK

Accountants on Call
8000 Towers Crescent Dr.
Vienna, VA 22182
703-525-6100
Temporary and permanent jobs in accounting.

Accountemps
7200 Wisconsin Ave.
Bethesda, MD 20814
301-652-1960
Accounting jobs in big accounting firms for high school graduates with experience, college graduates through CPA level.

Alexandria Diamond/Yellow Cab
3025 Mt. Vernon Ave.
Alexandria, VA 22305
703-549-2500

Barwood Taxi
4925 Nicholson Court

Kensington, MD 20848
301-984-1900

Capitol Cab
1023 3rd St. N.E.
Washington, DC 20002
202-546-2400

CDI
14120 Parke Long Court, Suite 204
Chantilly, VA 22021
703-222-0700
Most fields of work. One of the oldest in the area.

Core Personnel
4001 N. 9th St., Suite 104A
Arlington, VA 22203
703-243-6600
Office support, general. Two other Virginia locations.

Diamond Cab
1528 11th St. N.W.
Washington, DC 20009
202-387-6200

Don Richards Associates
1717 K St. N.W., Suite 1000
Washington, DC 20006
202-463-7210
Accounting, Finance. Locations in Rockville, MD, and McLean, VA.

Help Unlimited
1634 I St. N.W.
Washington, DC 20006
202-296-0200
Most areas, including legal and marketing.

Kelly Services
1300 I St. N.W., Suite 1070 West
Washington, DC 20005
202-371-9290
Secretarial, word processing, light industrial. 11 locations.

Key Temporaries
2101 Wilson Blvd., Suite 1120
Arlington, VA 22201
703-243-3600
Accounting, finance.

Manpower Temporary Services
1130 Connecticut Ave. N.W., Suite 530
Washington, DC 20036
202-331-8300
Word processing, secretarial. 10 Maryland and 8 Virginia locations.

Norrell
1901 L St. N.W., Suite 630
Washington, DC 20036

202-659-4013
Office support staff. 5 area locations.

Personnel Pool
1025 Connecticut Ave. N.W., Suite 214
Washington, DC 20036
202-293-9370
Office support, clerical, word processing. Also has 1 Virginia location.

Red Top Cab
1200 N. Hudson St.
Arlington, VA 22201
703-522-3333

TAD Technical Services
1400 Shepherd Drive
Sterling, VA 22170
703-450-5577
Computer programmers, technicians, tech writers. Largest in Washington area.

Talent Tree
1130 Connecticut Ave. N.W., Suite 425
Washington, DC 20036
202-331-8367
Office support, including medical.

Technical Aid
2095 Chain Bridge Rd.
Vienna, VA 22182
703-893-5260
All areas.

Telemarketing Temporaries
P.O. Box 7103
Arlington, VA 22207
703-237-8383
Telemarketing only.

TempWorld
800 Towers Crescent Drive
Tysons Corner, VA 22182
703-847-6310
Light industrial, word processing, clerical. Also sales personnel. 3 other area offices.

Wells Fargo Guard Services
7300 Pearl St., Suite 230
Bethesda, MD 20850
301-961-8660
Security guards.

How to Get a Job

Part-time work available for college students

Margaret Bunnell, the Career Information Coordinator at the George Washington University's Career and Cooperative Education Center, suggests that Washington is an ideal place for college students to find part-time work during the school academic year. She reports that their office receives hundreds of listings for part-time jobs from local employers interested in this enthusiastic, and often untapped, source of intelligent workers.

While many of these positions are not of a professional nature, often students who do part-time work make invaluable contacts in organizations that may hire new college graduates. "If an office already knows an individual," Bunnell comments, "there is no question that he or she would have a leg up in applying for a permanent position." ■

Unemployment Compensation

If you find yourself unemployed through no fault of your own (for example, you were laid off because your company lost several large accounts), then you may be eligible to collect unemployment benefits. The first step is to go to your nearest District of Columbia, Maryland, or Virginia Office of Unemployment and apply. You must apply in person and bring copies of W-2 forms and pay stubs. It will take up to 3 weeks for the claim to be processed. You will then receive written notification of the amount for which you are eligible. There are procedures for appeal.

You can also apply for partial unemployment benefits if you're working part time—provided you're earning less than what your unemployment claim would be.

Your claim, or the amount of unemployment you can collect, is based on the amount of money you earned during the first four of the past five calendar quarters. You need to show earnings in at least two of these quarters to establish a claim.

If you were fired, rather than laid off, or if you quit your job, you may still be able to collect unemployment. It just might take a little longer to get it. Getting fired or walking out on a job are situations that require evaluation before a claim can be processed.

AREA UNEMPLOYMENT COMPENSATION OFFICES

DISTRICT OF COLUMBIA

Northeast Employment Center
25 K St. N.E.
Washington, DC 20001

Petworth Employment Center
4120 Kansas Ave. N.W.
Washington, DC 20008

NORTHERN VIRGINIA

Employment Commission
386 S. Pickett St.
Alexandria, VA 22304
703-823-4155

Employment Commission
13135 Lee Jackson Hwy., #340
Fairfax, VA 22033
703-803-1100

Employment Services
14569 D. Jefferson Davis Highway
Woodbridge, VA 20082
703-494-2184

MARYLAND

Montgomery County Employment Services
Wheaton Plaza
South Office Bldg.
Wheaton, MD 20915
301-949-5624

Prince George's County
6321 Greenbelt Road
Greenbelt, MD 20840
301-441-2137

Sources of Emergency Help

FINANCES/TRANSPORTATION

Associated Catholic Charities
1438 Rhode Island Ave. N.E.
Washington, DC 20018
202-526-4100
Hours: 9:00 a.m.-5:00 p.m., Monday through Friday.
Central office and information and referral service for multi-service program. Local offices offer financial help. Call: 202-332-8666.

Community Family Life Services
305 E St. N.W.
Washington, DC 20001
202-347-0511
Hours: 10:00 a.m.-3:00 p.m., Monday and Friday; 10:00 a.m.-12:30 p.m., Tuesday and Thursday.
Emergency food for families with children, senior citizens, and disabled. Clothing and counseling for city residents.

Consumer Credit Counseling and Educational Service
1120 G St. N.W., Suite 885
Washington, DC 20005
202-682-1500

How to Get a Job

Hours: 9:00 a.m.-5:00 p.m., Monday through Friday.
Financial counseling. 4 other offices in metropolitan area.

Traveller's Aid Society of Washington
512 C St. N.E.
Union Station, National and Dulles Airports
202-546-3120
Hours: Main office 9:00 a.m.-5:00 p.m.; other locations vary, most have evening hours, 7 days/week.
Crisis intervention, case work service, protective travel assistance. Information and referrals for travelers, newcomers, transients. Limited financial assistance for travelers.

FOOD/CLOTHING

Anna B. Johanning Baptist Church
4025 9th St. S.E.
Washington, DC 20032
202-561-2095/202-651-5200
Hours: 11:00 a.m.-2:00 p.m., Monday and Tuesday: food; 9:00 a.m.-12:00 p.m., Monday and Wednesday: clothing.
Provides free food and clothing for those in crisis situations.

Arlington Community Action
1415 S. Queen St.
Arlington, VA 22206
703-979-2400
Hours: 9:00 a.m.-5:00 p.m., Monday through Friday.
Emergency food bank. Employment counseling.

Bread For The City
1305 14th St. N.W.
Washington, DC 20005
202-332-0440/202-332-8631
Hours: 10:00 a.m.-4:00 p.m., Monday through Friday.
Emergency food for families, elderly, and disabled. Also clothing.

Christian Action Center
1201 T St. N.W.
Washington, DC 20009
202-332-3721
Hours: 10:00 a.m.-3:00 p.m., Monday, Wednesday, and Friday.
Emergency food, clothing.

Community For Creative Non-Violence
425 2nd St. N.W.
Washington, DC 20001
202-393-4409
Hours: 8:00 a.m.-10:00 p.m., daily.
Day and overnight shelter, supper and clothing.

Foggy Bottom Food Pantry
1920 G St. N.W.
Washington, DC 20006
202-331-1495

Hours: 10:00 a.m.-12:00 noon, second and fourth Saturday.
Non-perishable foods to local residents.

So Others Might Eat
71 O St. N.W.
Washington, DC 20001
202-797-8806
Hours: 9:00 a.m.-5:00 p.m., Monday through Friday, office. Services offered at meal times.
Soup kitchen: breakfast and lunch daily. Food stamps, housing, and employment counseling. Two other sites in District.

HOUSING

Christ House
131 South West St.
Alexandria, VA 22314
703-549-8644
Hours: 24 hours.
Emergency shelter and three meals a day. For single men and families only. For non-addicted people.

House of Imogene
214 P St. N.W.
Washington, DC
202-797-7460
Hours: 24 hours, Monday through Sunday.
Shelter and meals for families and individuals. Job and housing referrals.

Luther Place Shelter
1226 Vermont Ave. N.W.
1335 N St. N.W., basement door (day center)
Washington, DC 20005
202-387-5464
Hours: 8:00 a.m.-7:00 p.m., 7 days/week; doors close at 10:00 p.m. Appointment necessary: Tuesday 10:00 a.m.-noon; Thursday 2:00 p.m.-4:00 p.m.
Evening meal and breakfast.

North County Emergency Shelter
11975 Bowman Towne Dr.
Reston, VA 22090
703-437-1975
Hours: 24 hours.
Emergency shelter for men, women, and families. Three meals a day. Job and mental health counselors available. Maximum stay limit.

Rainbow Place
215 West Montgomery Ave.
Rockville, MD 20850
301-762-3363
Hours: 7:00 p.m.-7:00 a.m.
Emergency shelter. Breakfast, dinner and bag lunch. Laundry facilities.

How to Get a Job

Fast talk nets big part-time $$$

People who need to earn money while job hunting might consider the telemarketing, or telephone sales, industry. Debbie Schwartz, who has worked as a telemarketing manager, feels that the field offers a variety of challenges and rewards.

"Being a telemarketer is almost like being an actor in a radio play," says Debbie. "Your success depends on how well you control your voice. You also have to be able to receive feedback from people without the benefit of eye contact or body language."

We asked Debbie what telemarketing managers look for in the people they hire. "The crucial element is the person's voice. Telemarketers must speak clearly and have pleasing voices. They also must use standard English grammar. Previous sales experience is a plus, although it's not necessary. Managers also look for people who can handle rejection. A person might get rejected 25 or 30 times before making a sale."

According to Debbie, most telemarketers work in four-hour shifts. "You can't work on the phone for more than four hours without becoming ineffective. Also, many firms operate only in the afternoons and evenings. But some firms do have morning hours—those involved in corporate sales, for example."

How much can a telemarketer expect to make?

"Top people can make over $10 per hour," says Debbie. "The average telemarketer makes about $4-$8 per hour. The pay varies depending on whether you are working on a straight commission basis or are being paid a base hourly wage plus commissions."

Debbie suggests investigating a telemarketing firm carefully before accepting a job since there are quite a few fly-by-night operations. But she emphasizes the many benefits to working for a reputable firm: "Telemarketing is a great experience for job hunters. Many of the basic sales techniques that you learn are usable when promoting yourself to a potential employer."

Getting a part-time job in telemarketing requires persistence since managers receive hundreds of calls and applications. "Don't give up," advises Debbie. "Have your sales pitch ready when you call. Sell yourself on the phone in the same way that you would sell a product once you're hired." ■

Where To Turn If Your Confidence Wilts

Recently a bank fired a loan officer who had worked there for more than ten years. The employee was 58 years old, about five-feet, six-inches tall, weighed almost 300 pounds, and did not have a college degree. His written communication skills were negligible. His poor attitude and appearance, lack of enthusiasm, and dismal self-esteem suggested he would be unemployed a long time.

The bank decided to use Tom Camden and Associates' outplacement service to help the person get another job. "There wasn't much we could do about changing his age, education, size, or communication skills," Tom recalls. "But we certainly could—and did—work with him on improving his self-esteem and changing his attitude toward interviewing for new jobs."

After a four-month search, the loan officer succeeded in landing a position that exactly suited his needs. His new job even was located in the neighborhood where he lived. It seemed like a typical success story—until the bank informed Tom Camden about how dissatisfied that person was with the counsel he had received. The man told the bank that they would have been better off paying *him* the consulting fee instead of retaining outside help.

"He was really angry," Tom recalls. "And also full of stress, guilt, fear, anxiety, desire for vengeance, and a host of other emotions."

If you've read Chapter 5, you know that you may speak with up to 300 people on a formal or informal basis while you're looking for suitable work—and a healthy percentage of those people will be unable or unwilling to help you. Every job seeker must anticipate rejection—it comes with the territory. Being turned down in an interview is a painful experience, and it's normal to feel hurt. The trick is to keep those hurt and angry feelings from clouding your judgment or affecting your behavior.

If you're beginning to feel your confidence wilt, reread the tips for treating yourself well in Chapter 5. Put yourself on a regular schedule. And stick to it. If you've always worked for others, you're probably used to working within a structured situation. Now you're out of a job, and you've got nobody to give you assignments, no colleagues for support, no supervisor to tell you what you're doing right and wrong. This is very stressful for some people. The more stressful you find it, the more important it is for you to create your own structure by working full time in a systematic way to find the right job. In addition to that, make sure you're eating healthy foods and getting enough rest and exercise. Don't punish yourself for being unemployed or losing a job offer by abusing your health!

One of the worst things that can happen in any job search is to let rejection undermine your self-confidence. Like the little boy at the door who asks, "You don't want to buy a magazine, do you?" a person who doesn't feel good about him- or herself will not easily convince an employer that he or she should be hired. Each new rejection further erodes self-esteem, and the job search stalls or takes a nose dive: "Maybe I *am* a loser. Perhaps I was lucky to have had my old job as long as I did. Maybe my sights are set too high. I suppose I should look for something less responsible at a lower salary."

Thoughts such as these cross most people's minds at some time or other in the job search. As we've said, it's normal to feel hurt, angry, and depressed after a series of rejections. It's important, however, to recognize these feelings and learn to work them out in some non-destructive way. It is *not* normal to let such feelings sabotage your job search. Just because you're unemployed or looking for a new job doesn't mean you're a bad or worthless person. The only thing "wrong" with you is that you haven't yet found the offer you want.

When your confidence starts to wilt, turn to trusted friends or relatives to be your huggers or your kickers: huggers to pat you on the back and with whom you can talk about your feelings frankly, get mad or sad or vengeful; kickers to help you get back to work on your job search. Don't let fear of rejection keep you from making that next call. It may be just the lead you're looking for.

There are no hard and fast rules on when to seek professional counseling and support, but we can offer certain guidelines. If you seriously think you need professional help, you ought to investigate two or three sources. Besides the ones we've listed below, check with your minister, priest, or rabbi. Many clerics are trained counselors, and their help is free.

If you feel you have nowhere else to turn, or if you don't want to share your feelings with anyone you know, you should consider psychiatric or psychological counseling. If you're not making calls, not preparing for interviews, or not doing what you know you have to do to get the job you want, you could probably use some counseling.

Everybody feels bad about being rejected. But if you allow those feelings to overwhelm you, or if they're interfering with finding a job, it's probably time to talk with a professional. Another sure sign of trouble is waking up most mornings too sick or lethargic from overeating, overdrinking, or abusing some other substance to do what you have to do.

The following organizations license psychologists:

Who's good?
Who's not?

Virginia State Board of Psychology
1601 Rolling Hills Dr.
Richmond, VA 23229-5005
804-662-9913

Maryland Board of Psychology
4201 Patterson Ave.
Baltimore, MD 21215
301-764-4787

District of Columbia Board of Psychology
1614 H St. N.W., Rm. 904
Washington, DC 20001
202-727-7468

How to Choose a Therapist

Psychotherapist Mary Lee Palmer recommends that you interview several therapists before you enter therapy—even if you have to buy 15 minutes of their time. Ask about cost, credentials, whether your health insurance covers their fees, the type of therapy they practice, the length of time they anticipate would be required to deal with your concerns. The answers to all of these questions are important. But equally important is the sense of rapport you feel. It is vital that you feel comfortable confiding in this person.

There are a number of professions that practice counseling and therapy. A psychiatrist is an M.D. and is able to prescribe medication. A psychologist usually has a Ph.D. and has gone through an internship. A clinical social worker has an M.S.W. and has conducted therapy under supervision while in training. There are also psychiatric nurses, pastoral counselors, and guidance counselors.

One of the best ways to find out who might be good for you to work with is to ask your friends. If someone you know well has been helped and swears by a therapist, that's a strong recommendation. There are, unfortunately, a bewildering variety of schools of therapy. Each one has its detractors and its supporters. What worked for your friend might not work for you. Ask your friend how the therapist worked, and try to envision yourself going through a similar process.

TELEPHONE CRISIS LINES

Crisis Center (DC)
202-965-8400

Dominion Hospital
703-538-2872

Family Crisis Center of Prince George's County
301-864-9101

Montgomery County Hotline
301-738-2255

Northern Virginia Hotline
703-527-4077

Psychiatric Institute of Montgomery County
301-251-4500

Psychiatric Institute of Washington
202-965-8500

Samaritans of Washington
202-362-8100

COMMUNITY MENTAL HEALTH CENTERS

There are many services available to those undergoing stress and anxiety that they can not handle alone. A physician is always a good source for referrals. The organizations listed below provide counseling, free consumer information concerning mental health problems as well as referrals. The Yellow Pages list a wide range of other private and public mental health services.

The **D.C. Hotline**, 202-223-0020, provides a variety of services, including crisis intervention for the hearing impaired and support groups. They publish an excellent directory of free, low-cost services throughout the metropolitan area.

Arlington Counseling Center
5319 Lee Highway
Arlington, VA 22207
703-533-1038
Short-term crisis intervention and long-term psychotherapy.

DC Institute for Mental Health
3000 Connecticut Ave. N.W., #436
Washington, DC 20008
202-462-2992
Psychiatric evaluation, psychological testing, individual, couple, group, and family psychotherapy. Two other district locations.

Fairfax County Mental Health Center
3340 Woodburn Road
Annandale, VA 22033
703-573-0523

Staffed by psychologists, psychiatrists, and social workers. Evening hours for ongoing clients. Referrals to other centers based on location. Sliding scale fee.

George Washington University Counseling Laboratory
801 22nd St. N.W., #T-407
Washington, DC 20052
202-994-8645
Inexpensive counseling in all areas for individuals, groups, and couples.

Mental Health Association of Montgomery County
1000 Twinbrook Pkwy.
Rockville, MD 20851
301-424-0656
Educational programs only; no therapy here. Referrals to other sources.

Mental Health Association of Northern Virginia
7630 Little River Trnpk., #206
Annandale, VA 22003
703-642-0800
Information and referrals to self-help support groups and community agencies in area. Addresses unemployment and career concerns.

Mental Health Association of Prince George's County
96 Harry S Truman Drive
Largo, MD 20772
301-499-2107
Information and referrals to counseling services in area. Community education in schools and other groups. Hotline for latch-key children.

Mental Health Association of the District of Columbia
1628 16th St. N.W.
Washington, DC 20009
202-265-6363
Referral agency for professional counseling services.

Pastoral Counseling Centers
P.O. Box 39
Oakton, VA 22124
703-281-1870
Individual, group, family, adolescent and child counseling. 27 centers in Greater Washington Area; 2 locations in Capitol Hill.

Women in transition

Psychotherapist Susan Levine has worked extensively with women in transition. She has noted that "it makes a lot of difference whether the transition is chosen or forced upon the woman. A woman who has chosen to go back to school, look for a 'real job,' or move up the career ladder will probably have fewer problems dealing with identity, self-esteem, and dependency. She has already sorted through her priorities and has a better idea of who she is as an individual. She will, of course, be susceptible to all the difficulties any job seeker must face. But the woman who is widowed or divorced must first struggle with her identity and somehow regain a sense of control over her life.

"Support groups are especially helpful for women whose transition has been forced upon them. Together with others who face similar issues, they can often more quickly redefine themselves and regain control over their lives."

Psychologist Angie Benham, who went through a midlife transition of her own choosing, has observed that "the biggest obstacle for women in transition is their fear that they lack competence. A big help for such women is to increase their self-confidence one small step at a time. This way they'll always be meeting challenges but won't feel overwhelmed." ■

FREE EMPLOYMENT SUPPORT GROUPS

Artists' Support Network
Georgetown Lutheran Church
1556 Wisconsin Ave.
Washington, DC 20007
202-783-4747/202-338-1443
Hours: Mondays, 6:30 p.m.-8:30 p.m.
Support group for persons interested in the arts.

Employment Support Network
Church of the Epiphany
1317 G St. N.W.
Washington, DC 20005
202-347-2635
Hours: 5:45 p.m.-7:45 p.m.
Free self-help group for professionals.

Georgetown Career Group
Georgetown Presbyterian Church
3115 P St. N.W.
Washington, DC 20007
202-783-4747
Hours: 12 noon-2:00 p.m. every Tuesday
Self-help employment group for professionals.

Reston Employment Assistance Program
Christ the Servant Lutheran Church
Hunters Woods Shopping /Community Center
Reston, VA 22091
703-476-6452
Hours: Wednesdays, 12 noon-2:00 p.m.
Support group for professionals.

Third Base
10010 Fernwood Rd.
Bethesda, MD 20814
301-258-9197
Hours: 9:00 a.m.-5:00 p.m., office; 9:00 a.m.-11:30 a. m., Tuesday; 7:30 p.m.-9:00 p.m., Wednesday
Free support group for professionals. Seminars offered weekly.

What To Do If You Get Fired

Being fired ranks just after the death of someone you love, or divorce, when it comes to personal traumas. But it's unwise to panic. Here are a few important tips on dealing with your employer after receiving notice of termination.

Take time to evaluate the bad news before accepting a settlement offer. If you quickly accept what your employer has to offer, it will be much more difficult to change your situation later. Tell the boss you want some time to think about a settlement. Then go back in a day or two and negotiate.

Stay on the payroll as long as you can, even if your pride hurts. Find out if you are eligible for part-time work or consulting jobs to tide you over until you find your new job. You may be able to hang on to insurance and other benefits until you've found new employment.

Try to negotiate a generous severance payment. In the last five years, severance agreements have risen dramatically in some industries. What the company offers at first may not be the maximum. Negotiation doesn't always work, but you certainly ought to try to get the most for your years of service.

Check with your personnel office to make sure you're getting all the benefits to which you are entitled, such as vacation pay and profit sharing. Check your eligibility for unemployment compensation before you accept an offer to resign instead of being terminated.

Don't attack management during your termination interview. It may cost you good references and hurt your chances of finding a new job.

Take advantage of any outplacement assistance that is offered. OK, so maybe the company shouldn't have let you go, and you feel utterly betrayed. Don't reject the company's offer to help. Chances are the outplacement counselor has been hired on a contractual basis and owes the company nothing more than to do his or her level best to help you find a suitable position.

Career Transition Issues

For most people, conducting a job search constitutes a crisis of sorts. Strong feelings will be aroused, and action must be taken if the crisis is to be resolved.

While it's normal to have all of the following emotional responses during the course of your job search, you must manage your emotions or they'll manage you.

Anger—You must not let the fact that you were fired or treated indifferently by some interviewer make you hostile on your next interview. Be aware of the object of your anger. Don't displace it onto someone else.

Depression—Of course, you're going to get disappointed and frustrated at times, but don't give in to self-pity. Your next employer wants a go-getter, not a poor-me-er.

Social withdrawal—When you're down and out it's very tempting to avoid others. Don't become a hermit. You need all the friends and contacts you can maintain. Don't apologize for being out of work. It has happened to most people.

The best antidote against getting bogged down in your own emotional turmoil is to take action:

1. *Stay physically active.* Research has shown that regular, vigorous aerobic activity combats depression and anxiety.

2. *Come up with a good plan* for finding a job, and stick to it. Give yourself lots to do every day. Impose deadlines on yourself. As you start making progress, you'll start feeling better

3. *Join a support group* for other job seekers. Not only will you get encouragement, you'll get leads and advice.

4. *Make finding a good job a full-time job.* You'll feel better and find the right position quicker.

Beating the Job Hunt Blues

Although it's not easy to relax when you're worried about dwindling savings, professional identity, and an uncertain future, even the most dedicated job hunter sometimes needs to take a breather. An afternoon off the beaten job search path can help clear your head of the job-hunt blues. Giving yourself a vacation day in the midst of your job search can revive flagging confidence. A selection of free or cheap Washington-area diversions follows.

So many of Washington's daytime activities are free that you could actually spend weeks wandering the Smithsonian museums and galleries. In fact, so many tourists actually do that that you often encounter more crowds than at a *Washington Post* Job Fair.

Most of the **Smithsonian** buildings are listed in the Cultural Institutions section of Chapter 12. Admission is always free and the hours are generally 10:00 a.m. to 5:30 p.m., with evening hours in the summer. Most of the museums have cafeterias, but they are pricey and very crowded. Try instead some of the federal government building cafeterias, where you might avoid the pricey part if not the lines.

Two smaller museums are sometimes missed by the hoards of tourists, and they can be quiet spots away from the bustle of official Washington. The **Phillips Collection**, 1600 21st St. N.W., 202-387-0961, has recently redone its newer wing and is in great form. The Phillips, which was one of the first museums to show modern art, also has Sunday afternoon concerts in the original ballroom of the house. The **Corcoran Gallery of Art**, 17th St. and New York Ave. N.W., 202-638-3211, is a nice, manageable collection, with frequently unusual special exhibits. Both have small admission fees and are easily reached by public transportation.

The **Dumbarton Oaks Collection and Gardens**, 1703 32nd St. N.W., 202-342-3200, are in upper Georgetown. Actually owned by Harvard University, the house contains a research library and recently redone gallery containing Byzantine art. The large grounds are best in spring and summer but are peaceful at any time. A modest fee is charged.

The **Washington (National) Cathedral**, Wisconsin and Massachusetts Aves. N.W., 202-537-6200, is open daily. Officially Episcopalian, it has no local congregation and is the setting for services of all denominations. Finally completed in late 1990, it sits atop the city's highest point. Don't miss the bookstore.

Washington abounds with great shopping areas, **Georgetown**, **Union Station**, Alexandria's **Old Town**, and **Dupont Circle**, to name a few. Since you are job hunting, however, you will want to avoid these great temptations. The neighborhoods nearby often provide great spots for walking and learning the character of the city, once you get off the beaten path. This goes for **Adams Morgan**, **Capitol Hill**, and **Foggy Bottom** as well, particularly if architectural diversity appeals to you. Speaking of architecture, the **Washington Building Museum** and the **Old Post Office Building** are sights to behold; and looking doesn't cost a cent!

Rock Creek Park, with over 1,700 acres in the District and Maryland, is run by the National Park Service. It contains miles of hiking, biking, and nature trails. The **National Zoo**, 3001 Connecticut Ave. N.W., 202-673-4800, sits right in the middle of it and is a great place to enjoy the outdoors. Easily reached by Metro or buses, the Zoo is free and open from 8 a.m. to 5 p.m., with longer summer hours.

We have listed mostly in-town diversions because these are accessible by public transportation. To get to many spots out in the country a car is essential. But there is a bike path you can take from the Washington Monument area, over Memorial Bridge, along the Potomac, through Alexandria, all the way to **Mt. Vernon**. There, you can tour George Washington's home and gardens and see the way a typical gentleman farmer lived in the 18th century. It is a lovely bike trail, flat and scenic; however, count on a couple of hours each way, even for regular bikers.

Other parks to hit, closer to the District, are **Roosevelt Park** (on its own island, right in the city!) and **Hain's Point** with its controversial sculpture (you gotta see it to believe it). While you're being physically active, don't forget in the winter to check out the **Ice Skating Rink** on the mall; it's a Washington thing to do.

Volunteer!

There are a number of organizations in Washington that help potential volunteers learn about opportunities to lend a hand. Sometimes the best way to get out of job-hunting doldrums is to help someone else:

The **National Volunteer Center**
1111 19th St. N.W.
Washington, DC 20036
202-408-5162

Volunteer Clearinghouse
1313 New York Ave. N.W., Suite 303
Washington, DC 20005
202-638-2664

(Ask here about **Doing Something**, an incredible network for group volunteer projects and an excellent way to meet other professionals in town. Call them at 202-393-5051). ∎

Selecting the Right Job
for You

Welcome to the most pleasant chapter of this book. You've figured out what you want to do, developed an acceptable resume, and used your network of contacts and other resources to research the job market and generate all sorts of interviews. At this point in the process you've probably received or are pretty close to landing at least a couple of offers that come fairly close to your objective.

You have a dilemma if one of your possibilities demands an immediate response to a firm offer while you're still investigating other promising leads. The employer making this offer is essentially telling you, "We think you have everything we're looking for, and we want you to start as soon as possible." It is difficult to stall or delay your acceptance just because other promising leads still haven't yielded firm offers. You have to use your best judgment in such a case, but try to delay a final decision until all likely offers are in. Unless you're absolutely desperate, there's no reason to jump at the first offer you receive.

You owe it to both yourself and the people who interviewed you to bring in all outstanding possibilities and *then* make your decision. Tell the employer who gave you the offer the truth—that you need more time to review the offer against all the situations that are outstanding and pending. Agree upon a period of time—five days, two weeks, a month—during which they won't offer the position to anyone else. Obviously, the more time you can get, the better for you, but they may have pressing needs to have someone in place pronto. If the offering company refuses to wait at all, that tells you a great deal about the atmosphere in which you'd be working.

If a company wants you badly enough, they'll wait a reasonable length of time for you to decide. In the meantime, use your offer to "encourage" other companies to reach a decision about your candidacy. We're not suggesting that you play hardball. That probably won't work and might even work against you. But it makes perfect sense to inform other companies who are interested in you that you have an offer. If you're sure you'd rather work for one of them, say so. But also say that you'll have to accept the first offer if you don't hear from them within the allotted time. Don't lie about your intentions. If you don't intend to accept the first offer, don't say that you do. Otherwise, the second (and perhaps better) company might write you off, assuming that you won't be available by the time they're ready to decide.

A job involves much more than a title and base salary. For any firm offer, be sure you understand what your responsibilities will be, what benefits you'll receive besides salary (insurance, vacation, profit sharing, training, tuition reimbursement, and the like), how much overtime is required (and whether you'll be paid for it), how much travel is involved in the job, who your superior will be, how many people you'll be supervising, and where the position might lead. (Is it a dead-end job, or are people in this slot often promoted?) In short, find out anything and everything you need to know to evaluate the offer.

For many positions, especially those requiring several years' experience, it's appropriate to ask for an offer in writing. Such a document would specify the position's title, responsibilities, reporting relationship, compensation, and include a statement of company benefits.

At the very least, before you make a firm decision, be sure to obtain a copy of the organization's personnel policy. It will fill you in on such details as the number of paid sick days, overtime and vacation policy, insurance benefits, profit sharing, and the like. These so-called fringe benefits can really add up. It's not a bad idea to try to assign a dollar value to them to help you evaluate the financial pros and cons of each offer.

It seems obvious to us that it is unwise to choose a job exclusively on the basis of salary and benefits. You spend more of your waking hours at work than at any other activity. Don't condemn yourself to working with colleagues and subordinates you can't stand, doing work that you find boring to accomplish goals you don't believe in.

Finding the Right Culture

Career counselors often rightly warn you that ignoring or failing to learn about a company's culture can put your job satisfaction or your chances of employment at great risk. You can find a position that suits you to a T but still be unhappy if you don't fit the culture of the employer that hires you. It takes some doing to assess an organization's culture, but it's worth your while.

Some signs are fairly obvious: What do people wear? What is the furniture like? Are office doors kept open or closed? Are there any minorities or women in positions of power? How friendly are people to you? To each other? Does anybody laugh? A very important question to ask—Do I feel comfortable here?

There are five aspects of an organization's culture to consider. Try to find out as much as you can about each.

1. What is the relationship between a company and its environment? Does it control its own destiny, or must it depend on the mood of an adversarial home office? You probably wouldn't be wise to work for the Department of Defense under a pacifist administration.

2. How does a company view human nature? Good or evil? Changeable or immutable? Answers to these questions determine how employees are treated, how much supervision and control is exerted. How openly will employees communicate? Will there be opportunities for training and development?

3. What are the philosophy and mission of an organization? Printed brochures are often good indicators. A good employer is clear on what it stands for.

4. How do people relate to each other in an organization? Is there a formal flow chart? Are there many vertical levels (the military)? Or is power more evenly and horizontally spread out (some new high-tech firms)? The more horizontal, the more informal and the easier it is to get things done, generally through relationships.

5. How are decisions made, who makes them, and upon what basis? Facts and reason? Politics? Ideology? Good-old-boy or old-girl network? The whims of an autocrat at the top?

The answers to these questions will determine the working atmosphere within almost any company.

Top Salary Strategy

Before you accept an offer—or dicker over salary—you need to know what other people who fill similar positions are making. The *Occupational Outlook Handbook,* put out by the U.S. Department of Labor every two years, cites salary statistics by field. Probably a better source of information is *The American Almanac of Jobs and Salaries* by John Wright, published by Avon.

What you really need to know is what other people with your qualifications and experience are making in the Washington area for working the job you're considering. Professional societies and associations frequently provide this sort of information. It's one more good reason to belong to one. Probably the best source of all for salary orientation is—you guessed it—your network of contacts.

For advice on compensation scales and how to get the salary you want, we recommend these books:

Chapman, Jack. *How to Make $1000 a Minute.* Berkeley, CA: Ten Speed Press, 1987.
Cohen, Herb. *You Can Negotiate Anything.* New York: Bantam Publishing Co., 1982.
Fisher, Roger, and William Ury. *Getting to Yes.* New York: Penguin Books, 1983.
Greater Washington Board of Trade. *The Greater Washington Board of Trade Compensation Survey.* Washington, DC: The Wyatt Co., 1989.

Krannich, Ronald L., and Caryl Rae Krannich. *Salary Success*. Manassas, VA: Impact Publications, 1990.

Savage, Kathleen, and Charity Anne Dorgan. *Professional Careers Sourcebook*. Detroit, MI: Gale Research.

U.S. Department of Labor. *Area Wage Survey: Washington, DC, Virginia, Metropolitan Area*. Washington, DC: Superintendent of Documents, 1991.

U.S. Department of Labor. *White-collar Pay: Private Service-Producing Industries*. Washington, DC: Superintendent of Documents, 1989-90.

Wright, John W., and Edward J. Dwyer. *The American Almanac of Jobs and Salaries*. New York: Avon Books, 1991.

Compare the Offers on Paper

You've talked with each employer and taken notes about the responsibilities and compensation being offered. Where possible, you've obtained a job offer in writing. You have also read through the company's personnel policy.

Now make yourself a checklist for comparing the relative merits of each offer. We've provided a sample here, but if another format suits your purposes better, use it. The idea is to list the factors that you consider important in any job, and then assign a rating for how well each offer fills the bill in each particular area.

We've listed some of the factors that we think ought to be considered before you accept any offer. Some may not be relevant to your situation. Others that we've left out may be of great importance to you. So feel free to make any additions, deletions, or changes you want.

Once you've listed your factors, make a column for each job offer you're considering. Assign a rating (say, 1 to 5, with 1 the lowest and 5 the highest) for each factor and each offer. Then, total the scores for each offer.

The offer with the most points is not necessarily the one to accept. The chart doesn't take into account the fact that "responsibilities" may be more important to you than "career path," or that you promised yourself you'd never punch a time clock again. Nevertheless, looking at the pros and cons of each offer in black and white should help you make a much more methodical and logical decision.

Factor	Offer A	Offer B	Offer C
Responsibilities	_____	_____	_____
Company reputation	_____	_____	_____
Salary	_____	_____	_____
Insurance	_____	_____	_____
Paid vacation	_____	_____	_____
Pension	_____	_____	_____
Profit sharing	_____	_____	_____
Tuition reimbursement	_____	_____	_____

On-the-job training	_____	_____	_____
Career path (where can you go from this job?)	_____	_____	_____
Company future	_____	_____	_____
Quality of product or service	_____	_____	_____
Location (housing market, schools, transportation)	_____	_____	_____
Boss(es)	_____	_____	_____
Other workers	_____	_____	_____
Travel	_____	_____	_____
Overtime	_____	_____	_____
Other	_____	_____	_____
_____	_____	_____	_____
_____	_____	_____	_____
TOTAL POINTS	_____	_____	_____

A Final Word

Once you have accepted a job, it's important that you notify each of the people in your log of your new position, company, address, and phone number. Be sure to thank these people; let them know you appreciated their assistance. After all, you never know when you may need to ask them to help you again. You've spent weeks building up a network of professional contacts. *Keep your network alive.*

On each anniversary date of your new job, take the time to run through the self-appraisal process to evaluate your situation and the progress you are making (as measured by increased responsibilities, salary, and abilities). Consider how they compare with the objectives you set at the start of your search. Although you may be completely satisfied in your new assignment, remember that circumstances can change overnight, and you must always be prepared for the unexpected. So make an employment "New Year's Resolution" to weigh every aspect of your job annually and compare the result with what you want and expect from your life's work.

We hope that you have made good use of the job-search techniques outlined in this book. Indeed, we hope that the resulting experiences not only have won you the job you want but—equally important—also have made you a better person. Perhaps the next time you talk to an unemployed person or someone who is employed but seeking a new job, you will look at that person with new insight gained from your own search experiences.

We hope you'll gladly share what you've learned about how to get a job in Washington.

Zeroing in on a great place to work

How do you know when you've found a great place to work? We asked business writer Robert Levering, co-author of *A Great Place to Work: What Makes Some Employers So Good and Some So Bad* and *The 100 Best Companies to Work for In America*, what he considered the key to evaluating a job proposal.

"Before you accept a job," Levering insists, "you ought to ask yourself, 'What kind of relationship am I going to have with the people I work for, with the people I'm going to work with, and with my work itself?'"

When he was tracking down "the 100 best employers in America," the rankings were based on five tangibles: pay, benefits, job security, opportunities for promotion, and ambiance. Now, however, he believes the values that rest behind the perks may be more significant than the perks themselves. Levering states, "You must trust the people you work for, have pride in what you do, and enjoy the people you work with. Simply put, the criteria for a great place to work are trust, pride, and fun.

"Let's face it, a happy marriage isn't defined by a house in the suburbs, two cars in the garage, 2.5 children, and a dog. When you find a great job, it's more than the result of just pay scales, benefits, and a chance to move up."

That doesn't mean that salary range, stock options, or a gourmet corporate cafeteria are irrelevant. Levering explains, "If you feel either you're being cheated or that the company is not paying you as much as it could, that's not just an issue of money. How your employer compensates you for your time tells you about how your employer values you, and that is about trust. Similarly, pride translates into systems that let people develop their skills. Pride ensures that employees have the tools they need to do their jobs. Pride means workers get credit for their accomplishments. And if your co-workers are relaxed, pleasant to be with, and basically compatible, work is fun. Often that comes down to how much corporate politics permeates the office."

Are companies—other than the 100 best—willing to create a corporate culture based on trust, pride, and fun?

"There are positive signs," Levering says. "Businesses know that the work force has changed. Employees are now highly educated and looking for the best job possible. Employers want to attract and retain the best people, so they want to treat their employees well. A hell of a lot of companies would like to be on the list of the 100 best places to work."

How To Get a Job in Government

Public service is the largest category of employment in America's labor market. Within this division, government is the biggest employer (18 million nationwide, 600,000 in the DC metropolitan area). This means there are a lot of jobs available in each of the three levels, federal, state, and local. While state and local jobs typically outnumber federal positions, in this area there are more federal jobs. For job hunters looking to work here, that is encouraging since greater opportunities exist (which means more hiring is being done) at the federal level.

Fourteen percent of all federal jobs are located in the Washington area. That accounts for approximately 300,000 people largely in white collar positions. With this many people in the area, a regular job turnover rate of 14%, and an average annual rate of increase of 1%, nearly 45,000 job opportunities become available each year! Even more interesting is that in some months the federal government hires as many as 70,000 new workers. This is good news, and with the information that follows, you will see that the government as an employer offers you a world of great career possibilities.

151

PLUSES

Besides these numbers, why consider government employment? Several reasons. First, there is wide variety in the types of jobs available. Just like the private sector, the U.S. government is divided into several occupational areas, each one varying again according to the size, structure, and mission of the organization or agency.

Another reason is the opportunity to have an impact on policies and programs that affect millions of people across the country and the world. Government employees often describe the reward of being involved with issues they believe in and consider important for the well-being of other people.

Finally, working for government is attractive because of the job security and opportunity for professional development, advancement, and mobility. Pay, benefits, and training are becoming more and more competitive in private industry, and greater attention is being paid to making public service as prestigious, exciting, and appealing to professionals as possible. The government sector no longer needs to be considered a job hunter's "last resort."

GRIPES

Drawbacks still exist, however. The biggest complaint is that of the "bureaucracy" involved in both getting and doing your job with government. Other criticisms include a sense of feeling lost or anonymous due to the overwhelming size of the agencies and poor physical environments. In each case, while these may be true of some agencies, environments vary and the job hunter is encouraged to proceed with caution, clarity about their own criteria, and an active approach to getting information about a particular office and position.

TIPS

For the job hunter, the good news is that the process for landing a job with government is becoming very similar to that of the private sector. Just as Chapter 2 says, you must focus and get clear your objective. Government employers who interview you want to know just as much about *what* you want to do and *why* you think you can do it as private employers. Then, the word on the streets is *networking*. This means getting out there and getting to know the agencies and people in them, just as you would in the private sector. Everyone you talk to can provide a different perspective that, when put together, can give you a pretty complete look at the job situation.

How to get a job in government

3 keys to a federal Job

Rich Bowie, Chief of Executive Employment at the U.S. Department of Energy, says: "There are 3 keys to getting a job with the federal government: 1) develop a thorough understanding of the application process and requirements for the particular job for which you are applying; 2) tailor your SF-171 to the job you're pursuing; and 3) be persistent. Don't just try once and give up. Keep trying. It's difficult to get a job anywhere these days, and this holds true for the government." ■

The following information should assist you in navigating your way through the various government offices and agencies and in making the right connections. How you function once you make them will determine your success.

Federal Government Employment

The federal government is divided into three branches: executive, legislative, and judicial and is represented by more than 100 agencies. The executive branch is the largest, employing more than 90% of all federal government employees. The second largest is the legislative branch, with approximately 37,000 workers, followed by the judicial branch and about 24,000 staff. While smaller than the executive branch, the legislative and judicial branches have experienced more significant job growth over the past several years.

While government budgets continue to increase, they are doing so at a much slower rate. Cutbacks in new hiring continues, too, though many of the positions being "cut" are actually jobs that are being vacated and not re-filled. In particular, the Department of Defense has experienced significant cutbacks and will continue to do so for the next several years.

Jobs that often go unnoticed or uncounted as government or government-related jobs are those filled by contracting or consulting firms. Large numbers of these services exist in the Washington area and continue to do strong business with government agencies.

EXECUTIVE

This branch consists of: the Executive Office of the President, the Departments, and independent agencies. Other corporations, committees, commissions, and quasi-agencies also belong to the executive branch and employ a significant number of people. (See chart.) Recent statistics indicate the following as the top 5 executive agencies employing the largest number of workers in the Washington area: Departments of Defense, Health and Human Services, Treasury, Justice, and Commerce.

LEGISLATIVE

The House of Representatives and the Senate together comprise this branch of government. While the House offers more employment opportunities

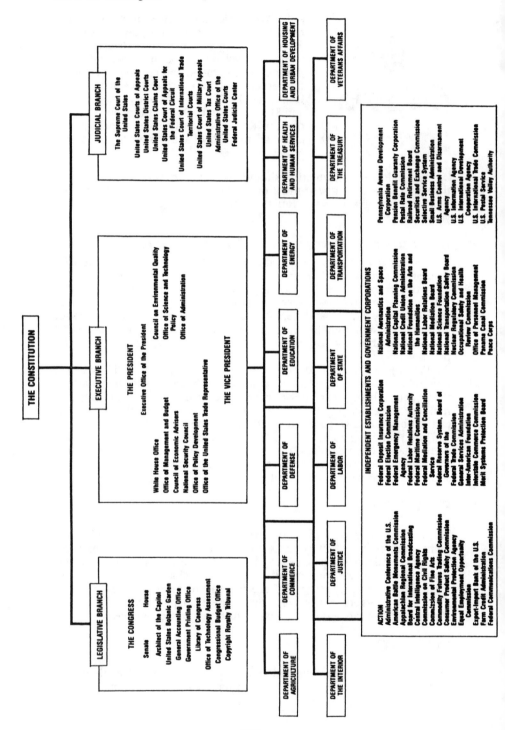

(about 12,000) than the Senate (7,000), both areas are quite competitive and require aggressive networking techniques.

In the House, jobs can be found in two areas in Washington: personal staffs of Representatives, and staffs of congressional committees. House leadership offices and support organizations also employ staff-level personnel.

Personal staff sizes vary but most employ between 6 and 9 people who work "on the Hill" (Capitol Hill office location). Many people enter "Hill jobs" through entry-level positions such as secretaries, receptionists, or staff assistants. While these may not be your dream job, hang in there. Familiarity pays off as many people move up the ranks within a few years. Successful job hunting in this setting rests squarely on your ability to connect with the Representative or a key staff member (like the administrative assistant or chief of staff) and doing everything possible to communicate and keep communicating with them until you influence the person with the power to hire.

Committees and subcommittees each hire between 5 and 70 staff members. These committees tend to hire people experienced on the Hill or those with special expertise in relevant policy areas. Again, the best way to get into this area is to network with key staff people. The larger committees include those on: Appropriations, Armed Services, and Budget.

The Senate offers the same two areas of employment in DC: personal staffs, committees and subcommittees, and the third area of leadership and support organizations. Senate personal staffs are larger than those of the House, between 20 and 30 people per Senator. Positions vary similarly to House positions, with opportunities to get in as office support personnel and then move up to Legislative Director, Assistant, or Administrative Assistant positions. Again, the networking or direct-job-search approach applies, and the Administrative Assistant or Chief of Staff is your target.

Committee staffs range from 5 to 80 employees. Partisan lines dictate number of positions, so the majority party gets most of the positions and the minority gets the rest. To land this kind of staff job, you'll need some prior experience or expertise. Direct your efforts to the committee Chair or Staff Director. The committees with the most staff include committees on Appropriations, Taxation, Commerce, Science, and Technology.

Congressional agencies are organizations that support Congress in a variety of capacities. While much smaller than their executive agency counterparts, each of the following agencies hires its own staff and has its own procedures and pay systems. They are arranged according to size, the largest first:

General Accounting Office

Government Printing Office

Library of Congress

Architect of the Capitol

Congressional Budget Office

Office of Technology Assessment

Botanic Garden

Copyright Royalty Tribune

How to Get a Job

If interested in a job with any of these agencies, contact the personnel office regarding openings, qualifications, and application procedures.

The Capitol Hill area is actually a fun place to go, even if you're not working or looking for a job. Some of the best networking spots continue to be the Hawk n'Dove, Bullfeathers, Tune Inn, Tortilla Coast, Irish Times, the Dubliner, and places in Union Station and on Massachusetts Avenue. ■

Networking hangouts on the Hill

JUDICIAL

This branch, considered the fastest growing branch of the federal government, is made up of the Supreme Court, various U.S. Courts, and several support organizations and personnel. Most growth has taken place, however, in regions other than Washington, DC, occurring within the U.S. Court system nationwide.

In the Supreme Court, most employees are appointed. Support organization personnel work directly with the court but are not court employees. The U.S. Court System, located in courts nationwide, employs 98% of all judiciary personnel. Each of the courts and related organizations employs legal specialists as well as administrative support staff. Starting out in a support position makes it easier to land a job within the court system.

Job hunting for professional positions requires the same if not more energetic networking as emphasized throughout the government sector. The legal network of schools, alumni, and law firms can make the competition pretty tough. Jobs in support are less difficult and require the more typical strategies and levels of effort.

The organization with the largest number of hired staff is the Administrative Office of the U.S. Courts. More than 650 employees are hired to work in the DC office. This office, as the name suggests, provides the administrative support for the federal court system, including financial and technical assistance.

The Federal Judicial Center does the research, training and development work for the judiciary branch and has a staff of about 120. Vacancies are advertised through *The Post* or can be found at the addresses given below.

A related organization is the Supreme Court Historical Association, a small non-profit group with the mission of educating the public about the federal judiciary.

Applying for Federal Employment

Most government jobs are classified as civil service positions, for which two kinds of hiring regulations exist: competitive and excepted service. Eighty percent of federal government positions are competitive service positions, which means that job announcements are made public, job candidates must be evaluated by the Office of Personnel Management (OPM) or by individual agencies, and applicants must compete with each other in open competition. (See "Hiring Procedures" below.)

Excepted (or exempted) service positions are not subject to these regulations or to the authority of OPM. Excepted positions, therefore, are regulated by individual agency policies and procedures. Job applicants interested in these types of positions must apply directly to the personnel office of their targeted agency. Here's the list of excepted service agencies.

Major Excepted Service Agencies*

Agency for International Development

Board of Governors of the Federal Reserve System

Central Intelligence Agency

Defense Intelligence Agency

Federal Bureau of Investigation

General Accounting Office

National Security Agency

Nuclear Regulatory Commission

Postal Rate Commission

Tennessee Valley Authority

U.S Postal Service

U.S. Department of State (Foreign Service Positions)

In addition, the following areas are filled largely according to excepted service standards:

For positions within the judiciary branch:
    Contact: **Personnel Office**
        U.S. Supreme Court Bldg.
        1 First St. N.W.
        Washington, DC 20543
        202-479-3000

For positions with the Administrative Office and the U.S. Claims Court:
    Contact: **Personnel Division**
        Administrative Office of the United States Courts
        Room L701
        Washington, DC 20544

    or: **United States Claims Court**
        717 Madison Place N.W.
        Washington, DC 20005

For positions within the legislative branch:
    Contact: **Placement Office**   **Placement Office**
        U.S. Senate   U.S. House of Representatives
        Washington, DC 20510   Washington, DC 20515
        202-224-9167   202-226-6731

How to Get a Job

Certain positions within Department of Veterans Affairs are excepted.
 Contact: **Recruitment and Examining Division (O54E)**
 Department of Veterans Affairs
 810 Vermont Ave. N.W.
 Washington, DC 20420

*In agencies where most jobs are part of competitive service, some are excepted by law. Policy-making and related positions are also excepted.

Hiring Procedures

Role of Office of Personnel Management (OPM)

OPM is divided into: 1) the Central Office, or Headquarters, located in Washington, DC; 2) 5 regional offices and the Washington Area Service Center (WASC), which serves the federal agencies in the DC area and some other locations; and 3) the Federal Job Information Centers (FJICs).

Applicants should contact the Regional Office or Federal Job Information Center nearest the location where they desire work for information on career and employment opportunities in that area and the necessary application forms. This means that *if you want to work in Washington, DC, call the Washington Area Service Center*. The center is located at the **OPM Headquarters building, 1900 E St. N.W., Washington, DC 20415-0001, 202-606-2700**, and it also maintains the FJIC for the DC area.

Regional OPM offices throughout the country can provide limited information about Washington area job openings. To learn about the FJIC nearest you, contact one of these **regional offices:**

Atlanta: Office of Personnel Management
75 Spring Street
Atlanta, GA 30303-3109
404-331-3459

Chicago: Office of Personnel Management
John C. Kluczynski Building
230 South Dearborn Street
Chicago, IL 60604-1687
312-353-2901

Dallas: Office of Personnel Management
1100 Commerce
Dallas, TX 75250
214-767-8227

Philadelphia: Office of Personnel Management
Federal Building
600 Arch Street
Philadelphia, PA 19106
215-597-4543

San Francisco: Office of Personnel Management
211 Main Street

San Francisco, CA 94105
415-744-7237

The folks at OPM recommend 5 ways to land a government job: 1) direct application; 2) ACWA exam; 3) Outstanding Scholar Program; 4) clerical and administrative support occupations; and 5) special occupations.

Direct Application

This is the typical process encouraged for most applicants. The following steps are recommended:

a) Locate job openings through FJIC, networking, or other published sources (see "Publications Listing Federal Job Openings" farther on).

b) Contact the FJIC or the personnel office of the federal agency at which you are seeking employment to determine whether applications are being accepted and to obtain required forms. For certain positions, schedule a written test.

c) Submit required paperwork. Standard Form 171 is typically required; however, some agencies prefer to use resumes.

The SF (Standard Form)-171

The SF-171 is the official application form for all federal government employment. It is used just like a resume for screening and hiring purposes. Therefore, you must take your time in planning and organizing your written responses to each of its 47 questions. Be especially clear when stating your strengths and abilities in the experience blocks provided. This is where you must describe and show relevance of all previous employment and volunteer experience. You can obtain the SF-171 from any Federal Job Information Center.

When submitting your SF-171, be sure to provide any additional information requested. These attachments can put you ahead, as they allow space to highlight unique experience and training (including self-study). Together these constitute your SF-171 package—your first impression on government agency personnel.

Two final tips: 1) make a master copy; then use specific agency copies related to actual jobs for which you are applying. Leave items 1, 11, and 12 blank on the master copy. These will be tailor-written for specific job openings; 2) Don't sign items 48 and 49 on your master copy. Each photocopied form you send to an agency requires an original signature.

Because this form is so important, several books and software packages have been developed to assist you. Here are a few helpful resources: *Your Application for Federal Government Employment*, a booklet available from the Office of Personnel Management (see address and phone number above); and *The 171 Reference Book, New Edition*, by Patricia B. Wood.

Software packages available include: the *SF-171-Template* for *FormWorx*, 1601 Trapelo Rd., Waltham, MA 02154, 800-992-0085.

Also: *Fedform 171 Laser*, The Arumon Group, P.O. Box 25090-CJF, Arlington, VA 22202, 703-751-6549; *Quick & Easy 171's*, Data Tech Distributors, 4820 Derry St., Harrisburg, PA 17111, 717-561-1335; and *SF-171 Automated*, The Software Den, 103 Loudon St., SW, Historic Leesburg, VA.

How to Get a Job

Application for Federal Employment—SF 171

Read the instructions before you complete this application. *Type or print clearly in dark ink.*

Form Approved
OMB No. 3206-0012

GENERAL INFORMATION

1 What kind of job are you applying for? *Give title and announcement no. (if any)*

2 Social Security Number

3 Sex ☐ Male ☐ Female

4 Birth date *(Month, Day, Year)*

5 Birthplace *(City and State or Country)*

6 Name *(Last, First, Middle)*

Mailing address *(include apartment number, if any)*

City   State   ZIP Code

7 Other names ever used *(e.g., maiden name, nickname, etc.)*

8 Home Phone — Area Code | Number

9 Work Phone — Area Code | Number | Extension

10 Were you ever employed as a civilian by the Federal Government? If "NO", go to Item 11. If "YES", mark each type of job you held with an "X".

☐ Temporary   ☐ Career-Conditional   ☐ Career   ☐ Excepted

What is your highest grade, classification series and job title?

Dates at highest grade: FROM   TO

DO NOT WRITE IN THIS AREA

FOR USE OF EXAMINING OFFICE ONLY

Date entered register

Form reviewed:
Form approved:

Option	Grade	Earned Rating	Veteran Preference	Augmented Rating
			☐ No Preference Claimed	
			☐ 5 Points (Tentative)	
			☐ 10 Pts. (30% Or More Comp. Dis.)	
			☐ 10 Pts. (Less Than 30% Comp. Dis.)	
			☐ Other 10 Points	

Initials and Date

☐ Disallowed   ☐ Being Investigated

FOR USE OF APPOINTING OFFICE ONLY

Preference has been verified through proof that the separation was under honorable conditions, and other proof as required.

☐ 5-Point   ☐ 10-Point- 30% or More Compensable Disability   ☐ 10-Point- Less Than 30% Compensable Disability   ☐ 10-Point- Other

Signature and Title

Agency   Date

AVAILABILITY

11 When can you start work? *(Month and Year)*

12 What is the lowest pay you will accept? *(You will not be considered for jobs which pay less than you indicate.)*

Pay $ _____ per _____ OR Grade _____

13 In what geographic area(s) are you willing to work?

14 Are you willing to work:

	YES	NO
A. 40 hours per week *(full-time)*?		
B. 25-32 hours per week *(part-time)*?		
C. 17-24 hours per week *(part-time)*?		
D. 16 or fewer hours per week *(part-time)*?		
E. An intermittent job *(on-call/seasonal)*?		
F. Weekends, shifts, or rotating shifts?		

15 Are you willing to take a temporary job lasting:

A. 5 to 12 months *(sometimes longer)*?		
B. 1 to 4 months?		
C. Less than 1 month?		

16 Are you willing to travel away from home for:

A. 1 to 5 nights each month?		
B. 6 to 10 nights each month?		
C. 11 or more nights each month?		

MILITARY SERVICE AND VETERAN PREFERENCE

17 Have you served in the United States Military Service? If your only active duty was training in the Reserves or National Guard, answer "NO". If "NO", go to item 22.

YES	NO

18 Did you or will you retire at or above the rank of major or lieutenant commander?

MILITARY SERVICE AND VETERAN PREFERENCE

19 Were you discharged from the military service under honorable conditions? *(If your discharge was changed to "honorable" or "general" by a Discharge Review Board, answer "YES". If you received a clemency discharge, answer "NO".)* If "NO", provide below the date and type of discharge you received.

YES	NO

Discharge Date *(Month, Day, Year)*	Type of Discharge

20 List the dates *(Month, Day, Year)*, and branch for all active duty military service.

From	To	Branch of Service

21 If all your active military duty was after October 14, 1976, list the full names and dates of all campaign badges or expeditionary medals you received or were entitled to receive.

22 **Read the instructions** that came with this form **before** completing this item. When you have determined your eligibility for veteran preference from the instructions, place an "X" in the box next to your veteran preference claim.

☐ NO PREFERENCE

☐ 5-POINT PREFERENCE -- You must show proof when you are hired.

10-POINT PREFERENCE -- If you claim 10-point preference, place an "X" in the box below next to the basis for your claim. To receive 10-point preference you must also complete a Standard Form 15, Application for 10-Point Veteran Preference, which is available from any Federal Job Information Center. ATTACH THE COMPLETED SF 15 AND REQUESTED PROOF TO THIS APPLICATION.

☐ Non-compensably disabled or Purple Heart recipient.

☐ Compensably disabled, less than 30 percent.

☐ Spouse, widow(er), or mother of a deceased or disabled veteran.

☐ Compensably disabled, 30 percent or more.

THE FEDERAL GOVERNMENT IS AN EQUAL OPPORTUNITY EMPLOYER
PREVIOUS EDITION USABLE UNTIL 12-31-90

NSN 7540-00-935-7150   171-109

Standard Form 171 (Rev. 6-88)
U.S. Office of Personnel Management
FPM Chapter 295

Page 1

160

ACWA (Administrative Careers With America)

This is an avenue into entry-level professional and administrative jobs. With a college degree or equivalent experience, interested applicants take an exam that allows them to compete for various positions at the GS-5 and GS-7 grade levels. (See General Schedule table later in this chapter.) Six occupational groups are open to applications in the DC area. These represent nearly 100 occupations, most of which occur in Groups III-VI:

Group I	Health, Safety, and Environmental
Group II	Writing and Public Information
Group III	Business, Finance, and Management
Group IV	Personnel, Administration, and Computers
Group V	Benefits Review, Tax, and Legal
Group VI	Law Enforcement and Investigation

A written test is required for each of the above groups. In Washington, DC, tests are given on a walk-in, space-available basis. Call the DC FJIC (Federal Job Information Center) at 1-900-990-9200 for exam schedule. To take tests in other areas, contact your nearest FJIC. If you pass the test, your name may be referred for employment consideration to agencies as vacancies occur. Your rating must place you among the best qualified to be considered for appointment.

Outstanding Scholar Program

This program is being used more and more by federal agencies. To qualify you must be a college graduate with a 3.5 grade-point average (on a 4.0 scale) for all undergraduate work, or have graduated in the upper 10% of your class or major. Applicants who meet these criteria are given special consideration for government positions at the GS-5 and GS-7 levels. Specifically, qualified applicants are not required to take a written test and may apply directly to agencies at any time.

Clerical and Administrative Support Occupations

This category is for those who take seriously their desire to get into an agency any way possible and then work their way up or around. Positions in this category are misleading, as 64 of them are covered under one exam and only 4 are typically clerical (typing). Exams are offered weekly, and with a qualifying score, you can apply directly to an agency in DC. Positions in this category are at the GS2-GS4 levels and represent the largest number of government employees.

Special Occupations

Certain high demand occupations have special application procedures. You must inquire at the FJIC for the guidelines that apply for each at any given time.

Federal Job Information Center

The FJIC is located at 1900 E St. N.W., Room 1416, Washington, DC 20415-0001 and is open 8:00 a.m–4:00 p.m., Monday–Friday.

The primary function of the FJIC is to provide assistance to anyone interested in federal employment. This valuable office provides job information and application forms, keeps abreast of which applications are being accepted, advises applicants on how and where to apply for jobs, and refers candidates to testing sites or employing agencies. (See "Specific FJIC Services" below.) For anyone wishing to work in the Washington, DC, area, it is important to contact the Washington FJIC since not all DC area government positions are advertised through other FJIC offices.

Specific FJIC Services

■ Personal counter service.

■ Self-service Touch Screen Computers with current job vacancy listings grouped by occupation.

■ Self-service Job Information Telephones with facts on federal employment process and job listings.

■ Postings of Job Vacancies, Qualifications Requirements, Veterans' Information, and other listings.

■ Federal College Hotline (free if calling from center, otherwise 40 cents/minute): 1-900-990-9200), 7 days/week, 24 hours/day.

■ Recorded Job Information: 202-606-2700, 7 days/week, 24 hours/day.

■ Veterans' Employment Seminar every Thursday, 4:30 p.m.; counseling available by appointment, call 202-606-1848.

■ General Employment Seminar first Tuesday each month, 3:00 p.m.

■ Federal Job Information via Telephone Device for the Deaf (TDD), call 202-606-0591.

■ Arrangements for special testing for people with disabilities, call 202-606-2528.

FJIC Self-Service Telephone System:
202-606-2700, 24 hrs./day, 7 days/week

The following are the topics available on a recorded phone message; to speak with an Information Specialist, M-F, 8:00 a.m.-4:00 p.m., dial 000.

1   General Job Information
101   How Jobs Are Filled
102   Competitive Service
103   Excepted Service
104   How Jobs Are Advertised
105   How Your Application is Rated
106   The Rule of Three
107   Chances for Employment
108   How to Obtain Temporary Employment

Job Types in the Federal Government

The federal government hires people within five groups of job types:

Professional occupations: require knowledge of science or specialized education and training equivalent to bachelor's degree or higher; engineers and nurses are the largest professional groups within the federal government.

Administrative occupations: require increasingly responsible experience or general college level education; examples include personnel specialists and administrative officers.

Technical occupations: associated with a professional field; non-routine in nature; examples: computer or electronics technician.

163

Clerical occupations: involve work which supports office, business, or fiscal operations; examples include clerk typist or mail clerk.

Other occupations: all others not classified above; includes many blue-collar and trade occupations, such as painters and carpenters.

As already mentioned, the federal government is quite diverse and has as many occupations as the private sector. The groups mentioned here are considered to be the major classifications. Further information and subdivisions for federal occupations are available in the *Handbook X-118*, one of the government's personnel reference books. This and other helpful references can be used at the Washington FJIC or any federal agency library.

White-collar professional, administrative, technical, and clerical employees are paid according to the *General Schedule (GS)*.

GENERAL SCHEDULE (JAN. 1, 1992) SALARY RANGE

GS-1	$11,478	$14,356	GS-9	$26,798	$34,835
2	12,905	16,237	10	29,511	38,367
3	14,082	18,303	11	32,423	42,152
4	15,808	20,551	12	38,861	50,516
5	17,686	22,996	13	46,210	60,070
6	19,713	25,626	14	54,607	70,987
7	21,906	28,476	15	64,233	83,502
8	24,262	31,543			

All GS positions are classified by OPM into 21 occupational groups and families. Each classification is further subdivided into additional classifications. The primary groups include:

GS-0000 Miscellaneous Occupational Group

GS-0100 Social Science, Psychology, and Welfare Group

GS-0200 Personnel Management and Industrial Relations Group

GS-0300 General Administrative, Clerical, and Office Services

GS-0400 Biological Sciences Group

GS-0500 Accounting and Budget Group

GS-0600 Medical, Hospital,Dental, and Public Health Group

GS-0700 Veterinary Medical Science Group

GS-0800 Engineering and Architecture Group

GS-0900 Legal and Kindred Group

GS-1000 Information and Arts Group

GS-1100 Business and Industry Group

GS-1200 Copyright, Patent, and Trademark Group

GS-1300 Physical Sciences Group

GS-1400 Library and Archives Group

GS-1500 Mathematics and Statistics Group

GS-1600 Equipment, Facilities, and Services Group

GS-1700   Education Group

GS-1800   Investigation Group

GS-1900   Quality Assurance, Inspection, and Grading Group

GS-2000   Supply Group

GS-2100   Transportation Group

Classification of GS Positions

The following table indicates the amount of education and experience required for certain administrative and managerial positions. Certain added criteria apply to some of these areas. Check with the Federal Job Information Center for additional information. Remember, too, that classifications are further subdivided.

Grade	Education	OR	Experience
		(or/and Equivalent) Combination	
		General	**Specialized***
GS-5	4-yr. course of study above high school, leading to a bachelor's degree	3 yrs., 1 yr. equivalent to GS-4	None
GS-7	1 full academic year of graduate-level education or superior academic achievement**	None	1 yr. at least equivalent to GS-5
GS-9	2 full academic years of graduate-level education or master's degree	None	1 yr. at least equivalent to GS-7
GS-11	3 full academic years of graduate-level education or Ph.D.	None	1 yr. at least equivalent to GS-9
GS-12	None (experience considered prime factor, regardless of education)	None	1 yr. at least equivalent to next lower grade level

*Specialized experience is that which is in or directly related to the duties of the positions being filled.

**College graduates who stand in the upper third of their graduating class, have a grade point average of 3.0 or better (4.0 scale), or belong to a national scholastic honor society are eligible for GS-7 positions.

Hotlines for Federal Job Openings

Federal jobs are advertised through the Federal Job Information Center. Vacancy information is also available through personnel departments at individual agencies. Many agencies have jobline phone numbers (hotlines) with recorded job listing information. Jobline phone numbers for selected agencies are as follows:

Action	**202-606-5263**
	202-606-5000
Agency For International	**202-663-1401**
Development	**202-663-1396**
Agriculture:	**202-720-5626**
Agriculture Research Service	**301-344-1518**
	301-344-1124/344-2288
Farmers Home Administration	**202-245-5561**
Food & Nutrition Service	**703-756-3351**
Forest Service Personnel	**703-235-8145**
Management Staff	**703-235-2730**
Soil Conservation Service	**202-720-4264**
	202-720-6365
Central Intelligence Agency	**703-874-4400**
	703-351-2028
Commerce:	
Office of Personnel &	**202-377-4807**
Civil Rights	**202-377-4285/377-5138**
Bureau of the Census	**301-763-7470**
	301-763-5537
International Trade	**202-377-1533**
Administration	
National Institute of	**301-975-3007**
Standards & Technology	**703-538-3344**
National Oceanic &	**301-713-0520**
Atmospheric Administration	
Office of Inspector General	**202-377-4661**
Patent and Trademark Office	**703-557-1244**
Commodity Futures Trading	**202-254-3275**
Commission	
Defense:	
Air Force	**703-695-4389**
	703-693-6550

Army	703-325-8840
Consolidated Civilian Personnel Office	202-433-5370 202-433-4931
David Taylor Research Center	202-227-4160
Defense Investigative Service	202-475-1116
Marine Corps	703-640-2048
Military District of Washington (Ft. Myer Civilian Personnel)	202-696-3035
National Naval Medical Center (Civilian Personnel)	202-295-6800
Naval Research Laboratory	202-767-3030
Navy	703-697-6181
One Stop Employment Information Center	703-780-4655 703-780-4677
Walter Reed Army Medical Center	202-576-0546
Defense Logistics Agency	703-274-7088
Defense Mapping Agency	703-285-9148 301-227-2130
District of Columbia Government	202-727-6406 202-727-9726
Education	202-401-0559
Energy	202-586-8580 202-586-4333
Environmental Protection Agency	202-260-2090 202-260-5055
Equal Employment Opportunity Commission	202-663-4264
Export-Import Bank of the U.S.	202-566-8834
Federal Bureau of Investigation	202-324-4981
Federal Communications Commission	202-632-7106
Federal Deposit Insurance Corporation	202-898-8890
Federal Emergency Management Agency	202-646-3970 202-646-3244

167

Federal Energy Regulatory	202-357-0992
Commission	202-219-2791
Federal Labor Relations Authority	202-382-0751
Federal Trade Commission	202-326-2022
	202-326-2020
General Accounting Office	202-275-6092
	202-275-6017 (GS-1/12)
	202-275-6361 (GS-13/above)
General Services Administration	202-501-0370
Government Printing Office	202-512-0000
Health and Human Services:	202-619-2123
Alcohol, Drug Abuse &	301-443-4826
Mental Health	301-443-2282
Food and Drug Administration	301-443-1970
	301-443-1969
National Institute of Health	301-496-2403
	301-496-9541
Social Security Administration	301-965-4506
	301-965-4404
Housing & Urban Development	202-708-0416
	202-708-3203
Interior:	
Minerals Management Service	703-787-1414
	703-787-1402
National Park Service	202-619-7256
	202-619-7111/619-7364
U.S. Geological Survey	703-648-6131
	703-648-7676
Justice:	202-514-6813
	202-514-6818
Bureau of Prisons	202-307-1304
	202-514-6388
Drug Enforcement	202-307-4055
Administration	
Immigration & Naturalization	202-514-2690
Service	202-514-4301
U.S. Marshal Service	202-307-9629
International Trade Commission	202-205-2651

Interstate Commerce Commission	**202-275-7288**
Merit Systems Protection Board	**202-653-5916** **202-254-8013**
NASA	**202-453-8478** **202-755-6299**
NASA Goddard Space Flight Center	**301-286-7918** **301-286-5326**
National Archives & Records Administration	**202-501-6100**
National Endowment For The Arts	**202-682-5405** **202-682-5700**
National Endowment For The Humanities	**202-786-0415**
National Labor Relations Board	**202-254-9044**
National Library of Medicine	**301-496-4943** **301-496-9541**
National Office of Management & Budget	**202-395-3765** **202-395-5892**
National Science Foundation	**202-357-7602**
Office of Personnel Management	**202-606-2424**
Peace Corps	**202-606-3336** **202-775-2214** **1-800-424-8580 ext.2214**
Securities and Exchange Commission	**202-272-2550**
Small Business Administration	**202-653-6504**
Smithsonian Institution	**202-287-3100** **202-287-3102**
U.S. Information Agency	**202-619-4659** **202-619-4539**
U.S. Postal Service	**202-268-3646** **202-268-3218**
U.S. Soldiers and Airmens Home	**202-722-3215**

Voice of America   **202-619-3117**
                                        202-619-0909

Publications Listings Federal Job Openings

Of course the best source of job opening information is through the grapevine. Besides keeping in touch with people employed at government agencies (or their friends), other sources of job openings are also useful. These include the following published sources:

Periodicals

Federal Career Opportunities—(Federal Research Service, 243 Church St. N.W., Vienna, VA 22180, 703-281-0800). Bi-weekly, $38/three-month subscription. Information on about 4,000 federal job vacancies from GS-5 to Senior Executive levels.

Federal Job Matching Service—(Breakthrough Publications, P.O. Box 594, Millwood, NY 10546, 1-800-824-5000). $30 fee ($25 for Federal Jobs Digest subscribers); fee refunded if found unqualified for any federal job. Service matches candidate's education and experience to federal job requirements and gives candidate a list of job titles and grade levels offering best chance of success. Candidate must consult sources to determine whether job is open.

Federal Jobs Digest—(Breakthrough Publications, P.O. Box 594, Millwood, NY 10546, 1-800-824-5000). Bi-weekly, $29/three-month subscription. Up to 30,000 federal positions listed with job title, grade, closing date, announcement, number and application address.

Federal Times—(6883 Commercial Dr., Springfield, VA 22159, 703-750-8920). Weekly, $48/annual subscription. Brief descriptions of several hundred federal positions, including the military. GS-7 and above.

Directories

Many directories have been compiled with invaluable information about key offices and staff within all branches of the federal government. These are critical tools for government job seekers. The following resources are available at most public and many college or university, general, or career libraries. (For descriptions and publisher information, see Chapter 4, "Researching the Washington Job Market.")

Almanac of American Government Jobs and Careers (Impact Publications, Manassas, VA)
America's Federal Jobs: A Complete Directory of Federal Career Opportunities (JIST WORKS, Indianapolis, IN)
The American Lobbyist's Directory (Gale Research, Detroit, MI)
Capitol Jobs: An Insider's Guide to Finding a Job in Congress (Tilden Press, Washington, DC)
The Capitol Source (National Journal, Washington, DC)
The Complete Guide to Public Employment (Impact Publications, Manassas, VA)

Congressional Staff Directory (Staff Directories, Mt. Vernon, VA)
Congressional Yellow Book (Monitor Publishing, Washington, DC)
Federal Career Directory (Superintendent of Documents, Washington, DC)
Federal Jobs for College Graduates (Prentice Hall, New York)
Federal Personnel Office Directory (Federal Reports, Washington, DC)
Federal/State Executive Directory (Carroll Publishing, Washington, DC)
Finding a Federal Job Fast (Impact Publications, Manassas, VA)
Government Job Finder (Planning Communications, River Forest, IL)
Government Research Directory (Gale Research, Detroit, MI)
Great Careers (Garrett Park Press, Garrett Park, MD)
Judicial Staff Directory (Staff Directories, Mt. Vernon, VA)
Political Resource Directory (Political Resources, Rye, NY)
U.S. Government Manual (Office of the Federal Register, Washington, DC)
Washington '92 (Columbia Books, Washington, DC)
Washington Information Directory (Congressional Quarterly, Washington, DC)
Washington Representatives (Columbia Books, Washington, DC)
Who's Who in Congress (Congressional Quarterly, Washington, DC)

Professional Organizations for Networking in Federal Government

Government employees also belong to a wide variety of occupational-specific organizations and societies. Here are a few you might investigate for networking possibilities in your job hunt.

American Federation of Government Employees
80 F St. N.W.
Washington, DC 20001-1525
202-737-8700

American Public Works Association
1313 E. 60th St.
Chicago, IL 60637
312-667-2200

American Society for Public Administration
1120 G St. N.W., Suite 700
Washington, DC 20005-3885
202-393-7878

Assembly of Governmental Employees
655 15th St. N.W.
Washington, DC 20005
202-371-1123

Civil Service Employees Association
143 Washington Ave.
Albany, NY 12210
518-434-0191

Federal Executive and Professional Association
15535 New Hampshire Ave.
Silver Spring, MD 20904
301-384-2616

Federally Employed Women
1400 I St. N.W., Suite 425

How to Get a Job

Washington, DC 20005
202-898-0994

Federal Women's Interagency Board
P.O. Box 14166
Washington, DC 20004
202-267-3884

National Association of Government Employees
1313 L St. N.W.
Washington, DC 20005
202-371-6644

National Federation of Federal Employees
1016 16th St. N.W.
Washington, DC 20036
202-862-4400

State and Local Government Employment

In most areas state and local governments employ the largest number of public service employees. Nationally this represents employment for more than 14 million people. Within this group, more than half of these individuals are employed in the field of education. State and local governments in the DC area (the district itself is considered state government) account for approximately 224,000 employees, 78,000 state and 146,000 local.

While this part of the labor market is large, cutbacks have been most severe on state and local levels. Figures indicate that employment in state government has increased overall over the past two decades. But these increases have been offset by the fact that certain state functions have actually decreased. Serious social problems and the recent economic recession continue to decrease the number of jobs available. Nevertheless, normal labor market turnover due to retirement, death, and career changes does create vacancies which need to be filled.

State government is largely concerned with the provision of higher education, health, highway, and correctional services. It is divided into the same three categories as the federal: executive, legislative, and judicial. Job-hunting strategies differ slightly between these areas as well as between organizations, depending on the type of position you are seeking. Therefore, the best overall approach to take is the tried and true method of researching your targeted agency(ies) for their recommended procedures and making contacts with as many knowledgeable people as possible. There is no substitute for being prepared with thorough knowledge of the state agency and people for whom you would like to work.

EXECUTIVE

This branch of state government hires people in positions similar to those in local and federal offices. The range of white-collar jobs is diverse, as indicated by the following sample of job areas:

Aeronautics	Air Quality
Aging	Banking

Child Labor
Civil Rights
Corrections
Developmental Disabled
Disaster Preparedness
Educational Television
Ethics
Foreign Trade
Geology
Historic Preservation
Human Resources

Juvenile Delinquency
Libraries
Lotteries
Mental Health
Natural Resources
Parks and Recreation
Social Services
Tourism
Veterans Affairs
Water Supply

LEGISLATIVE

Typically, each state legislature creates legislative agencies that hire varying numbers of staff.

The most common agencies include:

Legislative Reference Services

Bill Drafting Services

Legislative Councils

Budgeting and Audit Staffs

Consult the Blue Pages of the phone book for the state you are targeting, where a thorough listing of departments and locations is provided.

Specialized staffs are also created around a variety of policy issues for standing committees and within the personal staffs of legislators. These challenging jobs are largely advertised through word-of-mouth and, therefore, call forth your greatest networking abilities. Contacting a state legislator or key staff members is still the best way to get in. And if vacancies are not available when you make your connection, don't be discouraged. These kind of openings can occur with little advance notice so it pays to be persistent. By staying in touch, you may have just the visibility you need to get noticed when the time is right.

A related area to consider when job hunting in the legislature is that of private organizations that do business with the state. These jobs are often just as interesting and still provide the government connection you may be seeking. Use local directories (see end of chapter listings) to identify these agencies, or ask around when doing your networking at the legislature.

JUDICIAL

This area offers fewer job opportunities than the other two branches. It is typically divided into four levels of courts: Supreme Court, Intermediate Appellate Courts, Trial Courts of General Jurisdiction, and Trial Courts of Limited Jurisdiction. (The Blue Pages of the phone book will indicate which courts operate in Maryland, DC, and Virginia.) While hiring practices vary, many of these offices use county or city personnel offices to advertise administrative or support positions. Professional positions are often filled informally through networking and referrals from schools or professional associations.

State and DC Hiring Procedures

Most states do have a central personnel department or merit system that coordinates the formal hiring functions such as announcing vacancies, accepting applications, administering tests, screening candidates, and forwarding eligible applicants to the hiring person(s). Through this system, generally, the steps to follow in applying for state jobs include:

1. Identify and keep abreast of job vacancies at the personnel office.
2. Learn about and complete necessary application forms.
3. Take any required tests.

HIRING FOR DISTRICT OF COLUMBIA

To learn about job openings in DC,

Contact: Department of Employment Services
Job Information Center
500 C St. N.W., Room 102
Washington, DC 20001
202-727-9726

Publishes "Job Opportunities Bulletin," bi-weekly, one free copy available for non-residents; may write for job descriptions; jobs posted on bulletin boards at all DC personnel offices and city agencies.

Servicing Personnel Offices operate in 8 District locations. Employment assistance is available to local residents. Call this recorded directory, **202-630-1000,** to learn about the services nearest your zip code area.

DC Government Department Joblines: These offices assist those already employed but wishing to change positions within DC (you may contact them to learn about the status of your application):

Human Services & Recreation:
801 N. Capitol St. N.E.
202-727-0803

Consumer and Regulatory Affairs, Public Works,
Administrative Services, D.C. Energy Office:
2000 14th St. N.W.
202-939-8700

Police, Fire, Corrections, Board of Patrol:
300 Indiana Ave. N.W.
202-727-4272

Other District Agencies:
1133 North Capitol St. N.E.
202-525-1050

HIRING FOR MARYLAND

Department of Personnel
301 W. Preston St., Room 609
Baltimore, MD 21201
301-225-4715

For **Job Services Offices,** contact:
Department of Economic and Employment Development
1100 N. Eutaw St., Room 700
Baltimore, MD 21201
301-333-5070
This office also operates a free job-matching service. Call: 301-333-7574.
Matches your skills to job vacancies in government, private, and non-profit
sectors.
State Agency Locator: 301-974-2000

HIRING FOR VIRGINIA

State Employment Service Office:
Department of Personnel & Training
James Monroe Bldg.
101 North 14th St.
Richmond, VA 23219

Publishes bi-weekly statewide job listing, available at main office and libraries.

For **Job Services Offices** (42 locations) contact:
Virginia Employment Commission
703 E. Main St.
Richmond, VA 23219
804-786-3001

State, local, and federal vacancy announcements are available through this office.
ALEX, a newly established computerized statewide job listing service, is also
available and will be coming soon to shopping malls, libraries, and schools.

Local office for state employment:
13135 Lee Jackson Memorial Hwy., Suite 340
Fairfax, VA 22033
703-803-0000

Assists with state and federal jobs, free counseling, job listings.
State Agency Locator: 804-786-0000

Helpful Resources for State Employment

In addition to the newspapers and trade magazines listed in Chapter 4, the
following resources are available:

Opportunities in State Government (ACCESS: Networking in the Public
Interest, 50 Beacon St., Boston, MA 02108, 617-720-5627). Three issues/
year, $250 annual subscription. Listings of over 450 new jobs in all aspects
of state government nationwide.

Public Administration Times (American Society for Public Administration, 1255 Connecticut Ave. N.W., Washington, DC 20036, 202-785-
3255).

Public Allies Program (National Center for Careers in Public Life, 1225
15th St. N.W., Washington, DC 20005, 202-232-6800). Free; new placement service for young adults wishing to enter non-profit jobs. Placements
in jobs nationwide; program defers cost of student loans and provides
stipend to supplement salaries.

Public Service Minority Resume Bank (ACCESS, see above contact information). Available only to persons of color or who speak a language other

than English. Free. Submit resume to computerized job bank for match with employers. Call or write to obtain resume form.

The State Recruiter (Clearinghouse for Government Personnel, P.O. Box 2400, Station B, Lincoln, NE 68502). Bi-weekly listing of jobs in many areas within state agencies.

Employment with Local Government

Local governments employ more than 10 million workers nationally, 146,000 in the DC metropolitan area, who work in a variety of disciplines and types of organizations. Although tough times recently have taken a larger toll on this level of employment than the others, job hunters need to get past the big picture and focus on what's happening in the particular organizations of greatest interest.

This level of government is highly decentralized. In fact, there are five categories of governing authorities: counties, municipalities, townships, school districts, and special districts. (Only some of these categories apply to the District of Columbia.)

Counties are the largest governing unit next to state governments. Municipalities are units of government incorporated for urban areas. Usually, municipalities are political subdivisions of counties, but in Virginia certain municipalities are independent of counties. They are referred to differently, sometimes as cities, towns, villages, or boroughs. Townships are also political subdivisions of counties and share in governing power with them.

School districts are either independent or dependent. Those in Maryland, Virginia, and the District of Columbia are dependent, which means they are partly under the control of state, county, and municipal governments.

Special districts are those which provide special services otherwise not provided by local government. They are sometimes also referred to as authorities, boards, or commissions.

The best opportunities will be within the larger (more than 10,000 residents) counties, municipalities, and school districts. (In Virginia, Prince William County is considered the fastest growing; and in Maryland, eyes are on Prince George's County for an increase in commercial activity.) However, the greatest number of jobs and openings will be found in areas such as teaching, police, fire and rescue, health, social services, finance, development, libraries, parks and recreation, and general services. While many of these are support-level positions, white collar jobs exist in these and many other areas within local government. (For a complete listing of departments and offices, see the Blue Pages in the appropriate phone book.)

Local Government Hiring Procedures

Both formal and informal systems for hiring exist on the local levels. Like federal and state government, the job hunter is encouraged to look for jobs using both approaches. The formal approach again involves 3 main steps: 1) familiarize yourself with the main personnel office as well as the personnel department of the organization with the job opening; 2) monitor the job vacancies as advertised; 3) complete an application and take any tests required for the specific positions of interest to you.

It is a good idea to also make use of the informal job search method, where you research the organization and make contact with the person with the power to hire. Once your test results come in, if you receive a good score, your personal contact can go a long way in helping you land that job.

MARYLAND

See the Blue Pages in the phone book for directory of departments, offices, and phone numbers for state and local governments.

Personnel Offices:

Montgomery County
101 Monroe St., 7th floor
Rockville, MD 20850
301-217-2240

Publishes "Employment Opportunities," available at main office and libraries.

Also: Wheaton Plaza
South Office Bldg.
Wheaton, MD 20915
301-949-5624

Prince George's County
6321 Greenbelt Rd.
Greenbelt, MD 20740
301-441-2137

Maryland Local Government Job Hotlines:

Maryland National Capital Parks and Planning Commission—
301-927-5101
Montgomery County—301-217-2240
Prince George's County—301-952-3408

NORTHERN VIRGINIA

Alexandria, City of
Personnel Services Department
City Hall, Room 2500
301 King St.
Alexandria, VA 22314
703-838-4422

Publishes "Job Opportunities," available at main offices and libraries.

Arlington County
Personnel Department
#1 Courthouse Plaza
2100 Clarendon Blvd., Suite 511
Arlington, VA 22201
703-358-3500

Publishes "Job Opportunities," available at main offices and libraries.

How to Get a Job

Fairfax County
Office of Personnel
12000 Government Center Parkway
Fairfax, VA 22035
703-222-5872

Publishes "Job News," a bi-weekly. Also provides "Job News" on Cable Channel 16.

Virginia Local Government Job Hotlines:

Alexandria City—703-838-4422
Arlington County—703-538-3363
Fairfax City—703-385-7860
Fairfax County—703-246-4600
Falls Church—703-241-5130

Helpful Resources for Local Employment

General Resources

The Job Opportunities Bulletin for Minorities and Women in Local Government. Published every three weeks, free, by International City Management Association, 777 North Capitol St. N.E., #500, Washington, DC 20002, 202-962-3650.

The City-County Recruiter (Clearinghouse for Government Personnel, P.O. Box 2400, Station B, Lincoln, NE 68502). Bi-weekly listing of local jobs in many areas.

Resources for Maryland

Maryland Municipal League Information Bulletin (Maryland Municipal League, 1212 West St., Annapolis, MD 21401, 301-268-5514). Bi-weekly, $50/year non-member subscription, $25/members. Lists a small number of positions in all aspects of local government.

Also: *Maryland Municipal League Personnel Exchange Program.* $5/six months; submit resume for six months on file for match with local government job announcement; job seeker must contact agency for follow-up.

The Maryland National Capital Park & Planning Commission Job Opportunities Bulletin (6609 Riggs Rd., Hyattsville, MD 20782, 301-853-4816; 24-hr. hotline: 301-538-3361). Lists positions, locations, and salaries for local jobs.

Resources for Virginia

Virginia Town and City (Virginia Municipal League, 13 E. Franklin St., P.O. Box 12164, Richmond, VA 23241, 804-649-8471). Monthly, $8/ annual subscription for non-members, $4/members. Lists local jobs.

Also: *Virginia Municipal League Letter:* bi-weekly, $25/annual subscription. Lists local jobs.

Professional Organizations for Networking in State and Local Government

STATE

American Federation of Government Employees
80 F St. N.W.
Washington, DC 20001-1525
202-737-8700

Council of State Community Affairs Agencies
444 N. Capitol St. N.W.
Washington, 20001
202-393-6435

Council of State Governments
P.O. Box 11910
Iron Works Pike
Lexington, KY 40578
606-252-2291

National Association of State Boards of Education
1012 Cameron St.
Alexandria, VA 22314
703-684-4000

National Association for State Information Systems
P.O. Box 11910
Iron Works Pike
Lexington, KY 40578
606-231-1870

National Governors' Association
Hall of the States, Suite 250
444 N. Capitol St. N.W.
Washington, DC 20001-1572
202-624-5300

LOCAL

American Planning Association
1776 Massachusetts Ave. N.W.
Washington, DC 20036-1997
202-872-0611

American Public Welfare Association
810 First St. N.E., Suite 500
Washington, DC 20002-4205
202-682-0100

International City Management Association
1120 G St. N.W.
Washington, DC 20005
202-626-4600

National Association of Counties
444 First St. N.W.
Washington, DC 20001
202-393-6226

National Association of County Training and Employment Professionals
440 First St. N.W.
Washington, DC 20001
202-393-6226

National Association of Regional Councils
1700 K St. N.W., Rm. 1300
Washington, DC 20006
202-457-0710

National Association of Towns and Townships
1522 K St. N.W., Suite 600
Washington, DC 20005
202-737-5200

National League of Cities
1301 Pennsylvania Ave. N.W, 6th Fl.
Washington, DC 20004
202-626-3000

United States Conference of Mayors
1620 I St. N.W., 4th Fl.
Washington, DC 20006
202-293-7330

Directories for State and Local Government Jobs

BNA's Directory of State Courts, Judges, and Clerks (Bureau of National Affairs Books Distribution Center, Edison, NJ)
The Book of States (Council of State Governments, Lexington, KY)
Braddock's Federal-State-Local Government Directory (Braddock Communications, Alexandria, VA)
The Capitol Source (National Journal, Washington, DC)
Directory of Maryland Municipal Officials (Maryland Municipal League, Annapolis, MD)
Municipal/County Executive Directory (Carroll Publishing, Washington, DC)
The Municipal Yearbook (International City Management Association, Washington, DC)
Municipal Yellow Book (Monitor Publishing, New York, NY)
National Organizations of State Government Officials Directory (The Council of State Governments, Lexington, KY)
Regional, State and Local Organizations (Gale Research, Detroit, MI)
State Elected Officials and the Legislatures (The Council of State Governments, Lexington, KY)
State Executive Directory (Carroll Publishing, Washington, DC)
State Government Research Directory (Gale Research, Detroit, MI)
State Legislative Leadership, Committees, and Staff (The Council of State Governments, Lexington, KY)
State Yellow Book (Monitor Publishing, New York, NY)
Virginia Municipal League Directory (Virginia Municipal League, Richmond, VA)

Virginia Review Directory of State and Local Government Officials (County Publications, Chester, VA)
Washington '92 (Columbia Books, Washington, DC)

Where Washington Works

FOR GOVERNMENT EMPLOYMENT OPPORTUNITIES, SEE CHAPTER 11

This chapter contains the names, addresses, and phone numbers of the Washington area's top 1,400 employers of non-governmental white-collar workers. The companies are arranged in categories according to the major products and services they manufacture or provide. Where appropriate, entries contain a brief description of the company's business and the name of the personnel director or other contact.

This listing is intended to help you survey the major potential employers in fields that interest you. It is selective, not exhaustive. We have not, for example, listed all the advertising agencies in the area as you can find that information in the Yellow Pages. We have simply listed the top twenty-five or so, that is, the ones with the most jobs.

The purpose of this chapter is to get you started, both looking and thinking. This is the kickoff, not the final gun. Browse through the whole chapter, and take some time to check out areas that are unfamiliar to you.

Many white-collar skills are transferable. People with marketing, management, data processing, accounting, administrative, secretarial, and other talents are needed in a huge variety of businesses as well as government.

Ask yourself in what areas your skills could be marketed. Use your imagination, especially if you're in a so-called specialized field. A dietitian, for instance, might look first under Health Care, or perhaps Hospitality. But what about Insurance, Cultural Institutions, Financial Institutions, or the scores of other places that run their own dining rooms for employees or the public? What about Food and Media? Who invents all those recipes and tests those products?

The tips and insider interviews that are scattered throughout this chapter are designed to nudge your creativity and suggest additional ideas for your job search. Much more detailed information on the area's top employers and other, smaller, companies can be found in the directories and other resources suggested in Chapter 4. We can't stress strongly enough that *you have to do your homework when you're looking for a job,* both to unearth places that might need a person with your particular talents, and to succeed in the interview once you've lined up a meeting with the hiring authority.

A word about hiring authorities: if you've read Chapter 5, you know the name of the game is to meet the person with the power to hire you, or to get as close to that person as you can. You don't want to go to the chairman or the personnel director if the person who actually makes the decision is the marketing manager or customer service director.

Obviously, we can't list every possible hiring authority in the area's "Top 1,400." If we tried, you'd need a wagon to haul this book around. Besides, printed directories go out of date—even those that are regularly and conscientiously revised. So always double-check a contact whose name you get from a book or magazine, including this one. If necessary, call the company's switchboard to confirm who heads a particular department or division.

Here, then, are Washington's greatest non-government opportunities. Happy hunting!

The Washington area's top 1,400 employers are arranged in the following categories:

Accounting/Auditing Firms
Advertising/Public Relations
Aerospace and Aircraft
Architectural Firms
Associations
Book Publishers
Broadcasting
Computers: Data Processing
Computers: Hardware and Software
Contractors and Construction
Cultural Institutions
Educational Institutions
Electronics/Telecommunications
Engineering
Environmental Consulting Firms

> **Financial Institutions/Credit Unions**
> **Food/Beverage Producers and Distributors**
> **Foundations**
> **Health Care**
> **Hospitality/Caterers**
> **Human Services**
> **Instruments**
> **Insurance**
> **International Organizations**
> **Investment Banking/Stock Brokers**
> **Labor Unions**
> **Law Firms**
> **Media: Print**
> **Office Supplies and Equipment**
> **Political Consultants**
> **Printing**
> **Public Interest Groups**
> **Real Estate Developers and Brokers**
> **Recreation/Fitness**
> **Research & Development/Technical Services**
> **Retailers**
> **Think Tanks**
> **Travel and Transportation**
> **Utilities**

Accounting/Auditing Firms

Be sure to keep in mind that almost any organization with a reasonable size staff employs accountants. You should not limit yourself to the firms listed below.

For networking in accounting and related fields, check out these professional organizations listed in Chapter 5:

PROFESSIONAL ORGANIZATIONS:

American Institute of Certified Public Accountants/ Washington Office
District of Columbia Institute of CPAs

For additional information, you can write or call:

American Institute of CPA's
1211 Ave. of the Americas
New York, NY 10036
(212) 575-6200

American Society of Women Accountants
35 E. Wacker Drive

Chicago, IL 60601
(312) 726-9030

Institute of Management Accountants
10 Paragon Drive
Montvale, NJ 07645-1760
(201) 573-9000

National Association of Black Accountants
200 I St. N.E., #150
Washington, DC 20002
(202) 546-6222

National Association of Minority CPA's
1625 I St. N.W.
Washington, DC 20006

National Society of Public Accountants
1010 N. Fairfax St.
Alexandria, VA 22314
(703) 549-6400

PROFESSIONAL PUBLICATIONS:

Accounting News
The CPA Journal
Journal of Accountancy
National Public Accountant

DIRECTORIES:

Accountants Directory (American Business Directories, Inc., Omaha, NE)
Accounting Firms Directory (American Business Directories, Inc., Omaha, NE)
International Guide to Accounting Journals (Weiner Publications, Inc., New York, NY)
National Society of Public Accountants—Yearbook (National Society of Public Accountants, Alexandria, VA)
Who Audits America (Data Financial Press, Menlo Park, CA)

EMPLOYERS:

Arthur Anderson & Co.
1666 K St. N.W.
Washington, DC 20006
202-862-3100

Aronson, Fetridge, Weigle & Schimel
6116 Executive Blvd.
Rockville, MD 20852
301-231-6200

BDO Seidman
1707 L St. N.W.
Washington, DC 20036
202-833-2280

Beers & Cutler
1250 Connecticut Ave. N.W.
Washington, DC 20036
202-331-030

Berlin, Karam & Ramos
8484 Georgia Ave.
Silver Spring, MD 20910
301-589-9000

Bond, Beebe, Barton & Muckelbauer
5301 Wisconsin Ave. N.W.
Washington, DC 20015
202-244-6500

Coopers & Lybrand
1800 M St. N.W.
Washington, DC 20036
202-822-4000

Councillor Buchanan & Mitchell
7101 Wisconsin Ave.
Bethesda, MD 20814
301-986-0600

Deloitte & Touche
1001 Pennsylvania Ave. N.W.
Washington, DC 20004
202-879-5600

Dembo, Jones & Healy
7250 Woodmont Ave.
Bethesda, MD 20814
301-718-0900

Ernst & Young
1225 Connecticut Ave. N.W.
Washington, DC 20036
202-862-6000

Grant Thornton
1850 M St. N.W.
Washington, DC 20036
202-296-7800

K.P.M.G.-Peat Marwick
2001 M St. N.W.

Washington, DC 20036
202-467-3000

Keller, Zanger, Bissell & Co.
6000 Executive Blvd.
Rockville, MD 20852
301-770-7730

Pannell, Kerr & Forster
1199 N. Fairfax St.
Alexandria, VA   22314
703-549-6920

Price Waterhouse
1801 K St. N.W.
Washington, DC 20006
202-296-0800

Regardie, Brooks & Lewis
7101 Wisconsin Ave.
Bethesda, MD 20814
301-654-9000

Reznick Fedder & Silverman
4520 East-West Highway
Bethesda, MD 20814
301-652-9100

Snyder, Newrath and Co.
4520 East-West Highway
Bethesda, MD 20814
301-652-6700

Stoy, Malone & Co.
7315 Wisconsin Ave.
Bethesda, MD 20814
301-652-6300

Thomas Havey & Co.
900 17th St. N.W.
Washington, DC 20006
202-331-9880

Thompson, Greenspon & Co.
3930 Walnut St.
Fairfax, VA 22030
703-385-8888

Watkins, Meegan, Drury & Co.
4800 Hampden Lane
Bethesda, MD 20814
301-654-7555

**Auditing a
candidate's
prospects**

We asked Dick Jensen, former personnel director for a Big Eight accounting firm, what he was looking for in an interview.

"A combination of things," says Jensen. "Intelligence, of course. Also business presence, by which I mean not only appearance and communication skills but listening skills as well. We try to get a sense of the person's judgment, maturity, and independence. Then there is leadership potential—how well is this person respected by his or her peers?

"It's not just what a person says in an interview that counts. We try to tie what they say to whay they've done. I look for patterns of success and try to get a sense of the history of a person's accomplishments, sometimes going all the way back to grammar school. I'm likely to ask questions that don't seem at first to relate to working at a large accounting firm— such as, "What was your standing in the Eagle Scouts?" ■

Advertising/Public Relations

For networking in advertising and public relations, check out the following organizations listed in Chapter 5:

PROFESSIONAL ORGANIZATIONS:

**Advertising Club of Metropolitan Washington
Art Directors Club of Metropolitan Washington
Arts Club of Washington
Direct Marketing Association of Washington**

For additional information, you can write or call:

The Advertising Council
261 Madison Ave.
New York, NY 10016
(212) 922-1500

American Advertising Federation
1400 K St. N.W.
Washington, DC 20005
(202) 898-0089

American Association of Advertising Agencies
666 Third Ave.

New York, NY 10017
(212) 682-2500

Public Relations Society of America
33 Irving Place
New York, NY 10003

PROFESSIONAL PUBLICATIONS:

Advertising Age
Adweek
American Demographics
Direct Marketing Magazine
Journal of Advertising Research
Madison Avenue
Marketing/Communications
PR Reporter
Public Relations Journal
Public Relations Review

DIRECTORIES:

Advertising Career Directory (Career Press, Inc., Hawthorne, NJ)
Bradford's Directory of Marketing Research Agencies (Bradford Publishing
    Co., Fairfax, VA)
International Membership Directory and Marketing Services Guide (American
    Marketing Association, Chicago, IL)
O'Dwyer's Directory of Public Relations Firms (J.R. O'Dwyer Co., New York,
    NY)
Standard Directory of Advertising Agencies (National Register Publishing
    Co., Skokie, IL)
Target Marketing—Who's Who of Direct Marketing (North American
    Publishing Co., Philadelphia, PA)

EMPLOYERS:

Abramson Associates
1275 K St. N.W.
Washington, DC 20005
202-289-6900
Contact: David Abramson

John Adams Associates
1825 K St. N.W.
Washington, DC 20006
202-466-8320
Contact: Kris Ludwig

The Adams Group
1901 Research Blvd.
Rockville, MD 20850

301-279-5555
Contact: Kevin O'Keefe, Pres.

Bomstein Agency
2201 Wisconsin Ave. N.W.
Washington, DC 20007
202-965-6470
Contact: Howard Bomstein

Burson-Marsteller
1850 M St. N.W.
Washington, DC 20036
202-833-8550
Contact: John Cogman

The Canzeri Company
3240 Prospect St. N.W.
Washington, DC 20007
202-965-7320
Contact: Joseph W. Canzeri

DDB Needham Worldwide
8300 Greensboro Drive
McLean, VA 22102
703-790-4800
Contact: Joseph P. Landy

Susan Davis Companies
1146 19th St. N.W.
Washington, DC 20036
202-775-8881
Contact: Susan Davis

Demaine, Vickers & Associates
427 N. Lee St.
Alexandria, VA 22314
703-836-0505
Contact: Windsor Demaine

Doremus Porter Novelli
1001 30th St. N.W.
Washington, DC 20007
202-342-7000
Contact: Melissa Visaker

Earle Palmer Brown
6935 Arlington Blvd.
Bethesda, MD 20814
301-657-6000
Contact: Jeremy Brown

Daniel J. Edelman
1420 K St. N.W.
Washington, DC 20006
202-371-0200
Contact: Richard Edelman

Ehrlich-Manes & Associates
1275 K St. N.W.
Washington, DC 20005
202-289-6900
Contact: David Abramson

Fleishman Hillard
1301 Connecticut Ave. N.W.
Washington, DC 20036
202-659-0330
Contact: Richard J. Sullivan

Goldberg/Marchesano & Associates
927 15th St. N.W.
Washington, DC 20005
202-789-2000
Contact: Norman Goldberg

Govatos & Associates
6715 Little River Tnpk.
Annandale, VA 22003
703-914-8770
Contact: John Govatos

Greer Margolis Mitchell & Associates
2626 Pennsylvania Ave. N.W.
Washington, DC 20007
202-338-8700
Contact: Frank Greer

Hager, Sharp & Abramson
1090 Vermont Ave. N.W.
Washington, DC 20005
202-842-3600
Contact: Susan Hager

The Hannaford Company
655 15th St. N.W.
Washington, DC 20005
202-638-4600
Contact: Peter D. Hannaford

E. Bruce Harrison Co.
1440 New York Ave. N.W.
Washington, DC 20005

202-638-1200
Contact: E. Bruce Harrison

Hill and Knowlton
901 31st St. N.W.
Washington, DC 20007
202-333-7400
Contact: Robert Gray

Jaffe Associates
1700 Pennsylvania Ave. N.W.
Washington, DC 20006
202-383-6633
Contact: Jay M. Jaffe

Ernest S. Johnston Advertising Agency
1156 15th St. N.W.
Washington, DC 20005
202-223-3660
Contact: Ernest Johnston

The Kamber Group
1920 L St. N.W.
Washington, DC 20036
202-223-8700
Contact: Victor Kamber

Henry J. Kaufman & Associates
2233 Wisconsin Ave. N.W.
Washington, DC 20007
202-333-0700
Contact: Michael Carberry

Keene, Shirley & Associates
919 Prince St.
Alexandria, VA 22314
703-684-0550
Contact: David A. Keene

Ketchum Public Relations
1201 Connecticut Ave. N.W.
Washington, DC 20036
202-835-8800
Contact: Lorraine Thelian

Breaking into advertising or public relations

"Look at the job search like an agency looks at its new business development," suggests Wendy Atkins-Pattenson, former executive of a full-service advertising and public relations agency with divisions in advertising, PR, direct marketing, and Yellow Pages.

"Preparation really makes a big difference. It's a real plus on a resume if you have interned in the industry. Internships are available at local agencies. In advertising, your academic background can be liberal arts. In public relations, we're looking for a journalism background plus an internship in PR.

"Figure out where you fit in the agency before the interview. Entry-level positions include assistant media planner, assistant media buyer, assistant account executive, and traffic coordinator. You need to research the agency beforehand and know who their clients are. Subscribe to *Ad Week* and *Ad Age* to track what is happening in the marketplace. Talk to people in the trenches to get a real sense of what people feel it takes to succeed.

"Interviews are very telling. Be natural and straightforward. Come in with a long list of intelligent questions about the agency. Ask questions of everyone in every interview so you can determine the consistency of response.

"In an interview you can tell a lot about how intelligent a person is by the questions they ask. I've seen people blow job interviews simply because they didn't bother to ask any questions."

We asked Wendy what she looked for in someone applying for a job. "We ask for a lot: excellent verbal as well as presentation skills, someone who creates powerful first impressions but also has substance. You need the discipline to sit at a desk for hours at a time and grind out numbers. You must be detail-oriented. You need superb interpersonal skills, an ability to think on your feet, and an ability to engender confidence in the client." ■

KSK Communications
8618 Westwood Center Drive
Vienna, VA 22182
703-734-1880
Contact: Karen Kennedy

Nancy Low & Associates
5454 Wisconsin Ave.
Bethesda, MD 20815
301-951-9200
Contact: Nancy Low

Madison Public Affairs Group
2033 M St. N.W.
Washington, DC 20036
202-223-0030
Contact: Ed Gabriel

J. Thomas Malatesta & Co.
1000 Thomas Jefferson St. N.W.
Washington, DC 20007
202-965-2582
Contact: J. Thomas Malatesta

Manning, Selvage & Lee
1250 I St. N.W.
Washington, DC 20005
202-682-1660
Contact: Joseph Gleason

Market Development Group
1200 Potomac St. N.W.
Washington, DC 20007
202-298-8030
Contact: W. Michael Gretschel

Marketing General
1613 Duke St.
Alexandria, VA 22314
703-549-4420
Contact: J. Scott McBride

Mitchell & Associates
7830 Old Georgetown Road
Bethesda, MD 20814
301-986-1772
Contact: Ronald Mitchell

Ogilvy & Mather
1901 L St. N.W.
Washington, DC 20036
202-466-7590
Contact: Marcia Silverman

Rogers & Cowan
2233 Wisconsin Ave. N.W.
Washington, DC 20007
202-338-1900

Ruder/Finn
1615 M St. N.W.
Washington, DC 20036
202-466-7800
Contact: Myra Peabody

Soghigian Marketing
1511 K St. N.W.
Washington, DC 20005
202-628-2050
Contact: Harry Soghigian

Stackig, Sanderson & White
7680 Old Springhouse Road
McLean, VA 22102
703-734-3300
Contact: Larry Rosenfeld

Weitzman/Livingston
4709 Montgomery Lane
Bethesda, MD 20814
301-951-4900
Contact: Rich Livingston

E. James White Company
151 Spring St.
Herndon, VA 22070
703-318-8000
Contact: E. James White

Williams Whittle Associates
711 Princess St.
Alexandria, VA 22314
703-836-9222
Contact: Andy Williams

Aerospace and Aircraft

Be sure also to check the **Electronics/Telecommunications** and
Research & Development/Technical Services sections.

To learn more about aerospace and related fields, you might want to
contact the following:

PROFESSIONAL ORGANIZATIONS:

Aerospace Industries Association of America
1250 I St. N.W.
Washington, DC 20005

American Institute of Aeronautics and Astronautics
370 L'Enfant Plaza S.W.
Washington, DC 20024

PROFESSIONAL PUBLICATIONS:

Aerospace America
Aviation Week & Space Technology
Business & Commercial Aviation

DIRECTORIES:

Aviation Week & Space Technology, Buyer's Guide (McGraw-Hill, New York, NY)

EMPLOYERS:

Allied Signal Aerospace
1530 Wilson Blvd.
Arlington, VA 22209
703-276-2000

Amecom Div.
5115 Calvert Road
College Park, MD 20740
301-864-5600
Search, navigation, and aeronautical systems.

Atlantic Research Corp.
5440 Cherokee Ave.
Alexandria, VA 22312
703-642-4000
Space propulsion units.

Boeing Company
1700 N. Moore St.
Arlington, VA 22209
703-558-9600
Aircraft.

British Aerospace
1101 Wilson Blvd.
Arlington, VA 22209
703-243-3939

Fairchild Space
20301 Century
Germantown, MD 20874
301-428-6000
Guided missiles and space vehicles.

General Dynamics
1745 Jefferson Davis Highway
Arlington, VA 22202
703-553-1200

General Electric. Space Systems Division
8080 Grainger Court
Springfield, VA 22153
703-866-3200

Grumman Corp.
1000 Wilson Blvd.
Arlington, VA 22209
703-875-8400

GTE Spacenet
1700 Old Meadow Rd.
McLean, VA 22102
703-848-1000

Gulfstream Aerospace
1000 Wilson Blvd.
Arlington, VA 22209
703-276-9500

Honeywell Aerospace and Defense Group
7900 Westpark Drive
McLean, VA 22102
703-734-7830

Kaman Aerospace Corp.
1111 Jefferson Davis Highway
Arlington, VA 22202
703-979-2500

Lockheed Missiles & Space
1735 Jefferson Davis Highway
Arlington, VA 22202
703-413-5900

Loral Corp.
1111 Jefferson Davis Highway
Arlington, VA 22202
703-685-5500

The Washington connection

Most of the aerospace and aircraft manufacturing companies included in this section do not, obviously, have their main manufacturing facilities located in the Washington metropolitan area. However, many of the major U.S. players, and several international ones as well, maintain sizable staff in their DC offices. These executives are the primary interface between the corporations and their Defense Department counterparts. With Defense budgets under increasingly greater scrutiny, and the spectre of scandal still lurking, these Washington offices will likely become even more important. ∎

LTV Aerospace
1725 Jefferson Davis Highway
Arlington, VA 22202
703-271-4900

Martin Marietta
6801 Rockledge Drive
Bethesda, MD 20817
301-897-6000

McDonnell Douglas Corp.
1735 Jefferson Davis Highway
Arlington, VA 22202
703-553-3800

Northrup
1000 Wilson Blvd.
Arlington, VA 22209
703-525-6767

OAO Corp.
7500 Greenway Center Drive
Greenbelt, MD 20770
301-345-0750
Aerospace manufacturing equipment.

Paramax Systems Corp.
12010 Sunrise Valley Drive
Reston, VA 22091
703-620-7000
Flight simulators and training equipment.

Rockwell International
1745 Jefferson Davis Highway
Arlington, VA 22202
703-553-6600

Architectural Firms

Be sure also to check the sections on **Contractors and Construction, Engineering,** and **Real Estate Developers and Brokers**.

For networking in architecture and related fields, check out the following professional organizations listed in Chapter 5:

PROFESSIONAL ORGANIZATIONS:

American Institute of Architects
American Society of Civil Engineers
American Society of Mechanical Engineers

For additional information, you can write or call:

American Institute of Architects
1735 New York Ave., N.W.
Washington, DC 20006
(202) 626-7300

Society of American Registered Architects
1245 S. Highland Ave.
Lombard, IL 60148
(708) 932-4622

PROFESSIONAL PUBLICATIONS:

AIA Journal
Architectural Forum
Architectural Record
Building Design and Construction
Inland Architect
Practicing Architect
Progressive Architecture

DIRECTORIES:

AIA Membership Directory (American Institute of Architects, New York, NY)
Architects Directory (American Business Directories, Inc., Omaha, NE)
Directory of Trade Associations Useful for Architectural Practice (Vance Bibliographies, Inc., Monticello, IL)
Society of American Registered Architects—National Membership Directory (Society of American Registered Architects, Lombard, IL)

EMPLOYERS:

Burt Hill Stinson Capelli
1056 Thomas Jefferson St. N.W.

Washington, DC 20007
202-333-2711

CHK Architects
1300 Spring St.
Silver Spring, MD 20910
301-588-4800

Cooper-Lecky Architects
1000 Potomac St. N.W.
Washington, DC 20007
202-333-2310

DMJM
1900 M St. N.W.
Washington, DC 20036
202-467-2000

Daly, Leo A.
1201 Connecticut Ave. N.W.
Washington, DC 20036
202-861-4600

Davis & Carter
8260 Greensboro Drive
McLean, VA 22102
703-556-9275

Dewberry & Davis
8401 Arlington Blvd.
Fairfax, VA 22031
703-849-0100

Donnally, Donnally, Soelin & Associates
9401 Key West Ave.
Rockville, MD 20850
301-590-9666

Ellerbe Becket
1875 Connecticut Ave. N.W.
Washington, DC 20009
202-986-2000

Gensler & Associates
1101 17th St. N.W.
Washington, DC 20036
202-887-5400

Gordon & Greenberg Architects
5707 Seminary Road
Bailey's Crossroad, VA 22041
703-845-0900

HDR Inc.
103 Oronoco St.
Alexandria, VA 22314
703-683-3400

Hellmuth, Obata & Kassabaum
1110 Vermont Ave. N.W.
Washington, DC 20005
202-457-9400

Kerns Group Architects
666 11th St. N.W.
Washington, DC 20001
202-393-2800

Keyes Condon Florance
1100 New York Ave. N.W.
Washington, DC 20005
202-842-2100

Maguire Group
5203 Leesburg Pike
Falls Church, VA 22041
703-998-0100

Mariani Associates
P.O. Box 510
Olney, MD 20830
202-462-5656

Oldham & Seltz
21 Dupont Circle N.W.
Washington, DC 20036
202-822-9797

Peck, Peck & Associates
1942 Davis Ford Road
Woodbridge, VA 22192
703-690-3121

RTKL
1140 Connecticut Ave. N.W.
Washington, DC 20036
202-833-4400

Sasaki Associates
1500 K St. N.W.
Washington, DC 20005
202-393-4300

Shalom Baranes Associates
1024 Wisconsin Ave. N.W.

How to Get a Job

Washington, DC 20007
202-342-2200

Sverdrup Corp.
1001 19th St. North
Arlington, VA 22209
703-351-4200

Ward/Hall Associates
12011 Lee Jackson Memorial Highway
Fairfax, VA 22033
703-385-5800

The Weihe Partnership
1666 K St. N.W.
Washington, DC 20006
202-857-8300

Wisnewski Blair & Associates
625 Slaters Lane
Alexandria, VA 22314
703-836-7766

**Architects—
getting in on the
ground floor**

John Christensen is an architect who has worked for a number of prominent firms since his Yale college days. We asked him for some advice on how to get that all-important first architectural job.

"Try to work as much as you can while you are in school. This builds up both your experience and your confidence and gives you a real feel for how to work successfully with clients. Working with faculty on projects is also important. Some of them might have excellent contacts within the industry, and you can benefit from this as much as you can from their teaching.

"As in most jobs, you have to put in your years doing less glamorous work. You will not start out meeting clients and doing important design work. But all the drafting and sketching will ultimately pay off.

"However, you have to remember that architecture and construction generally are very sensitive to the economic conditions. I have been laid off several times in my career, usually hired back by my original firm. Try to keep these fluctuations in mind and not get panicked if it happens to you." ■

Associations

Included in this section are the largest trade and professional associations in the Washington metropolitan area. Most are headquartered in the area, although some with headquarters elsewhere are listed because their Washington staffs and budgets are sizable. The directories listed below contain descriptions of the associations mentioned here, as well as hundreds of other organizations with varying-sized staffs.For networking in the association management field, check out the following organization listed in Chapter 5:

PROFESSIONAL ORGANIZATIONS:

Greater Washington Society of Association Executives

For additional information, you can write to:

American Society of Association Executives
1575 I St. N.W.
Washington, DC 20005

PROFESSIONAL PUBLICATIONS:

Association Executive

DIRECTORIES:

Encyclopedia of Associations (Gale Research, Detroit, MI)
National Trade & Professional Associations of the U.S. (Columbia Books, Washington, DC)
Who's Who in Association Management (American Society of Association Executives, Washington, DC)
World Guide to Trade Associations (K.G. Saur, New York, NY)

EMPLOYERS:

Aerospace Industries Association of America
1250 I St. N.W.
Washington, DC 20005
202-371-8400

Air Force Association
1501 Lee Highway
Arlington, VA 22209
703-247-5800

Air Transport Association of America
1301 Pennsylvania Ave. N.W.
Washington, DC 20004
202-626-4000

American Anthropological Association
1703 New Hampshire Ave. N.W.
Washington, DC 20009
202-232-8800

American Apparel Manufacturers Association
2500 Wilson Blvd.
Arlington, VA 22201
703-524-1864

Networking through associations

Many people who come to Washington hoping for a job on Capitol Hill soon realize that there are numerous other organizations involved in political or legislative issues. While many of these are public interest groups with very small staffs, others are large trade or professional organizations with huge budgets.

Kris Balderston, formerly on the staff of the National Governors Association, suggests that association work is invaluable for building up contacts in a city that thrives on "who you know." Getting your name and face known, attending issue-related hearings and meetings, and always working the network are essential career moves, Kris feels. Associations can be perfect for building this pyramid of contacts because of the wide variety of interactions most maintain. ■

American Association of Homes for the Aging
901 E St. N.W.
Washington, DC 20004
202-783-2242

American Association of School Administrators
1801 N. Moore St.
Arlington, VA 22209
703-528-0700

American Association of State Colleges and Universities
1 Dupont Circle N.W.
Washington, DC 20036
202-293-7070

American Association of University Women
11 16th St. N.W.
Washington, DC 20036
202-785-7700

American Astronomical Society
1630 Connecticut Ave. N.W.
Washington, DC 20009
202-328-2010

American Automobile Association
12600 Fair Lakes Circle
Fairfax, VA 22033
703-222-6000

American Bakers Association
1111 14th St. N.W.
Washington, DC 20005
202-789-0300

American Bankers Association
1120 Connecticut Ave. N.W.
Washington, DC 20036
202-663-5000

American Bar Association
1800 M St. N.W.
Washington, DC 20036
202-331-2200

American Chamber of Commerce Executives
4232 King St.
Alexandria, VA 22302
703-998-0072

American Chemical Society
1155 16th St. N.W.
Washington, DC 20036
202-872-4600

American College of Cardiology
9111 Old Georgetown Road
Bethesda, MD 20814
301-897-5400

American College of Health Care Administrators
325 S. Patrick St.
Alexandria, VA 22314
703-549-5822

American College of Obsetricians and Gynecologists
409 12th St. S.W.
Washington, DC 20024
202-638-5577

American Council on Education
1 Dupont Circle N.W.
Washington, DC 20036
202-939-9300

American Council of Life Insurance
1001 Pennsylvania Ave. N.W.

Washington, DC 20004
202-624-2000

American Counseling Association
5999 Stevenson Ave.
Alexandria, VA 22304
703-823-9800

American Forestry Association
1516 P St. N.W.
Washington, DC 20005
202-667-3300

American Gas Association
1515 Wilson Blvd.
Arlington, VA 22209
703-841-8400

American Geological Institute
4220 King St.
Alexandria, VA 22302
703-379-2480

American Geophysical Union
2000 Florida Ave. N.W.
Washington, DC 20009
202-462-6900

American Health Care Association
1201 L St. N.W.
Washington, DC 20005
202-842-4444

American Home Economics Association
1555 King St.
Alexandria, VA 22314
703-706-4600

American Horticultural Society
7931 East Blvd.
Alexandria, VA 22308
703-768-5700

American Hospital Association
50 F St. N.W.
Washington, DC 20001
202-638-1100

American Hotel and Motel Association
1201 New York Ave. N.W.
Washington, DC 20005
202-289-3132

American Institute of Aeronautics and Astronautics
370 L'Enfant Promenade S.W.
Washington, DC 20024
202-646-7400

American Institute of Architects
1735 New York Ave. N.W.
Washington, DC 20006
202-626-7300

American Insurance Association
1130 Connnecticut Ave. N.W.
Washington, DC 20036
202-828-7100

American Iron and Steel Institute
1101 17th St. N.W.
Washington, DC 20036
202-452-7100

American Medical Association
1101 Vermont Ave. N.W.
Washington, DC 20005
202-789-7400

American Medical Research Association
1230 17th St. N.W.
Washington, DC 20036
202-223-9485

American Petroleum Institute
1220 L St. N.W.
Washington, DC 20005
202-682-8000

American Pharmaceutical Association
2215 Connecticut Ave. N.W.
Washington, DC 20037
202-628-4410

American Physical Therapy Association
1111 N. Fairfax St.
Alexandria, VA 22314
703-684-2782

American Planning Association
1776 Massachusetts Ave. N.W.
Washington, DC 20036
202-872-0611

American Podiatric Medical Association
9312 Old Georgetown Road

Bethesda, MD 20814
301-571-9200

American Political Science Association
1527 New Hampshire Ave. N.W.
Washington, DC 20036
202-483-2512

American Production and Inventory Control Society
500 W. Annandale Road
Falls Church, VA 22046
703-237-8344

American Psychiatric Association
1400 K St. N.W.
Washington, DC 20005
202-682-6000

American Psychological Association
750 1st St. N.E.
Washington, DC 20002
202-336-5500

American Public Health Association
1015 15th St. N.W.
Washington, DC 20005
202-789-5600

American Public Power Association
2301 M St. N.W.
Washington, DC 20037
202-775-8300

American Public Transit Association
1201 New York Ave. N.W.
Washington, DC 20005
202-898-4000

American Public Welfare Association
810 1st St. N.E.
Washington, DC 20002
202-682-0100

American Society of Association Executives
1575 I St. N.W.
Washington, DC 20005
202-626-2723

American Society for Engineering Education
11 Dupont Circle N.W.
Washington, DC 20036
202-293-7080

American Society of Hospital Pharmacists
4630 Montgomery Ave.
Bethesda, MD 20814
301-657-3000

American Society of Internal Medicine
1101 Vermont Ave. N.W.
Washington, DC 20005
202-289-1700

American Society of Landscape Architects
4401 Connecticut Ave. N.W.
Washington, DC 20008
202-686-2752

American Society for Microbiology
1325 Massachusettes Ave. N.W.
Washington, DC 20005
202-737-3600

American Society for Training and Development
1640 King St.
Alexandria, VA 22313
703-683-8100

American Society of Travel Agents
1101 King St.
Alexandria, VA 22314
703-739-2782

American Sociological Association
1722 N St. N.W.
Washington, DC 20036
202-833-3410

American Trucking Associations
430 1st St. S.E.
Washington, DC 20003
202-544-6245

Associated Builders and Contractors
729 15th St. N.W.
Washington, DC 20005
202-637-8800

Association of American Medical Colleges
2450 N St. N.W.
Washington, DC 20037
202-828-0400

Association of American Railroads
50 F St. N.W.

Washington, DC 20001
202-639-2403

Association of General Contractors
1957 E St. N.W.
Washington, DC 20006
202-393-2040

Association of Trial Lawyers of America
1050 31st St. N.W.
Washington, DC 20007
202-965-3500

Association of the United States Army
2425 Wilson Blvd.
Arlington, VA 22201
703-841-4300

Building Owners and Managers Association International
1201 New York Ave. N.W.
Washington, DC 20005
202-408-2662

Chemical Manufacturers Association
2501 M St. N.W.
Washington, DC 20037
202-887-1100

Cosmetic, Toiletry and Fragrance Association
1101 17th St. N.W.
Washington, DC 20036
202-331-1770

Council of Better Business Bureaus
4200 Wilson Blvd.
Arlington, VA 22203
703-276-0100

Council on Foundations
1828 L St. N.W.
Washington, DC 20036
202-466-6512

Electronic Industries Association
2001 Pennsylvania Ave. N.W.
Washington, DC 20006
202-457-4900

Food Marketing Institute
800 Connecticut Ave. N.W.
Washington, DC 20006
202-452-8444

Grocery Manufacturers Association
1010 Wisconsin Ave. N.W.
Washington, DC 20007
202-337-9400

Independent Petroleum Association of America
1101 16th St. N.W.
Washington, DC 20036
202-857-4722

Information Industry Association
555 New Jersey Ave. N.W.
Washington, DC 20001
202-639-8262

Institute of Electrical and Electronics Engineers Computer Society
1730 Massachusettes Ave. N.W.
Washington, DC 20036
202-371-0101

International City Management Association
777 N. Capitol St. N.E.
Washington, DC 20002
202-289-4262

ITAA: The Computer Software and Services Industry Association
1616 N. Ft. Myer Drive
Arlington, VA 22209
703-522-5055

Mortgage Bankers Association of America
1125 15th St. N.W.
Washington, DC 20005
202-861-6500

National Association of Broadcasters
1771 N St. N.W.
Washington, DC 20036
202-429-5300

National Association of College and University Business Officers
1 Dupont Circle N.W.
Washington, DC 20036
202-861-2500

National Association of Home Builders of the United States
15th and M Sts. N.W.
Washington, DC 20005
202-822-0200

National Association of Life Underwriters
1922 F St. N.W.
Washington, DC 20006
202-331-6000

National Association of Manufacturers
1331 Pennsylvania Ave. N.W.
Washington, DC 20004
202-637-3000

National Association of Regulatory Utility Commissioners
1102 I.C.C. Building
Washington, DC 20044
202-898-2200

National Association of Secondary School Principals
1904 Association Drive
Reston, VA 22091
703-860-0200

National Association of Securities Dealers
1735 K St. N.W.
Washington, DC 20006
202-728-8000

National Association of Social Workers
750 1st St. N.E.
Washington, DC 20002
301-565-0333

National Automobile Dealers Association
8400 Westpark Drive
McLean, VA 22102
703-821-7000

National Cable Television Association
1724 Massachusetts Ave. N.W.
Washington, DC 20036
202-775-3550

National Coal Association
1130 17th St. N.W.
Washington, DC 20036
202-463-2625

National Electrical Contractors Association
7315 Wisconsin Ave.
Bethesda, MD 20814
301-657-3110

National Electrical Manufacturers Association
2101 L St. N.W.

Washington, DC 20037
202-457-8400

National Food Processors Association
1401 New York Ave. N.W.
Washington, DC 20005
202-639-5900

National Forest Products Association
1250 Connecticut Ave. N.W.
Washington, DC 20036
202-463-2700

National Governors' Association
444 N. Capitol St. N.W.
Washington, DC 20001
202-624-5300

National League of Cities
1301 Pennsylvania Ave. N.W.
Washington, DC 20004
202-626-3000

National Restaurant Association
1200 17th St. N.W.
Washington, DC 20036
202-331-5900

National School Supply & Equipment Association
8300 Colesville Road
Silver Spring, MD 20910
301-495-0240

National Soft Drink Association
1101 16th St. N.W.
Washington, DC 20036
202-463-6732

Newspaper Association of America
11600 Sunrise Valley Drive
Reston, VA 22091
703-648-1000

Pharmaceutical Manufacturers Association
1100 15th St. N.W.
Washington, DC 20005
202-835-3400

Retired Officers Association
201 N. Washington St.
Alexandria, VA 22314
703-549-2311

Savings and Community Bankers of America
1101 15th St. N.W.
Washington, DC 20005
202-857-3100

Society for Human Resource Management
606 N. Washington St.
Alexandria, VA 22314
703-548-3440

Society of the Plastics Industry
1275 K St. N.W.
Washington, DC 20005
202-371-5200

Transportation Institute
5201 Auth Way
Camp Springs, MD 20746
202-347-2590

United States Chamber of Commerce
1615 H St. N.W.
Washington, DC 20062
202-463-5731

United States Conference of Mayors
1620 I St. N.W.
Washington, DC 20006
202-293-7330

Book Publishers

For networking in book publishing and related fields, check out the following professional organization listed in Chapter 5:

PROFESSIONAL ORGANIZATIONS:

Washington Independent Writers

For additional information, you can write or call:

American Booksellers Association
560 White Plains Road
Tarrytown, NY 10591
(914) 631-7800

Association of American Publishers
220 E. 23rd St.
New York, NY 10010
(212) 689-8920

PROFESSIONAL PUBLICATIONS:

American Bookseller
Editor & Publisher
Library Journal
Publishers Weekly
Small Press

DIRECTORIES:

American Book Trade Directory (R.R. Bowker, New York, NY)
Literary Market Place (R.R. Bowker, New York, NY)
Publishers Directory (Gale Research, Detroit, MI)

EMPLOYERS:

Acropolis Books
13950 Park Center Road
Herndon, VA 22071
703-689-245

Catholic University of America Press
620 Michigan Ave. N.E.
Washington, DC 20064
202-319-5052

Columbia Books
1212 New York Ave. N.W.
Washington, DC 20005
202-898-0662

George Mason University Press
4400 University Drive
Fairfax, VA 22030
703-993-2185

Georgetown University Press
Georgetown University
Washington, DC 20057
202-687-6251

Government Printing Office
732 N. Capitol St. N.W.
Washington, DC 20401
202-512-0000

Howard University Press
2900 Van Ness St. N.W.
Washington, DC 20008
202-806-6100

Jane's Publishing Co.
1340 Braddock Place
Alexandria, VA 22314
703-683-3700

Johnson Publishing Co.
1750 Pennsylvania Ave. N.W.
Washington, DC 20006
202-393-5860

McGraw-Hill
1120 Vermont Ave. N.W.
Washington, DC 20005
202-463-1600

Smithsonian Institution Press
470 L'Enfant Plaza S.W.
Washington, DC 20560
202-287-3738

Time-Life Books
777 Duke St.
Alexandria, VA 22314
703-838-7000

Warren Gorham Lament
1340 Braddock Place
Alexandria, VA 22314
703-706-8260

Washington Researchers Publishing
2612 P St. N.W.
Washington, DC 20007
202-333-3499

Broadcasting

For networking in radio and television and related fields, check out the following professional organizations listed in Chapter 5:

PROFESSIONAL ORGANIZATIONS:

American Federation of Television & Radio Artists
American News Women's Club
Capital Press Women
National Press Club
Washington Press Club
White House Correspondents Association

For additional information, you can write or call:

American Federation of Television & Radio Artists
260 Madison Ave.
New York, NY 10016
(212) 532-0800

Broadcast Promotion Association
P.O. Box 5102
Lancaster, PA 17601

National Academy of Television Arts & Sciences
111 W. 57th St.
New York, NY 10019
(212) 586-8424

National Association of Broadcasters
1771 N St. N.W.
Washington, DC 20036
(202) 429-5300

National Association of Television Program Executives
P.O. Box 5272
Lancaster, PA 17601

National Cable Television Association
1724 Massachusetts Ave. N.W.
Washington, DC 20036
(202) 775-3550

National Radio Broadcasters Association
2033 M St. N.W.
Washington, DC 20036

Radio-Television News Directors Association
1717 K St. N.W.
Washington, DC 20006
(202) 659-6510

Television Information Office
745 Fifth Ave.
New York, NY 10022

PROFESSIONAL PUBLICATIONS:

Billboard
Broadcasting
Cable World
Communications News
Radio World
Television Broadcast

DIRECTORIES:

Broadcasting—Top 100 Companies in Electronic Communications Issue
(Broadcasting Publications, Washington, DC)
Broadcasting Yearbook (Broadcasting Publishing, Washington, DC)
Cable Programming Resource Directory: A Guide to Community TV Production Facilities and Programming Sources and Outlets (Broadcasting Publications, Washington, DC)
Cablevision—Top 50 Companies in Cable Issue (Diversified Publishing, Denver, CO)
Television Fact Book (Television Digest, Washington, DC)

EMPLOYERS:

ABC News
1717 DeSales St. N.W.
Washington, DC 20036
202-887-7777
Contact: George Watson, Bureau Chief

ABC Radio News
1717 DeSales St. N.W.
Washington, DC 20036
202-887-7630
Contact: Robin Sproul

Allbritton Communications
800 17th St. N.W.
Washington, DC 20006
202-789-2130

AP Broadcast Services
1825 K St. N.W.
Washington, DC 20006
202-955-7200
Contact: Jim Williams, Dir.

BizNet/ American Business Network
1615 H St. N.W.
Washington, DC 20062
202-463-5921

Black Entertainment Television
1232 31st St. N.W.
Washington, DC 20007
202-337-5260
Contact: Robert L. Johnson, Pres.

CBS News
2020 M St. N.W.
Washington, DC 20036

218

202-457-4321
Contact: Barbara Cohen, Bureau Chief

CBS Radio News
2020 M St. N.W.
Washington, DC 20036
202-457-4321
Contact: Evelyn Thomas

C-SPAN
400 N. Capitol St. N.W.
Washington, DC 20001
202-737-3220
Contact: Brian P. Lamb, CEO

Cable News Network
820 1st St. N.E.
Washington, DC 20002
202-898-7900
Contact: William W. Headline, Bureau Chief

Cable TV Arlington
2707 Wilson Blvd.
Arlington, VA 22201
703-358-2770
Contact: John Evans, Pres.

Cable TV Montgomery
20 West Gute Drive
Rockville, MD 20850
301-384-8646
Contact: John Eddy, Pres.

Corporation for Public Broadcasting
901 E St. N.W.
Washington, DC 20004
202-879-9600
Contact: Donald E. Ledwig, Pres.

District Cablevision
1232 31st St. N.W.
Washington, DC 20007
202-337-5260
Contact: Tyrone Brown, Pres.

E-Z Communications
10800 Main St.
Fairfax, VA 22030
703-591-1000
Contact: Alan L. Box, Pres.

First Media Corp.
6301 Ivy Lane
Greenbelt, MD 20770
301-441-3561
Contact: Dan Mason, Pres.

Gannett Co.
1100 Wilson Blvd.
Arlington, VA 22229
703-284-6000

Home Team Sports
1111 18th St. N.W.
Washington, DC 20036
301-718-3200
Contact: Bill Abe

Media General Cable
Chantilly, VA 22021
703-378-8400
Contact: Thomas Waldrop, CEO

Mutual Broadcasting
1755 S. Jefferson Davis Highway
Arlington, VA 22202
703-685-2073
Contact: John B. Clement, Pres.

NBC News
4001 Nebraska Ave. N.W.
Washington, DC 20016
202-885-4000
Contact: Timothy Russert, Bureau Chief

NBC Radio News
1755 S. Jefferson Davis Highway
Arlington, VA 22202
703-685-2000
Contact: Jack Clements

National Public Radio
2025 M St. N.W.
Washington, DC 20036
202-822-2000

Public Broadcasting Service
1320 Braddock Pl.
Alexandria, VA 22314
703-739-5000

UPI Radio
1400 I St. N.W.

Washington, DC 20005
202-898-8111
Contact: Mike Aulabaugh

Warner Cable Communications
P.O. Box 2400
Reston, VA 22090
703-471-1749
Contact: John Edwards

Washington Post Co.
1150 15th St. N.W.
Washington, DC 20071
202-334-6000

Broadcasting Stations—Television

WDCA-TV (20)
5202 River Road
Bethesda, MD 20816
301-986-9322
Contact: Richard Williams, G.M

WETA-TV (26)
Box 2626
Washington, DC 20013
703-998-2600
Contact: Sharon Rockefeller

WFTY-TV (50)
12276 Wilkins Ave.
Rockville, MD 20852
301-230-1550
Contact: Andrew M. Ockershausen, G.M.

WHMM-TV (32)
2222 4th St. N.W.
Washington, DC 20059
202-806-3012
Contact: Edward Jones, G.M.

WJLA-TV (7)
3007 Tilden St. N.W.
Washington, DC 20008
202-364-7777
Contact: John Sawhill, G.M.
ABC affiliate.

WNVT-TV & WNVC-TV (53 & 56)
8101 A Lee Highway
Falls Church, VA 22042
703-698-9682

WRC-TV (4)
4001 Nebraska Ave. N.W.
Washington, DC 20016
202-885-4000
Contact: Allan Horlick, G.M.
NBC affiliate.

WTTG-TV (5)
5151 Wisconsin Ave. N.W.
Washington, DC 20016
202-244-5151
Contact: Kim Montour
Fox.

WUSA-TV (9)
4100 Wisconsin Ave. N.W.
Washington, DC 20016
202-895-5999
Contact: Henry Yaggi, G.M.
CBS affiliate.

Broadcasting Stations—Radio

WAMU-FM
American University
Washington, DC 20016
202-885-1030

WASH-FM
3400 Idaho Ave. N.W.
Washington, DC 20016
202-895-5000

WAVA-FM
5232 Lee Highway
Arlington, VA 22207
703-534-0320

WCPT-AM
510 King St.
Alexandria, VA 22314
703-683-3000

WCUA-FM & AM
620 Michigan Ave. N.E.
Washington, DC 20064
202-319-5000

WCXR-FM
510 King St.
Alexandria, VA 22314
703-683-3000

WDCU-FM
4200 Connecticut Ave. N.W.
Washington, DC 20008
202-282-7588

WETA-FM
P.O. Box 2626
Washington, DC 20013
703-998-2600

WGAY-FM
8121 Georgia Ave.
Silver Spring, MD 20910
301-587-4900

WGMS-AM & FM
11300 Rockville Pike
Rockville, MD 20852
301-468-1800

WHUR-FM
529 Bryant St. N.W.
Washington, DC 20059
202-806-3500

WINX-AM
8 Baltimore Road
Rockville, MD 20850
301-424-9292

WJFK-FM
P.O. Box 3649
Washington, DC 20007
703-691-1900

WKYS-FM
4001 Nebraska Ave. N.W.
Washington, DC 20016
202-686-9300

WLTT-FM
5912 Hubbard Drive
Rockville, MD 20852
301-984-6000

WMZQ-AM & FM
5513 Connecticut Ave. N.W.
Washington, DC 20015
202-362-8330

WRQX-FM
4400 Jennifer St. N.W.

Washington, DC 20015
202-686-3100

WTOP-AM
3400 Idaho Ave. N.W.
Washington, DC 20016
202-895-5000

WXTR-FM
5210 Auth Road
Marlow Heights, MD 20746
301-899-3014

Breaking into broadcasting

Janet Worthing is an executive at a Washington radio station. We asked her how to get started in broadcasting.

"Persevere," she says. "One of my first interviews was with the personnel director of a station in DC. He said, 'Do you realize how many communications majors finished up this year? There is no way the market can absorb all of you.'

"That was a sobering thought. It discourages a lot of people. But you have to keep in there. Send out resumes, read the trades, see who is switching formats, and all that. Do anything on the side that might result in a good lead. The year after I graduated from college, I took a news writing course taught at American University by someone who had been in the industry for years; getting to know these people can lead to valuable contacts.

"Another point is to treat these contacts with respect. Broadcasting is a volatile business. You can't afford to burn a lot of bridges or alienate a lot of people. Somebody can be your assistant one day and your boss the next." ■

Computers: Data Processing

For information about the data processing industry, you can write to:

PROFESSIONAL ORGANIZATIONS:

Data Processing Management Association
505 Busse Highway
Park Ridge, IL 60068

PROFESSIONAL PUBLICATIONS:

Data Communications
Datamation

DIRECTORIES:

Data Communications Buyers Guide (McGraw-Hill, New York, NY)
Data Entry Services Directory (American Business Directories, Omaha, NE)
Data Processing Directory (American Business Directories, Omaha, NE)
Data-Sources (Ziff-Davis, Cherry Hill, NJ)
Engineering, Science and Computer Jobs (Peterson's Guides, Princeton, NJ)
Thomas Register's Guide to Data/Information Processing (Thomas Publishing Co., New York, NY)

EMPLOYERS:

American Management Systems
1777 N. Kent St.
Arlington, VA 22209
703-841-6000

Automated Business Systems
9475 Lottsford Road
Landover, MD 20785
301-386-2600

Birch & Davis Associates
8905 Fairview Road
Silver Spring, MD 20910
301-589-6760

CAP Gemini America
8391 Old Courthouse Road
Vienna, VA 22182
703-734-1511

CBIS Federal
12750 Fair Lakes Circle
Fairfax, VA 22033
703-222-1500

Computer Data Systems
1 Curie Court
Rockville, MD 20850
301-921-7215

Delta Research Corp.
1501 Wilson Blvd.
Arlington, VA 22209
703-841-1900

Syscon Corp.
1000 Thomas Jefferson St. N.W.
Washington, DC 20007
202-342-4000

Computers: Hardware and Software

Be sure also to check the **Electronics/Telecommunications** and **Research & Development/Technical Services** sections.

To learn more about the computer industry, you can write to or call the following professional organizations:

PROFESSIONAL ORGANIZATIONS:

Association for Computing Machinery
11 W. 42nd St.
New York, NY 10036
(212) 869-7440

IEEE Computer Society
1730 Massachusetts Ave. N.W.
Washington, DC 20036
(202) 371-0101

ITAA—Information Technology Assoc. of America
1616 N. Ft. Myer Drive
Arlington, VA 22209
(703) 522-5055

Semiconductor Industry Association
4300 Stevens Creek Blvd.
San Jose, CA 95129

PROFESSIONAL PUBLICATIONS:

Byte
Computerworld
Electronic Business
Electronic News
MIS Week
PC Magazine
Personal Computing

DIRECTORIES:

Data Sources: v.1 Hardware, v.2 Software (Ziff-Davis Publishing, Cherry Hill, NJ)
Directory of Computer Software and Services Companies (ITAA, Arlington, VA)
Engineering, Science and Computer Jobs (Peterson's Guides, Princeton, NJ)
ICP Software Directory (International Computer Programs, Indianapolis, IN)
Yearbook/Directory (Semiconductor Industry Association, San Jose, CA)
Who's Who in Electronics (Harris Publications, Twinsburg, OH)

EMPLOYERS:

AGS Genasys
11820 Parklawn Drive
Rockville, MD 20852
301-770-4600
Contact: Miki Carroll, Dir.
Applications software.

ANADAC, Inc.
2011 Crystal Drive
Arlington, VA 22202
703-685-0021
Software development.

ARC Information Systems
1375 Piccard Drive
Rockville, MD 20850
301-258-5300
Contact: Edward Jones
Software.

ARC Professional Services
1375 Piccard Drive
Rockville, MD 20850
301-670-2000
Contact: Ed Jones, Pres.

ATAC
950 Herndon Pkwy.
Herndon, VA 22070
703-834-3703
Contact: Harlon Reece, Dir.
Software engineering, facilities management.

AT&T Information Systems
3033 Chain Bridge Road
Oakton, VA 22185
703-691-5000

Advanced Systems Development
2800 Shirlington Road
Arlington, VA 22206
703-998-3900

American Management Systems
1777 N. Kent St.
Arlington, VA 22209
703-841-2000
Contact: Judy Blair, Dir.
Software applications, micrographics.

Analysas
1140 Connecticut Ave. N.W.
Washington, DC 20036
202-429-5653
Contact: Robin DuShole
Computer information services.

Aspen Systems
16000 Research Blvd.
Rockville, MD 20850
301-251-5000
Contact: A. Lampert
Information systems.

Automata Inc.
1200 Severn Way
Sterling, VA 20166
703-450-2600
Electronic components, printed circuit boards.

BBN Communications
1300 N. 17th St.
Arlington, VA 22209
703-848-4800
Contact: Rosanne Taugner
Packet switching networks.

BTG, Inc.
1945 Old Gallows Road
Vienna, VA 22182
703-556-6518
Contact: Winder Heller
Turnkey systems.

Baxter Health Care
12355 Sunrise Valley Drive
Reston, VA 22091
703-715-0193
Contact: Bruce Jones, Pres.
Software for hospital management.

Boeing Computer Services
7990 Boeing Court
Vienna, VA 22180
703-847-1100

Closing the deal on sales

Hadley Smith put in a long and successful career with Xerox, then got an MBA and decided to switch to a start-up, comparatively new computer company. We asked him the differences between selling for a giant and taking a risk with a relatively unknown firm.

"Xerox is probably fairly typical of any large corporation," says Hadley, in that they are very structured. It was a good place to work, but it didn't provide much opportunity for individual decision-making. A company like my new venture offers a fantastic chance to exercise some entrepreneurial skills. The corporation sets general goals, but it's up to me how I meet them. I can try out new marketing techniques, divide up the territory a new way, create teams, whatever. It's neat to have that flexibility."

We asked Hadley what it takes to be a good salesperson.

"A lot of people think that sales people are forever taking people to lunch or playing golf, but in order to be successful, you really do have to work hard. I don't necessarily mean 80 hours a week, but you need to put in sufficient time to do all the follow-up that is necessary. You have to have a thorough understanding not only of your own products but of your competitors as well.

"Communication and interpersonal skills are critical as well because people, as the old saying goes, buy from people, not companies. You have to develop a rapport so that the client knows you will be around even after the sale is completed. You have to not only look presentable but be able to convince the customer your product is the best." ■

CACI International
1100 N. Glebe Road
Arlington, VA 22201
703-841-7800
Analytical software, information systems, engineering support systems.

Comnet Corp.
6404 Ivy Lane
Greenbelt, MD 20770
301-220-5400
Contact: Robert Bowen
Service and software for marketing and management.

Compucare
12110 Sunset Hills Road

Reston, VA 22090
703-709-2300
Contact: Linda Oland
Information software for health care.

Computer Associates
12120 Sunset Hills Road
Reston, VA 22090
703-709-4500

Computer Based Systems (CBSI)
2750 Prosperity Ave.
Fairfax, VA 22031
703-849-8080
Contact: Dan Ryan
Office automation, systems integration, facilities management.

Computer Data Systems
1 Curie Court
Rockville, MD 20850
301-921-7000
Software.

Computer Sciences Corp
6565 Arlington Blvd.
Falls Church, VA 22042
703-237-2000
Design, engineer, and integrate computer-based systems.

Contol Data Corp.
6003 Executive Blvd.
Rockville, MD 20852
301-468-8000
Computer services to government and industry.

DBA Systems
11781 Lee Jackson Highway
Fairfax, VA 22033
703-934-6795
Contact: Gordon Deckman, Dir.
Systems that apply computers to government markets.

DHD, Inc.
2000 Corporate Ridge
McLean, VA 22102
703-560-3636
Contact: Tandy Harris
IBM mainframe applications.

Delta Research Corp.
1501 Wilson Blvd.
Arlington, VA 22209

703-841-1900
Contact: George M. Gingerelli, Pres.

Electronic Data Systems
136 EDS Drive
Herndon, VA 22071
703-742-2000
Contact: Paul J. Chiapparone, Sr. V.P.

G.E. Information Services
401 N. Washington
Rockville, MD 20850
301-340-4000
Software.

General Kinetics Inc.
12300 Parklawn Drive
Rockville, MD 20852
301-881-2044
Recertified computer tape.

Government Technology Services
4100 Lafayette Center Drive
Chantilly, VA 22021
703-631-3333
Computer hardware and software sales.

Group 1 Software
6404 Ivy Lane
Greenbelt, MD 20770
301-982-2000
Software for direct marketing.

Grumman Data Systems Division
2411 Dulles Corner Road
Herndon, VA 22071
703-713-4000

Hadron Inc.
9990 Lee Highway
Fairfax, VA 22030
703-359-6201
Contact: Edie Cardwell

Hewlett-Packard
2 Choke Cherry Road
Rockville, MD 20850
301-258-5983
Contact: Camille Borrelli
Landmark systems.

Honeywell Federal Systems
7900 Westpark Drive
McLean, VA 22102
703-827-3000
Contact: R.E. Cuneo
Peripheral equipment.

IBAX, Inc.
12355 Sunset Valley Drive
Reston, VA 22091
Hospital management software.

IBM
1301 K St. N.W.
Washington, DC 20005
202-515-5900

IBM Federal Systems Company
6600 Rockledge Drive
Bethesda, MD 20817
301-493-8100
Designs and supports federal government network.

Information Development Corp.
8455 Colesville Road
Silver Spring, MD 20910
301-565-4233
Micro-computer systems.

Intersolve Software
3200 Tower Oaks Blvd.
Rockville, MD 20852
301-230-3200
Contact: Kevin J. Burns
Advanced applications for IBM mainframes.

Iverson Technology
1356 Beverly Road
McLean, VA 22101
703-749-1200
Contact: Donald D. Iverson
Develops secure data transmission and computer services.

Kastle Systems
1501 Wilson Blvd.
Arlington, VA 22209
703-528-8800
Contact: A. Gene Samburg, Pres.
Central station automated security systems.

Legant Corp.
8615 Westwood Center Drive

Vienna, VA 22182
703-734-9494
Contact: John Burton, Pres.
Software programs for IBM mainframes.

MRJ Inc.
10455 White Granite Drive
Oakton, VA 22124
703-385-0745
Contact: Bob Rubinstein, Dir.
Systems engineering, software, value-added work stations.

Martin Marietta
6801 Rockledge Drive
Bethesda, MD 20817
301-897-6000
Integrated circuits, neural network systems.

National Capitol Systems
5205 Leesburg Pike
Falls Church, VA 22041
703-671-3360
Contact: Sandy MacIntosh, V.P.
Systems analysis, development, and implementation.

Network Management
11242 Waples Mill Road
Fairfax, VA 22030
703-359-9400
Contact: Human Resource Dept.
Electronic computing machinery.

Orkand Corp.
8484 Georgia Ave.
Silver Spring, MD 20910
301-585-8480
Contact: Mike Nelson
System operations and development.

Paramax Systems Corp.
2345 Crystal Drive
Arlington, VA 22202
703-471-0157

Penril Data Communications Network
1300 Quince Orchard Blvd.
Gaithersburg, MD 20878
301-921-8600
Contact: David Johnson, G.M.
Modems, multiplexers, data PBXs.

QuesTech Inc.
7600A Leesburg Pike
Falls Church, VA 22043
703-760-1000
Contact: Mark Hartung
Computer-integrated systems design.

RMS Technologies
1400 McCormick Drive
Landover, MD 20785
301-925-9760
Contact: David Huggins, Pres.
Software.

ST Research Corp.
8419 H Terminal Road
Newington, VA 22122
703-550-7000
Contact: S.R. Perrino, Pres.
Microprocessing, receiving systems, RF components.

Scope, Inc.
1860 Michael Faraday Drive
Reston, VA 22090
703-471-5600
Contact: Steve Lowe
Government research and development.

Sentech Group
4200 Wilson Blvd.
Arlington, VA 22203
703-525-5818

Social and Scientific Systems
7101 Wisconsin Ave.
Bethesda, MD 20814
301-986-4870
Contact: Herbert J. Miller, Pres.
Computer-related services.

Software AG of North America
11190 Sunrise Valley Drive
Reston, VA 22091
703-860-5050
Contact: Michael J. King, Pres.

Star Technologies
515 Shaw Road
Sterling, VA 20100
703-689-4400
Contact: Robert C. Compton, Pres.
Array processors.

Syntrex Technologies
8403 Arlington Blvd.
Fairfax, VA 22031
703-207-3000
Integration and networking.

Systemhouse Inc.
1010 N. Glebe Road
Arlington, VA 22201
703-276-0500
Contact: Peg Gamse
Software.

Systems Center
1800 Alexander Bell Drive
Reston, VA 22091
703-264-8000
Contact: Carla Mooris
Software for IBM VM system.

Systems Research and Applications Corp.
2000 N. 15th St.
Arlington, VA 22201
703-558-4700
Contact: Dr. Ernest Volgenau, Pres.

Tandem Computers
1200 Sunrise Valley Drive
Reston, VA 22091
703-476-0550
Contact: Nancy Sullivan
Electronic computing equipment.

Technalysis Corp.
7700 Leesburg Pike
Falls Church, VA 22043
703-821-3911
Systems development, software design.

Tempest, Inc.
112 Elden St.
Herndon, VA 22070
703-709-9543
Modifies computer components to Tempest standards.

Vanguard Technologies
12750 Fair Lakes Circle
Fairfax, VA 22033
703-222-1500
Information management services, custom software.

Wilson-Hill Associates
8401 Arlington Blvd.
Fairfax, VA 22031
703-207-3100
Contact: Loretta Williams, V.P.
Software for government clients.

Xerox Corp.
1616 N. Ft. Meyer Drive
Arlington, VA 22209
703-527-6400
Contact: Human Resources

XMCO
460 Spring Park Place
Herndon, VA 22070
703-709-5000
Integrated logistic support, artificial intelligence.

**High-tech job
fair spotlights
opportunities**

Each fall the *Washington Post* sponsors a High-Tech Job Fair where representatives of some of the area's largest and best known computer, electronics, and telecommunications companies gather to meet with potential employees. The companies usually offer a wide range of job opportunities for hardware designers, manufacturing engineers, logistics and facility management experts, and operations researchers. The great benefit to the job candidates, of course, is that they can meet with over 35 employment representatives in one location without making appointments.

There is no fee, and the Fair is usually held at a convenient suburban hotel. Check with the *Post* for dates, or keep your eyes out for the advertisements in the newspaper itself. ■

Contractors and Construction

Be sure to look at the **Real Estate**, **Engineering**, and **Architecture** sections as well.

For networking in the construction industry, check out the following professional organizations listed in Chapter 5:

PROFESSIONAL ORGANIZATIONS:

**American Society of Civil Engineers
District of Columbia Contractors Association**

For additional information, you can write or call:

Construction Products Manufacturers Council
1600 Wilson Blvd.
Arlington, Va 22209

National Asphalt Pavement Association
6811 Kenilworth Ave.
Riverdale, MD 20840

National Association of Home Builders of the U.S.
15th and M Sts. N.W.
Washington, DC 20005
(202) 822-0200

National Association of Minority Contractors
1333 F St. N.W., #500
Washington, DC 20004
(202) 347-8259

National Construction Industry Council
2000 L St. N.W., Suite 612
Washington, DC 20036

PROFESSIONAL PUBLICATIONS:

Builder
Building Design and Construction
Concrete Construction Magazine
Construction Review
Contractor
Masonry Construction
Modern Steel

DIRECTORIES:

Blue Book of Major Homebuilders (CMR Associates, Crofton, MD)
Construction Equipment, Construction Giants (Cahners Publishing, Des
    Plaines, IL)
Directory of Contract Service Firms (C.E. Publications, Kenmore, WA)
ENR Directory of Contractors (McGraw-Hill, New York, NY)
ENR Directory of Design Firms (McGraw-Hill, New York, NY)
Guide to Information Sources in the Construction Industry (Construction
    Products Manufacturers Council, Arlington, VA)
Peterson's Guide to Careers (Peterson's Guides, Princeton, NJ)
Who's Who in Technology (Gale Research, Detroit, MI)

EMPLOYERS:

Barber Construction Corp.
1340-F Charwood Road

237

Hanover, MD 21076
301-470-3244

Blake Construction Co.
1120 Connecticut Ave. N.W.
Washington, DC 20036
202-828-9000

Centennial Contractors Enterprises
1801 Alexander Bell Drive
Reston, VA 22091
703-264-0235

Clark Construction
7500 Old Georgetown Road
Bethesda, MD 20814
301-657-7100

James G. Davis Construction
12500 Parklawn Drive
Rockville. MD 20852
301-881-2990

The Donohoe Companies
2101 Wisconsin Ave. N.W.
Washington, DC 20007
202-333-0880

B. Joy Frank Co.
5355 Kilmer Place
Bladensburg, MD 20710
301-779-9400

Giant Construction
P.O. Box 1804
Washington, DC 20013
301-386-0439

Gilbane Building
7901 Sandy Spring Road
Laurel, MD 20707
301-317-6100

Glen Construction
9055 Comprind Court
Gaithersburg, MD 20872
301-258-2700

HITT Contracting
921 N. Quincy St.
Arlington, VA 22203
703-522-6937

Harkins Group
12301 Old Columbia Pike
Silver Spring, MD 20904
301-622-9000

Interstate General Co.
222 Smallwood Village Ctr.
St. Charles, MD 20602
301-843-8600

Lafarge Corp.
11130 Sunrise Valley Drive
Reston, VA 22091
703-264-3600

The Leapley Co.
1724 Kalorama Road N.W.
Washington, DC 20009
202-483-1800

Majestic Builders
5530 Wisconsin Ave.
Chevy Chase, MD 20815
301-951-0900

A.S. McGaughan Co.
4550 Montgomery Ave.
Bethesda, MD 20814
301-469-3030

NVR L.P.
7601 Lewinsville Road
McLean, VA 22102
703-761-2000

OMNI Construction
7500 Old Georgetown Road
Bethesda, MD 20814
301-657-6800

Richmarr Construction
5301 Wisconsin Ave. N.W.
Washington, DC 20015
202-686-8000

Ryland Group
7130 Minstrel Way
Columbia, MD 21045
410-290-7050

Sigal Construction
3299 K St. N.W.
Washington, DC 20007
202-944-6600

Tiber Construction
10461 White Granite Drive
Oakton, VA 22124
703-273-8200

Tompkins, Chas. H., Corp.
Chas. H. Tompkins Corp.
1333 H St. N.W.
Washington, DC 20005
202-789-0770

Turner Construction
4601 N. Fairfax Dr.
Arlington, VA 22203
703-841-5200

Williams Industries
2849 Meadow View Road
Falls Church, VA 22042
703-560-1505

Cultural Institutions

To help you learn more about opportunities with museums and other cultural organizations, you can write or call:

PROFESSIONAL ORGANIZATIONS:

American Association of Museums
1225 I St. N.W.
Washington, DC 20005
(202) 289-1818

American Federation of Arts
41 E. 65th St.
New York, NY 10021

Arts and Business Council
130 E. 40th St.
New York, NY 10016

National Assembly of State Art Agencies
1010 Vermont Ave. N.W.
Washington, DC 20005
(202) 347-6352

PROFESSIONAL PUBLICATIONS:

Artsbeat
Art World
Museum News
Symphony Magazine
Variety

DIRECTORIES:

NASAA Directory (National Assembly of State Art Agencies, Washington, DC)
Official Museum Directory (American Assoc. of Museums, Washington, DC)
Symphony Magazine's Annual Orchestra and Business Directory Issue (American Symphony Orchestra League, Washington, DC)

EMPLOYERS:

Alexandria Commission for the Arts
1108 Jefferson St.
Alexandria, VA 22314
703-838-6348

Alexandria Symphony Orchestra
P.O. Box 1035
Alexandria, VA 22313
703-548-0045

American Film Institute
John F. Kennedy Center
Washington, DC 20566
202-828-4000

American Folklife Center
Library of Congress
10 1st St. S.E.
Washington, DC 20540
202-707-6590

American Showcase Theatre Company
1822 Duke St.
Alexandria, VA 22314
703-548-9044

American Symphony Orchestra League
777 14th St. N.W.
Washington, DC 20005
202-628-0099

Anacostia Museum
1901 Fort Place S.E.

Washington, DC 20020
202-287-3306

Anderson House Museum
2118 Massachusetts Ave. N.W.
Washington, DC 20008
202-785-2040

Archives of American Art
8th and F St. N.W.
Washington, DC 20560
202-357-2781

Arena Stage
6th and Maine Ave. S.W.
Washington, DC 20024
202-554-9066

Arlington County Division of Cultural Affairs
2700 S. Lang St.
Arlington, VA 22206
703-358-6960

Art Barn Association
2401 Tilden St. N.W.
Washington, DC 20008
202-244-2482

Arts and Industries Building
900 Jefferson Drive S.W.
Washington, DC 20560
202-357-1300
Smithsonian Institution.

Arts Council of Montgomery County
Strathmore Hall Arts Center
10701 Rockville Pike
Rockville, MD 20852
301-530-6744

Bethune Museum—Archives
1318 Vermont Ave. N.W.
Washington, DC 20005
202-332-1233

Capital Children's Museum
800 3rd St. N.E.
Washington, DC 20002
202-543-8600

Capitol Hill Arts Workshop
545 7th St. S.E.

Washington, DC 20003
202-547-6839

Cathedral Choral Society at the Washington Cathedral
Wisconsin and Massachusetts Ave. N.W.
Washington, DC 20016
202-966-3423

Choral Arts Society of Washington
4321 Wisconsin Ave. N.W.
Washington, DC 20016
202-244-3669

Commission on Fine Arts
441 F St. N.W.
Washington, DC 20001
202-504-2200

Bright outlook for artisans in DC

Although Washington abounds in museums, many artists, restorers, and others interested in fine arts do not automatically think of this city as a culturally rich area. Many people assume that New York draws all the talent along the East Coast. However, the art scene in Washington has changed drastically in the past ten years and many of the artisans previously disdainful of the market here realize that there are things happening in the District.

It is not only the Smithsonian that provides an environment rich for the potential arts employee. There are other galleries, smaller museums, and even historical properties that hire artists, textile experts, woodworkers, designers, and even stone masons. Be creative, and don't fall into the "New York is the only place to be" trap. ■

Corcoran Gallery of Art
17th St. and New York Ave. N.W.
Washington, DC 20006
202-638-3211

Cultural Alliance of Greater Washington
410 8th St. N.W.
Washington, DC 20004
202-638-2406

D.C. Artwork
410 8th St. N.W.
Washington, DC 20004
202-727-3412

D.C. Commission on the Arts and Humanities
410 8th St. N.W.
Washington, DC 20004
202-724-5613

D.C. Community Humanities Council
1331 H St. N.W.
Washington, DC 20005
202-347-1732

Daughters of the American Revolution Museum
1776 D St. N.W.
Washington, DC 20006
202-879-3241

Decatur House
748 Jackson Place N.W.
Washington, DC 20006
202-842-0920

District of Columbia Community Orchestra Association
P.O. Box 9658
Washington, DC 20016
202-966-0772

Dumbarton House
c/o NSCDA
6723 Whittier Road
McLean, VA 22101
703-556-0881

Dumbarton Oaks
1703 32nd St. N.W.
Washington, DC 20007
202-338-8278

Explorers Hall—National Geographic Society
17th and M Sts. N.W.
Washington, DC 20036
202-857-7588

Fairfax County Council of the Arts
4022 Hummer Road
Annandale, VA 22003
703-642-0862

Fairfax County Department of Recreation & Community Services, Performing & Fine Arts Division
12011 Government Center Pkwy.
Fairfax, VA 22035
703-324-5515

Fairfax Symphony Orchestra
P.O. Box 1300
Annandale, VA 22003
703-642-7200

Folger Shakespeare Library
201 East Capitol St. S.E.
Washington, DC 20003
202-544-4600

Ford's Theatre Society
511 10th St. N.W.
Washington, DC 20004
202-638-2941

Freer Gallery
12th St. and Jefferson Drive S.W.
Washington, DC 20560
202-357-2104
Smithsonian Institution.

Friends of the Kennedy Center
John F. Kennedy Center
Washington, DC 20566
202-416-8300

Friends of the National Zoo (FONZ)
National Zoological Park
Washington, DC 20008
202-673-4950

Hillwood Museum
4155 Linnean Ave. N.W.
Washington, DC 20008
202-686-8500

Hirshorn Museum and Sculpture Garden
Independence Ave. and 8th St. S.W.
Washington, DC 20560
202-357-1300
Smithsonian Institution.

Historical Society of Washington, D.C.
1307 New Hampshire Ave. N.W.
Washington, DC 20036
202-785-2068

Kennedy Center for the Performing Arts
New Hampshire Ave. and Rock Creek Parkway
Washington, DC 20566
202-416-8015

Library of Congress
10 1st St. S.E.
Washington, DC 20540
202-707-5000

Montgomery County Historical Society
111 W. Montgomery Ave.
Rockville, MD 20850
301-762-1492

Mount Vernon
c/o Mount Vernon Ladies Association
Mount Vernon, VA 22121
703-780-2000

National Air and Space Museum
6th St. and Independence Ave. S.W.
Washington, DC 20560
202-357-2491
Smithsonian Institution.

National Arboretum
3501 New York Ave. N.E.
Washington, DC 20002
202-475-4815

National Archives and Records Administration
Pennsylvania Ave. and 8th St. N.W.
Washington, DC 20408
202-501-5000

National Building Museum
Judiciary Square
Pension Building N.W.
Washington, DC 20001
202-272-2448

National Chamber Orchestra Society
15209 Frederick Road
Rockville, MD 20850
301-762-8580

National Endowment for the Arts
1100 Pennsylvania Ave. N.W.
Washington, DC 20506
202-682-5400

National Endowment for the Humanities
1100 Pennsylvania Ave. N.W.
Washington, DC 20506
202-786-0438

National Gallery of Art
6th St. and Constitution Ave. N.W.
Washington, DC 20565
202-737-4215
Smithsonian Institution, but separately administered.

National Museum of African Art
950 Independence Ave. S.W.
Washington, DC 20560
202-357-4600
Smithsonian Institution.

National Museum of American Art
8th and G St. N.W.
Washington, DC 20560
202-357-1959
Smithsonian Institution.

National Museum of American History
Constitution Ave. and 12th St. N.W.
Washington, DC 20560
202-357-3129
Smithsonian Institution.

National Museum of Natural History
Constitution Ave. and 10th St. N.W.
Washington, DC 20560
202-357-2700
Smithsonian Institution.

National Museum of Women in the Arts
1250 New York Ave. N.W.
Washington, DC 20005
202-783-500

National Portrait Gallery
8th and F St. N.W.
Washington, DC 20560
202-357-2866
Smithsonian Institution.

National Symphony Orchestra
John F. Kennedy Center
Washington, DC 20566
202-416-8100

National Theatre
1321 Pennsylvania Ave. N.W.
Washington, DC 20004
202-628-6161

National Trust for Historical Preservation
1785 Massachusetts Ave. N.W.
Washington, DC 20036
202-673-4000

National Zoological Park
3000 Block of Connecticut Ave. N.W.
Washington, DC 20008
202-673-4717

Phillips Collection
1600 21st St. N.W.
Washington, DC 20009
202-387-2151

Renwick Gallery—National Museum of American Art
17th St. and Pennsylvania Ave. N.W.
Washington, DC 20560
202-357-2531
Smithsonian Institution.

Arthur M. Sackler Gallery
Smithsonian Institution
Washington, DC 20560
202-357-4880

Shakespeare Theatre at the Folger
301 East Capitol St. S.E.
Washington, DC 20003
202-547-3230

Smithsonian Institution
1000 Thomas Jefferson Dr. S.W.
Washington, DC 20560
202-357-1300

Textile Museum
2320 S St. N.W.
Washington, DC 20008
202-667-0441

United States Botanical Gardens
1st St. and Maryland Ave. S.W.
Washington, DC 20024
202-225-8333

United States Holocaust Memorial Museum
2000 L St. N.W.
Washington, DC 20036
202-653-9220

Washington Ballet
3515 Wisconsin Ave. N.W.
Washington, DC 20016
202-362-3606

Washington Chamber Symphony
1099 22nd St. N.W.
Washington, DC 20037
202-452-1321

Washington Opera
John F. Kennedy Center
Washington, DC 20566
202-244-0024

Washington Project for the Arts
400 7th St. N.W.
Washington, DC 20004
202-347-4813

Wolf Trap Farm Park for the Performing Arts
1624 Trap Road
Vienna, VA 22182
703-255-1900

Woodlawn Plantation
P.O. Box 37
Mount Vernon, VA 22121
703-780-4000

Woodrow Wilson House
2340 S St. N.W.
Washington, DC 20008
202-387-4062

Educational Institutions

For networking in education and related fields, check out the following professional organization listed in Chapter 5:

Washington Teachers Union

For additional information, you can write to:

American Association of School Administrators
1801 N. Moore St.
Arlington, VA 22209

Association of School Business Officials
11401 N. Shore Drive
Reston, VA 22090

National Association of College and University Business Officials
1 Dupont Circle N.W.
Washington, DC 20036

National Education Association
1201 16th St. N.W.
Washington, DC 20036

PROFESSIONAL PUBLICATIONS:

Chronicle of Higher Education
Instructor
School Administrator
Teaching Exceptional Children
Teaching K-8
Technology and Learning
Today's Catholic Teacher

DIRECTORIES:

Guide to Secondary Schools (Various Regions) (College Board, New York, NY)
Patterson's American Education (Educational Directories, Mt. Prospect, IL)
Peterson's Guide to Independent Secondary Schools (Peterson's Guides, Princeton, NJ)
Public Schools USA (Williamson Publications, Charlotte, NC)
QED's School Guide (Quality Education Data, Denver, CO)
Yearbook of Higher Education (Marquis Publishing Co., Chicago, IL)

EMPLOYERS:

Colleges and Universities

American University
4400 Massachusetts Ave. N.W.
Washington, DC 20016
202-885-1000
Approx. Enrollment: 12,000
Wide range of undergraduate and graduate programs. Individual schools include law, education, business, communications, public affairs, and international service.

Bowie State University
1400 Jericho Park Road
Bowie, MD 20715
301-464-3000
Approx. Enrollment: 4,000
Part of University of Maryland system. Offers 29 majors and several graduate programs.

250

Capitol College
11301 Springfield Road
Laurel, MD 20708
301-953-0060
Approx. Enrollment: 1,000
Four-year college of engineering and management.

Catholic University of America
620 Michigan Ave. N.E.
Washington, DC 20064
202-319-5000
Approx. Enrollment: 7,000
Full range of undergraduate and graduate programs in nine schools, including law, music, nursing, engineering and architecture, social service, philosophy, library and information science, and religious studies.

Columbia Union College
7600 Flower Ave.
Takoma Park, MD 20912
301-270-9200
Approx. Enrollment: 1,300
Liberal arts college owned by the Seventh-Day Adventist Church.

Corcoran School of Art
17th St. and New York Ave. N.W.
Washington, DC 20006
202-628-9484
Approx. Enrollment: 250
Four-year program in art.

Defense Intelligence College
Bolling Air Force Base
Washington, DC 20340
202-373-3344
Approx. Enrollment: 2,400
Graduate school sponsored by the government. Also runs various training programs for another 7,500 students.

Gallaudet University
800 Florida Ave. N.E.
Washington, DC 20002
202-651-5000
Approx. Enrollment: 2,200
Undergraduate programs are open primarily to the hearing impaired. Some graduate programs, as well as a wide range of majors.

George Mason University
4400 University Drive
Fairfax, VA 22030
703-993-1000

Approx. Enrollment: 18,200
State-operated institution with 50 undergraduate and 40 graduate programs.

George Washington University
2121 I St. N.W.
Washington, DC 20052
202-994-1000
Approx. Enrollment: 19,500
Undergraduate, graduate, and professional programs, including liberal arts, law, business, medicine, engineering, education, and international affairs.

Georgetown University
37th and O Sts. N.W.
Washington, DC 20057
202-687-4324
Approx. Enrollment: 12,000
Private Jesuit institution with four graduate and professional schools: medicine, foreign service, business, and law; and five undergraduate schools.

Graduate School, United States Department of Agriculture
14th and Independence Ave. S.W.
Washington, DC 20250
202-447-2187
Approx. Enrollment: 40,000
Continuing education school for adults. Non-credit courses. No degrees given.

Howard University
2400 6th St. N.W.
Washington, DC 20059
202-806-6100
Approx. Enrollment: 12,000
Private university, offering undergraduate, graduate, and professional programs. Maintains special responsibility for admission and education of black students.

Levine School of Music
1690 36th St. N.W.
Washington, DC 20007
202-337-2227
Approx Enrollment: 2,200
Pre-conservatory training.

Marymount University
Arlington, VA 22207
703-522-5600
Approx. Enrollment: 3,000
Graduate and undergraduate programs offered in arts and sciences, business, nursing, and education.

Montgomery College
900 Hungerford Drive
Rockville, MD 20850
301-279-5000
Approx. Enrollment: 21,600
Two-year associate degrees and many non-credit courses.

Mount Vernon College
2100 Foxhall Road N.W.
Washington, DC 20007
202-625-4682
Approx. Enrollment: 500
Private four-year college for women.

Nitze School of Advanced International Sudies/Johns Hopkins University
1740 Massachusetts Ave. N.W.
Washington, DC 20036
202-663-5600
Approx. Enrollmment: 400
SAIS offers masters and doctoral programs in international public policy.

Northern Virginia Community College
4001 Wakefield Chapel Road
Annandale, VA 22003
703-323-3000
Approx. Enrollment: 59,000
Two-year state institution with five permanent campuses.

Prince George's Community College
301 Largo Road
Largo, MD 20772
301-336-6000
Approx. Enrollment: 30,000
Offers two-year programs and technical and career education courses.

Southeastern University
501 I St. N.W.
Washington, DC 20024
202-488-8162
Approx. Enrollment: 800
College programs offered at times convenient for people who work.

Trinity College
125 Michigan Ave. N.E.
Washington, DC 20017
202-939-5000
Approx. Enrollment: 1,100
Private Catholic college for women.

University of Maryland. College Park Campus
College Park, MD 20742

301-405-4621
Approx. Enrollment: 35,000
Largest unit in Maryland system. Offers undergraduate and graduate
programs in most disciplines.

University of Maryland. University College
University Blvd. at Adelphi Road
College Park, MD 20742
301-985-7000
Approx. Enrollment: 14,500
Adult and continuing education programs throughout area and over-
seas.

University of the District of Columbia
4200 Connecticut Ave. N.W.
Washington, DC 20008
202-282-7300
Approx. Enrollment: 11,000
Public land-grant university, offering graduate and undergraduate
programs.

University of Virginia. Northern Virginia Center
2990 Telstar Court
Falls Church, VA 22042
703-876-6900
Approx. Enrollment: 12,000
Offers several master's programs and certificate course work in varied
subjects.

Major Public School Districts

Arlington County Public Schools
1426 N. Quincy St.
Arlington, VA 22207
703-358-6101

City of Alexandria Public Schools
Personnel Department
Howard Administration Building
3801 W. Braddock Road
Alexandria, VA 22302
703-824-6665
Jobline: 703-824-6624

District of Columbia Public Schools
415 12th St. N.W.
Room 706
Washington, DC 20004
202-724-4080
Jobline: 202-424-4054

Fairfax County Public Schools
Office of Personnel
6815 Edsall Road
Springfield, VA 22151
703-750-8400

Falls Church City School Board
210 E. Broad St.
Falls Church, VA 22046
703-241-7600

Montgomery County Public Schools
Division of Staffing
30 W. Gude Drive
Rockville, MD 20850
301-279-3940
Jobline: 301-279-3973

Prince George's County Public Schools
14201 School Lane
Upper Marlboro, MD 20772
301-952-6180

Electronics/Telecommunications

Be sure also to check the **Research & Development/Technical Services** and **Computers** sections as well.

To help you learn more about the electronics and telecommunications industries, you can write or call:

PROFESSIONAL ORGANIZATIONS:

Electronics Industries Association
2001 Pennsylvania Ave.
Washington, DC 20006
(202) 457-4900

Institute of Electrical & Electronics Engineers (IEEE)
345 E. 47th St.
New York, NY 10017
(212) 705-7900

North American Telecommunications Association
2000 M St. N.W.
Washington, DC 20036

PROFESSIONAL PUBLICATIONS:

Communications Week
Electronic Business

Electronic News
Telecommunications Reports
Telephone Engineer & Management
Telephony

DIRECTORIES:

Design News Electronic Directory (Cahner's Publishing Co., Boston, MA)
SIA Yearbook (Semiconductor Industry Association, Washington, DC)
Telecommunications Systems & Services Directory (Gale Research, Detroit, MI)
Telephone Engineer and Management Directory (Edgell Communications, Chicago, IL)
Telephony's Directory & Buyers Guide (Infertec, Chicago, IL)
U.S. Electronics Industry Directory (Harris Publications, Twinsburg, OH)
Who's Who in Electronics (Harris Publications, Twinsburg, OH)
Who's Who in Technology (Research Publications, Woodbridge, CT)

EMPLOYERS:

AT&T
3033 Chain Bridge Road
Oakton, VA 22185
703-691-5000

Aiken Advanced Systems
5901 Edsall Road
Alexandria, VA 22304
703-370-0900
Contact: Ronald E. Irons, G.M.
Multicouplers.

Allied Bendix Communications
1768 Old Meadow Road
McLean, VA 22102
703-790-5980
Electronic components.

Amstar Technical Products
5901 Edsall Road
Alexandria, VA 22304
703-370-0900
Contact: Ronald E. Irons, G.M.
Electronic surveillance equipment.

Applied Electro-Mechanics
4600 Duke St.
Alexandria, VA 22304
703-370-0510
Contact: Charles Banks, Pres.
High-powered PA systems.

Atlantic Research Corp.
5440 Cherokee Ave.
Alexandria, VA 22312
703-642-4000
Contact: A. Savoca, Pres.
Electronic systems.

Bell Atlantic Network Services
1310 N. Courthouse Road
Arlington, VA 22201
703-974-3000
Telecommunications.

Cable & Wireless
1919 Gallows Road
Vienna, VA 22182
703-790-5300
Communication services, fiber-optic, and digital equipment.

Commonwealth Scientific Corp.
500 Pendleton St.
Alexandria, VA 22314
703-548-0800

Communications Satellite Corp. (COMSAT)
950 L'Enfant Plaza S.W.
Washington, DC 20024
202-863-6800
International satellite communications.

Com-Site
12050 Baltimore Ave.
Beltsville, MD 20705
301-953-1202
Contact: Tom Rosato, Pres.
Electronic manufacturing and scientific equipment.

Delta Electronics
5730 General Washington Drive
Alexandria, VA 22312
703-354-3350
Contact: John Wright
Antenna systems for transmission and reception.

Digital Equipment Corp.
8181 Professional Place
Landover, MD 20785
301-306-6000
Terminal communications equipment.

Dynatech Laboratories
14340 Sullyfield

Chantilly, VA 22021
703-631-7800
Contact: Tim Ellis, Pres.
Telehone, telegraph apparatus.

Bell Atlantic to continue hiring grads

Jeanette Mobley, formerly with College Relations for Bell Atlantic Network Services, projects that telecommunications companies, particularly those also involved in providing service as well as products, will be hiring their usual mix of recent graduates during the 1990s: engineers, computer scientists, telemarketing personnel, business and marketing students, and information systems people.

Jeanette suggests that a job hunter make use of any contacts he or she might have with a particular company; this is a tried and true method of getting in to see the right person. However, she feels that a well written, personalized letter accompanying a clear and concise resume will often bring results, although she acknowledges that a follow-up phone call, allowing enough time for the letter to have been received, might ensure a more prompt response.

Interviews, even if they don't result in a job offer, can be important, Jeanette believes, because an impressed personnel department will often keep the resumes of those they would like to hire, frequently giving call-backs when new opportunities arise. ■

E-Systems. Melpar Division
11225 Walples Mill Road
Fairfax, VA 22030
703-385-5880
Contact: Talbot S. Huff Jr., V.P.

Electronic Data Systems
13600 E.D.S. Drive
Herndon, VA 22071
703-742-2000
Contact: Virgil Smith, V.P.
Computer systems.

ESCO Electronics Corp.
1235 Jefferson Davis Highway
Arlington, VA 22202
703-920-7600
Electronic equipment.

Fairchild Industries
300 W. Service Road

Chantilly, VA 22021
703-478-5800
Diversified electronics and aerospace.

Fairchild Industries. Space & Electronics Division
20301 Century Blvd.
Germantown, MD 20874
301-428-6000
Contact: Jack Frohbieter, Pres.
Technology center.

Fusion Systems Corp.
7600 Standish Place
Rockville, MD 20855
301-251-0300
Contact: Leslie S. Levine, Pres.
Factory automation, photo-electronic equipment.

GTE Communications
12490 Sunrise Valley Drive
Reston, VA 22096
703-709-8630
Contact: Paolo Guidi, Pres.

GTE Government Systems Corp.
1001 19th St. North
Arlington, VA 22202
703-247-9200
Contact: Phil Martin, V.P.
Diversified electronics for federal government.

GTE Federal Systems
15000 Conference Center Drive
Chantilly, VA 22021
703-818-4000
Contact: John Messier
Telecom services for the federal government.

Halifax Engineering
5250 Cherokee Ave.
Alexandria, VA 22312
703-750-2202
Electronics services.

Harvey Hubbell. Pulse Comunications Division
2900 Towerview Road
Herndon, VA 22071
703-471-2900
Telecommunications equipment.

Hekimian Laboratories
15200 Omega Drive

Rockville, MD 20850
301-590-3600
Contact: Dr. R.M. Ginnings, G.M.
Telecom testing apparatus.

Honeywell, Inc.
1766 Old Meadow Lane
McLean, VA 22102
703-749-2000
Contact: Pete Badali, V.P.
Diversified electronics.

Hughes Network Systems
11717 Exploration Lane
Germantown, MD 20874
301-428-5500
Satellite, microwave, telephone/voice equipment.

Ideas, Inc.
10741 Tucker St.
Beltsville, MD 20705
301-621-8766
Contact: Paige Reed, Pres.
Telecommunications.

Isomet Corp.
5263 Port Royal Road
Springfield, VA 22151
703-321-8301
Laser components.

Iverson Technology
1356 Beverly Road
McLean, VA 22101
703-749-1200
Contact: Donald D. Iverson, Pres.
Commercial grade microcomputers.

MCI Communications
1802 Pennsylvania Ave. N.W.
Washington, DC 20002
202-872-1600
Telecommunications.

Martin Marietta
6801 Rockledge Drive
Bethesda, MD 20817
301-897-6000
Diversified electronics.

Micro Systems
12000 Baltimore Ave.

Beltsville, MD 20705
301-490-2000
Contact: Bill Buckley, G.M.
Electronic cash registers.

Microlog
20270 Goldenrod Lane
Germantown, MD 20876
Steven Delmar, Pres.
Voice processing equipment.

MITRE Corp. The Washington Center
7525 Colshire Drive
McLean, VA 22102
703-883-6000
Diversified electronics and systems.

NEC America. Radio and Transmission Division
14040 Park Center Road
Herndon, VA 22071
703-560-2010
Contact: A. Tomozawa, V.P.
Fiber-optic and satellite communications systems, carrier transmission, and teleconferencing.

Northern Telecom
2010 Corporate Ridge
McLean, VA 22102
703-712-8000
Telecommunications.

Penril Corp.
1300 Quince Orchard Blvd.
Gaithersburg, MD 20878
301-417-0552
Contact: Henry D. Epstein, Pres.
Data transmission systems.

Pioneer Technology Group
9100 Gaither Road
Gaithersburg, MD 20877
301-921-0660
Contact: B.S. Tucker

RACAL Communications
5 Research Place
Rockville, MD 20850
301-948-4420
Communications receivers.

Radiation Systems
1501 Moran Road

Sterling, VA 22170
703-450-5680
Contact: Richard Thomas
Antenna products, radar platforms.

Raytheon
1215 Jefferson Davis Highway
Arlington, VA 22202
703-271-5800
Contact: Jerry Smith, V.P.
Diversified electronics.

Rolm Corp.
2070 Chain Bridge Road
Vienna, VA 22182
703-734-1200
Telecom equipment.

SACI
1500 Wilson Blvd.
Arlington, VA 22209
703-351-8200
Contact: Maurice N. Shriber
Radar equipment.

SSE TELECOM
1430 Springhill Road
McLean, VA 22102
703-790-0250
Satellite communications.

S T Research Corp.
8419 H Terminal Road
Newington, VA 22122
703-550-7000
Contact: S.R. Perrino, Pres.
Microprocessing systems, receiving systems.

Satellite Business Systems
12369 Sunrise Valley Drive
Reston, VA 22091
703-648-8000
Satellite communications systems.

Science Applications
11251 Roger Bacon Drive
Reston, VA 22090
703-318-4586
Contact: Larry Brown
Electronic components.

SCOPE Inc.
1860 Michael Faraday Drive
Reston, VA 22090
703-471-5600
Contact: Steven Lowe
Defense electronics, network interface systems.

Solarex Corp.
630 Solarex Court
Frederick, MD 21701
301-698-4200
Contact: J. Corsi, Pres.
Silicon solar cells, photovoltalc systems.

Systems Planning Corp.
1500 Wilson Blvd.
Arlington, VA 22209
703-351-8200
Contact: Ronald L. Easlay
Prototype radar systems.

TRW
101 19th St. North
Arlington, VA 22209
703-276-5000
Contact: John Castellani, V.P.
Diversified electronics.

TRW Defense Systems Group
1 Federal Systems Park Drive
Fairfax, VA 22033
703-734-6000

TVI Corp.
11431 Rockville Pike
Rockville, MD 20852
301-816-0300
Disposable infrared targets for military training.

Telecommunications Techniques Corp./Dynatech Corp.
20410 Observation Drive
Germantown, MD 20876
301-353-1550
Data transmission and monitoring equipment.

US SPRINT
2002 Edmund Halley Drive
Reston, VA 22091
703-264-4000
Telecommunications.

Vega Precision
800 Follin Lane
Vienna, VA 22180
703-938-6300
Command and control equipment and systems.

Verdix
14130-A Sullyfield Circle
Chantilly, VA 22304
703-318-5800
Secure communications.

Watkins-Johnson Co.
700 Quince Orchard Road
Gaithersburg, MD 20878
301-948-7550
Contact: Dr. D.A. Watkins
Communications equipment.

Zenith/INTEQ
13860 Redskins Drive
Herndon, VA 22071
703-471-1500
Contact: Hoy Y. Chang, Pres.
Data communications interface devices, Tempest devices.

Engineering

Be sure also to check the **Architecture, Contractors and Construction,** and **Real Estate** sections.

For networking in engineering and related fields, be sure to check out the following professional organizations listed in Chapter 5:

PROFESSIONAL ORGANIZATIONS:

American Society of Civil Engineers
American Society of Mechanical Engineers

For more information, you can write or call:

American Society of Civil Engineers
1 Walnut St.
Boston, MA 02108
(617) 227-5551

Institute of Industrial Engineers
25 Technology Park
Norcross, GA 30092

National Society of Professional Engineers
1420 King St.
Alexandria, VA 22314
(703) 684-2800

Society of Women Engineers
345 E. 47th St., #305
New York, NY 10017
(212) 705-7855

PROFESSIONAL PUBLICATIONS:

Building Design and Construction
Chemical Engineering News
Civil Engineering
ENR: Engineering News Record

DIRECTORIES:

Directory of Contract Service Firms (C.E. Publications, Kirkland, WA)
ENR Directory of Design Firms Official Register (American Society of Civil Engineers, New York, NY)
Professional Engineering Directory (National Society of Professional Engineers, Alexandria, VA)
Who's Who in Engineering (American Association of Engineering Societies, New York, NY)

EMPLOYERS:

Baker Engineers
3601 Eisenhower Ave.
Alexandria, VA 22304
703-960-8800
Contact: Richard L. Shaw

Bengtson, DeBall, Elkin & Titus
5900 Centreville Road
Centreville, VA 22020
703-631-9630
Contact: John T. DeBell

Leo A. Daly
1201 Connecticut Ave. N.W.
Washington, DC 20036
202-861-4600
Contact: Leo A. Daly III

Delon Hampton & Associates
800 K St. N.W.
Washington DC 20001

202-898-1999
Contact: Delon Hampton

Leland D. Eisenhower
8200 Greensboro Drive
McLean, VA 22102
703-448-4880
Contact: Leland D. Eisenhower

William H. Gordon Associates
4501 Daly Drive
Chantilly, VA 22021
703-263-1900
Contact: William H. Gordon

HDR Inc.
103 Oronoco St.
Alexandria, VA 22314
03-683-3400
Contact: Dina Hendrickson

ICF Technology
9300 Lee Highway
Fairfax, VA 22031
703-934-3000
Contact: Charles A. Debelius

Kamber Engineering
818 W. Diamond Ave.
Gaithersburg, MD 20878
301-840-1030
Contact: Dennis M. Kamber

Landmak Engineering
1751 Etan Road
Silver Spring, MD 20903
301-656-9550

Paciulli, Simmons & Associates
1821 Michael Faraday Drive
Reston, VA 22091
703-742-7870
Contact: Howell Simmons

Patton, Harris, Rust & Associates
3998 Fair Ridge Drive
Fairfax, VA 22030
703-273-8700
Contact: Charles R. Weber

Rinker, Detwiler & Associates
9240 B. Moseby Drive

Manassas, VA 22110
703-591-6812
Contact: Jack Rinker

RTKL
1140 Connecticut Ave. N.W.
Washington, DC 20036
202-833-4400
Contact: Harold L. Adams

Schnabel Engineering Associates
10215 Fernwood Road
Bethesda, MD 20817
301-564-9355
Contact: James J. Schnabel

Shefferman & Bigelson Co.
8455 Colesville Road
Silver Spring, MD 20910
301-587-4433
Contact: S.M. Shefferman

Environmental Consulting Firms

For additional information, you can write to:

PROFESSIONAL ORGANIZATIONS:

Institute of Hazardous Materials Management
5010 A. Nicolson Lane
Rockville, MD 20852

National Association of Environmental Professionals
815 Second Ave.
New York, NY 10017

Water Pollution Control Federation
601 Wyth St.
Alexandria, VA 22314-1994

PROFESSIONAL PUBLICATIONS:

Energy and Environment Alert
Environmental Analysis
Environmental Forum
Environmental Geology
Environmental Week
Pollution Engineering
Water and Wastes Digest

DIRECTORIES:

The Complete Guide to Environmental Careers (The CEIP Fund. Island Press, 1989)
Directory of Environmental Information Sources (Government Institutes, Rockville, MD)
Directory of Experts and Consultants in Environmental Science (Research Publications, Woodbridge, CT)

EMPLOYERS:

APEX Environmental
15850 Crabbs Branch Way
Rockville, MD 20855
301-417-0200

AWD Technologies
15204 Omega Drive
Rockville, MD 20850
301-948-0040

CH2M Hill
625 Herndon Pkwy.
Herndon, VA 22070
703-471-1441

Dames & Moore
7101 Wisconsin Ave.
Bethesda, MD 20814
301-652-2215

Dewberry & Davis
8401 Arlington Blvd.
Fairfax, VA 22031
703-849-0100

Engineering Science
10521 Rosehaven St.
Fairfax, VA 22030
703-591-7575

Halliburton & N.V.S.
910 Clopper Road
P.O. Box 6032
Gaithersburg, MD 20877
301-258-6000

ICF International
9300 Lee Highway
Fairfax, VA 22031
703-934-3600

Kamber Engineering
616 W. Diamond Ave.
Gaithersburg, MD 20878
301-840-1030

Kenron Environmental Services
7928 Jones Branch Drive
McLean, VA 22102
703-893-4106

Law Engineering
4465 Brookfield Corp. Drive
Chantilly, VA 22021
703-968-4700

Law Environmental
7375 Boston Blvd.
Springfield, VA 22153
703-912-9400

Risk Science International
1101 30th St. N.W.
Washington, DC 20007
202-342-2206

SAIC
1710 Goodridge Drive
McLean, VA 22102
703-749-8988

SCS Engineers
11260 Roger Bacon Drive
Reston, VA 22090
703-471-6150

Versar, Inc.
6850 Versar Center
Springfield, VA 22151
703-750-3000

DC a mecca for environmental work

With concern about and interest in environmental issues at an all-time high, the U.S. government has allocated billions of dollars toward environmental expenditures such as massive cleanups and water-and air-quality protection programs. Consequently, the demand for environmental consultants to help manage these environmental affairs has become quite high.

Donald Feliciano, Senior Policy Analyst within Versar, Inc.'s Waste Management Division, states that "Washington is largely a mecca for environmental work. Many of the environmental interest groups have offices here; and environmental think tanks and professional associations abound. Each of these organizations is a fertile area for young minds to get exposed to key environmental issues and acquire working knowledge for possible consultant careers later on."

Suitable work and academic backgrounds for environmental consulting careers tend to be technical in nature. Mr. Feliciano says: "Engineering and science degrees and experience are preferred by the federal agencies for their environmental consultants. Environmental, civil and chemical engineering and sciences like biology and chemistry seem to be in high demand. Additionally, there are a lot of very successful environmental consultants from a variety of other backgrounds who specialize in program management, policy and regulatory analysis, communications, and information management skills that help to keep the bureaucratic process moving. If you want to work in the environmental consulting field in the Washington area, you must recognize that this type of work is mainly pushing paper and helping federal agencies manage their programs. If you want to do environmental consulting where you roll up your sleeves and get dirty, you need to work in the field, where the problems are actually located—outside Washington." ■

Financial Institutions/Credit Unions

To learn more about banking and related fields, check out the following organization listed in Chapter 5:

Washington Area Bankers Association

For additional information, you can write or call:

American Bankers Association
1120 Connecticut Ave. N.W.
Washington, DC 20036
(202) 663-5000

Bank Marketing Association
309 W. Washington Blvd.
Chicago, IL 60606
(312) 782-1442

Mortgage Bankers Association of America
1125 15th St. N.W.
Washington, DC 20005
(202) 861-6500

Savings and Community Bankers of America
1101 15th St. N.W.
Washington, DC 20005
(202) 857-3100

PROFESSIONAL PUBLICATIONS:

American Banker
Bank Administration
Bank Marketing Magazine
Bankers Magazine
Bankers Monthly
Credit Union Magazine
Credit Union Management
Credit Union Report
Savings Institutions

DIRECTORIES:

American Bank Directory (McFadden Business Publications, Norcross, GA)
American Banker's Guides (American Banker, New York, NY)
Callahan's Credit Union Directory (Callahan and Associates, Washington, DC)
Directory of American Savings and Loan Associations (T.K. Sanderson, Baltimore, MD)
Money Market Directory (Money Market Directories, Charlottesville, VA)
Moody's Bank & Finance Manual (Moody's Investor Service, New York, NY)
Polk's Bank Directory (R.L. Polk, Nashville, TN)
Rand McNally Bankers Directory (Rand McNally, Chicago, IL)
U.S. Savings and Loan Directory (Rand McNally, Chicago, IL)

EMPLOYERS, BANKS and S&Ls:

Ameribanc Investors Group. Ameribanc Savings
7630 Little River Turnpike
Annandale, VA 22003
703-658-1170

American Security Bank
1501 Pennsylvania Ave. N.W.
Washington, DC 20013
202-624-4000

Central Fidelity
8100 Boone Blvd.

Vienna, VA 22182
703-827-1000

Chevy Chase Federal Savings Bank
8401 Connecticut Ave.
Chevy Chase, MD 20815
301-598-7100

Citicorp Savings of Washington DC
1775 Pennsylvania Ave. N.W.
Washington, DC 20006
202-857-6700

Citizens Bancorp
14401 Sweitzer Lane
Laurel, MD 20707
301-699-7000

Citizens National Bank
390 Main St.
Laurel, MD 20707
301-725-3100

Citizens Savings Bank
8485 Fenton St.
Silver Spring, MD 20910
301-565-8900

Columbia First Federal Savings & Loan
1560 Wilson Blvd.
Arlington, VA 22209
703-247-5000

Continental Federal Savings
4020 University Drive
Fairfax, VA 22030
703-691-4400

Crestar
1445 New York Ave. N.W.
Washington, DC 20005
202-879-6000

Dominion Bank of Washington
927 15th St. N.W.
Washington, DC 20005
202-624-0400

Equitable Bancorp.
11501 Georgia Ave.
Wheaton, MD 20902
301-949-6500

Federal Home Loan Mortgage Corp. (Freddie Mac)
8200 Jones Branch Drive
McLean, VA 22102
703-759-8000

Federal National Mortgage Association (Fannie Mae)
3900 Wisconsin Ave. N.W.
Washington, DC 20016
202-752-7000

First American Bankshares
15th & H Sts. N.W.
Washington, DC 20005
202-383-1400

First Virginia Banks
6400 Arlington Blvd.
Falls Church, VA 22046
703-241-4866

Government National Mortgage Association (Ginnie Mae)
451 7th St. S.W.
Washington, DC 20410
202-708-0926

Household Bank
119 N. Washington St.
Alexandria, VA 22314
703-765-2675

Meritor Savings Bank
2111 Wilson Blvd.
Arlington, VA 22201
703-525-3345

Nation's Bank
3401 Columbia Pike
Arlington, VA 22204
703-271-2201

NVR Federal Savings Bank
1451 Dolley Madison Blvd.
McLean, VA 22101
703-356-2290

Riggs National Bank
1503 Pennsylvania Ave. N.W.
Washington, DC 20013
202-835-6000

RTC/Perpetual
2034 Eisenhower Ave.

Alexandria, VA 22314
703-838-6000

Signet Banking Group
8330 Boone Blvd.
Vienna, VA 22182
703-734-7400

Student Loan Marketing Association (Sallie Mae)
1050 Thomas Jefferson St. N.W.
Washington, DC 20007
202-333-8000

EMPLOYERS, CREDIT UNIONS:

Andrews FCU
Andrews Air Force Base
Washington, DC 20331
301-702-5500

Apple FCU
9701 Main St.
Fairfax, VA 22030
703-323-0246

Bank Fund Staff FCU
1818 H St. N.W.
Washington, DC 20433
202-458-4300

NASA FCU
P.O. Box 1910
Bowie, MD 20717
301-249-1800

Naval Research Laboratories FCU
P.O. Box 1026
Oxon Hill, MD 20750
301-839-8440

Navy FCU
P.O. Box 3000
Merrifield, VA 22119
703-255-8904

Northwest FCU
200 Spring St.
Herndon, VA 22070
703-709-8900

Pentagon FCU
1001 N. Fairfax St.

Alexandria, VA 22314
703-838-1000

State Department FCU
1630 King St.
Alexandria, VA 22314
703-706-5000

Tower FCU
P.O. Box 123
Annapolis Junction, MD 20701
301-688-6486

Food/Beverage Producers and Distributors

For networking in the food products industry, check out the following professional organizations listed in Chapter 5:

PROFESSIONAL ORGANIZATIONS:

District of Columbia Dietetic Association
Washington DC Restaurant & Beverage Association
Washington DC Retail Liquor Dealers Association

For additional information, you can write to:

Distilled Spirits Council
1250 I St. N.W.
Washington, DC 20005

Food Marketing Institute
1750 K St. N.W.
Washington, DC 20006

National Food Brokers Association
1010 Massachusetts Ave. N.W.
Washington, DC 20001

National Food Distributors Association
401 N. Michigan Ave.
Chicago, IL 60601

National Food Processors Association
1401 New York Ave. N.W.
Washington, DC 20005

National Frozen Food Association
4755 Linglestown Road
P.O. Box 6069
Harrisburg, PA 17112

National Soft Drink Association
1101 16th St. N.W.
Washington, DC 20036

Wine & Spirits Wholesalers of America
1023 15th St. N.W.
Washington, DC 20005

PROFESSIONAL PUBLICATIONS:

Beverage World
Food and Beverage Marketing
Food Management
Foodservice Product News
Institutional Distribution
Progressive Grocer
Wines and Vines

DIRECTORIES:

Directory of the Canning, Freezing, Preserving Industry (J.J. Judge, Westminster, MD)
National Beverage Marketing Directory (Beverage Marketing Group, New York, NY)
NFBA Directory (National Food Brokers Association, Washington, DC)
Thomas Grocery Register (Thomas Publishing Co., New York, NY)

EMPLOYERS:

East Coast Ice Cream
9090 Whiskey Bottom Road
Laurel, MD 20723
301-776-7727
Contact: William L. Carter

Giant Food
6300 Sheriff Road
Landover, MD 20785
301-341-4100
Supermarkets, bakery, dairy.

Hills of Westchester
3400 Windom Road
Brentwood, MD 20722
301-864-4421
Cookies, confections.

ITT Continental Baking
2301 Georgia Ave. N.W.
Washington, DC 20001

202-797-2920
Bakery products.

Marriott Corp.
One Marriott Drive
Washington, DC 20058
301-380-9000
Huge food service operations.

Mars Inc.
6885 Elm St.
McLean, VA 22101
703-821-4900
Cady.

Maryland-Virginia Milk Producers
P.O. Box 184
Laurel, MD 20725
301-792-7960

Pepsi Cola Bottling
1 Pepsi Place
Cheverly, MD 20781
301-322-7000
Contact: C.B. Gillions

Pepsi-Cola Bottling of Washington DC
405 Fannon St.
Alexandria, VA 22301
703-549-0800

Safeway Stores
4551 Forbes Drive
Lanham, MD 20706
301-386-6500
Grocery stores.

Shenandoah's Pride
5325 Port Royal Road
Springfield, VA 22151
703-321-9500

Vie De France
8201 Greensboro Drive
McLean, VA 22102
703-442-9205
Bakery products.

Mouth-watering opportunities in food service management

Paula Hall, manager of the dietary department of a large DC hospital, sees the food service industry as a growing field with tremendous growth potential. The many hospitals in the area offer varied opportunities; some of the jobs, such as clinical or administrative dietitian, require a college degree. But many do not.

"Some employees have experience working in fast food restaurants," says Paula. "Others just learn on the job. Still others have completed one- or two-year programs in food service offered by various colleges."

Besides dietitians, Paula's staff includes food service supervisors, who manage the personnel who prepare food; diet technicians, who prepare and implement menus based on ₁ information about the patient; diet aides, who perform such tasks as delivering meals; a chef and cooking staff; and a food purchasing agent.

Paula is optimistic about employment prospects in the food service industry as a whole. "Opportunities exist in food equipment companies, public and private schools, contract food companies, and food service consulting firms.

"The nutritional needs of the growing elderly population," Paula adds, "will also create many new jobs as hospitals and other organizations become involved in the field of long-term care." ■

Foundations

To learn more about foundations and philanthropy, you can write to the following organization:

PROFESSIONAL ORGANIZATIONS:

Foundation Center
79 Fifth Avenue
New York, NY 10003

PROFESSIONAL PUBLICATIONS:

Foundation News
Fund Raising Management

DIRECTORIES:

Corporate Foundation Profiles (The Foundation Center, New York, NY)
Corporate Giving Yellow Pages (Taft Group, Washington, DC)
Foundation Directory (The Foundation Center, New York, NY)

EMPLOYERS:

Arca Foundation
1425 21st St. N.W.
Washington, DC 20036
202-822-9193

Bender Foundation
1120 Connecticut Ave. N.W.
Washington, DC 20036
202-828-9000

Benton Foundation
1710 Rhode Island Ave. N.W.
Washington, DC 20006
202-857-7829

Cafritz Foundation
1825 K St. N.W.
Washington, DC 20006
202-223-3100

Council on Foundations
1828 L St. N.W.
Washington, DC 20036
202-466-6512

Council on Library Resources
1785 Massachusetts Ave. N.W.
Washington, DC 20036
202-483-7474

Families USA Foundation
1334 G St. N.W.
Washington, DC 20005
202-628-3030

Freed Foundation
1202 Eaton Court
Washington, DC 20007
202-337-5487

Philip L. Graham Fund
1150 15th St. N.W.
Washington, DC 20071
202-334-6640

Gudelsky Family Foundation
11900 Tech Road
Silver Spring, MD 20904
301-622-0100

Hariri Foundation
1020 19th St. N.W.
Washington, DC 20036
202-659-9200

Higginson Trust, Corina
3400 Bryan Pt. Road
Accokeek, MD 20607
301-283-2113

Hitachi Foundation
1509 22nd St. N.W.
Washington, DC 20037
202-457-0588

Independent Sector
1828 L St. N.W.
Washington, DC 20036
202-223-8100

Johnston Trust for Charitable and Educational Purposes
1101 Vermont Ave. N.W.
Washington, DC 20005
202-289-4996

Kennedy Foundation, Joseph P., Jr.
1350 New York Ave. N.W.
Washington, DC 20005
202-393-1250

Kiplinger Foundation
1729 H St. N.W.
Washington, DC 20006
202-887-6537

Loyola Foundation
308 C St. N.E.
Washington, DC 20002
202-546-9400

The J. Willard Marriott Foundation
1 Marriott Drive N.W.
Washington, DC 20058
202-380-9000

Eugene and Agnes E. Meyer Foundation
1400 16th St. N.W.

Washington, DC 20036
202-483-8294

National Committee for Responsive Philanthropy
2001 S St. N.W.
Washington, DC 20009
202-387-9177

Public Welfare Foundation
2600 Virginia Ave. N.W.
Washington, DC 20037
202-965-1800

Alexander and Margaret Stewart Trust
c/o First American Bank
740 15th St. N.W.
Washington, DC 20005
202-637-7887

Hattie M. Strong Foundation
1735 I St. N.W.
Washington, DC 20006
202-331-1619

Truman Scholarship Foundation
712 Jackson Place N.W.
Washington, DC 20006
202-395-4831

Government

SEE CHAPTER 11 FOR GOVERNMENT EMPLOYMENT
OPPORTUNITIES

Health Care

For networking in health and medical care, check out the following
professional organizations listed in Chapter 5:

PROFESSIONAL ORGANIZATIONS:

**Dental Societies of the District of Columbia and Northern
    Virginia**
District of Columbia Hospital Association
District of Columbia Nurses Association
Medical Society of the District of Columbia
Montgomery County Medical Society
Washington Psychiatric Society

For additional information, you can write or call:

American Health Care Association
1201 L St. N.W.
Washington, DC 20005
(202) 842-4444

American Hospital Association
840 N. Lake Shore Drive
Chicago, IL 60611

American Psychiatric Association
1400 K St. N.W.
Washington, DC 20005

American Public Health Association
1015 15th St. N.W.
Washington, DC 20005
(202) 789-5600

National Association of Social Workers
750 1st St. N.E.
Washington, DC 20002

PROFESSIONAL PUBLICATIONS:

ADA News
American Journal of Nursing
American Journal of Public Health
The Dental Assistant
Health Care Financial Management
Health Care Strategic Management
Health Facilities Management
Health Industry Today
Hospital Materials Management
Hospitals
JAMA (Journal of the American Medical Association)
Laboratory Medicine
Modern Healthcare

DIRECTORIES:

Directory of Health Care Coalitions in the U.S. (American Hospital Association, Chicago, IL)
Directory of Hospitals (SMG Marketing Group, Chicago, IL)
Guide to the Health Care Field (American Hospital Association, Chicago, IL)
Saunders Health Care Directory (W.B. Saunders, Philadelphia, PA)

EMPLOYERS:

Alexandria Hospital
4320 Seminary Road
Alexandria, VA 22304
703-379-3000

Arlington Hospital
1701 N. George Mason Drive
Arlington, VA 22205
703-558-5000

Blue Cross and Blue Shield
550 12th St. S.W.
Washington, DC 20065
202-479-8000

CapitalCare
1921 Gallows Road
Tysons Corner, VA 22183
703-761-5599
HMO

Children's Hospital National Medical Center
111 Michigan Ave. N.W.
Washington, DC 20010
202-745-5000

Cigna Health Plan
9700 Patuxent Woods Drive
Columbia, MD 21046
800-542-2471
HMO

Clinical Center—National Institutes of Health
9000 Rockville Pike
Bethesda, MD 20892
301-496-3141

Columbia-Freestate Health System
10626 York Road
Cockeysville, MD 21030
410-683-0100

D.C. General Hospital
19th St. and Massachusetts Ave. S.E.
Washington, DC 20003
202-675-5000

Doctor's Community Hospital
8118 Lanham Road

Lanham, MD 20706
301-552-8118

Fairfax Hospital
3300 Gallows Road
Falls Church, VA 22046
703-698-1100

George Washington University Health Plan
1901 Pennsylvania Ave. N.W.
Washington, DC 20006
202-416-0440
HMO

George Washington University Medical Center
901 23rd N.W.
Washington, DC 20037
202-994-1000

Georgetown University Hospital
3800 Reservoir Road N.W.
Washington, DC 20007
202-784-3000

Greater Southeast Community Hospital
1310 Southern Ave. S.E.
Washington, DC 20032
202-574-6000

Group Health Association
4301 Connecticut Ave. N.W.
Washington, DC 20008
202-364-2000
HMO

Health Plus Option
7601 Ora Glen Drive
Greenbelt, MD 20770
301-441-1600
HMO

Holy Cross Hospital of Silver Spring
1500 Forest Glen Road
Silver Spring, MD 20910
301-905-0100

Howard University Hospital
2401 Georgia Ave. N.W.
Washington, DC 20060
202-865-6100

Kaiser Permanente
4200 Wisconsin Ave. N.W.
Washington, DC 20016
202-364-3400
HMO

MD-IPA Health Plan
4 Taft Court
Rockville, MD 20850
301-294-5100
HMO

Malcolm Grow United States Air Force Medical Center
Andrews Air Force Base
Camp Springs, MD 20331
301-981-3001

Manor Care
10750 Columbia Pike
Silver Spring, MD 20901
301-681-9400
Operator of nursing homes and retirement communities.

Mount Vernon Hospital
2501 Parker's Lane
Alexandria, VA 22306
703-664-7000

National Health Laboratories
139 Park Center Road
Herndon, VA 22071
703-742-3100
Clinical research.

National Naval Medical Center
8901 Wisconsin Ave.
Bethesda, MD 20889
301-295-5388

PHP Healthcare
4900 Seminary Road
Alexandria, VA 22311
703-998-7808
Provides health care facilities for federal and state agencies.

Prince George's Hospital Center
3001 Hospital Drive
Cheverly, MD 20785
301-618-2000

Providence Hospital
1150 Varnum St. N.E.

Washington, DC 20017
202-269-7000

Saint Elizabeth's Hospital
2700 Martin Luther King Ave. S.E.
Washington, DC 20032
202-562-4000

Shady Grove Adventist Hospital
9901 Medical Center Drive
Rockville, MD 20850
301-279-6000

Sibley Memorial Hospital
5225 Loughboro Road N.W.
Washington, DC 20016
202-537-4000

Suburban Hospital
8600 Old Georgetown Road
Bethesda, MD 20814
301-530-3100

Veteran's Affairs Medical Center
50 Irving St. N.W.
Washington, DC 20422
202-745-8000

Walter Reed Army Medical Center
6825 16th St. N.W.
Washington, DC 20307
202-576-3501

Washington Hospital Center
110 Irving St. N.W.
Washington, DC 20010
202-877-7000

Hospitality/Caterers

For networking in the hotel and restaurant industries, check out the following organizations listed in Chapter 5:

PROFESSIONAL ORGANIZATIONS:

Hotel Association of Washington
Restaurant Association of Metropolitan Washington

For additional information, you can also write or call:

American Hotel and Motel Association
1201 New York Ave. N.W.
Washington, DC 20005
(202) 289-3100

Hotel Sales Marketing Association International
1300 L St. N.W.
Washington, DC 20005
(202) 789-0089

National Restaurant Association
1200 17th St. N.W.
Washington, DC 20036
(202) 331-5900

PROFESSIONAL PUBLICATIONS:

Catering Today
Hotel Management
Hotel & Motel Management
Hotel & Resort Industry
Lodging Magazine
Meetings & Conventions
Restaurant Business
Restaurant Hospitality
Restaurants and Institutions

DIRECTORIES:

Directory of Hotel and Motel Systems (American Hotel & Motel
    Association,Washington, DC)
Hotel & Motel Redbook (American Hotel & Motel Association, Washing-
    ton, DC)
Restaurant Hospitality—500 Issue (Penton Publishing, Cleveland, OH)
Restaurants & Institutions—400 Issue (Cahners Publishing, Des Plaines, IL)
*Salesman's Guide: National Directory of Association Meeting Planners &
    Conference/Convention Directors* (National Register Publishing Co.,
    Wilmette, IL)

EMPLOYERS, HOTELS & RESTAURANTS:

Atlantic Restaurant Ventures
7700 Old Branch Ave.
Clinton, MD 20735
301-868-7614
Fudruckers, Little Tavern.

Bethesda Marriott
5151 Pooks Hill Road

Bethesda, MD 20814
301-897-9400

Burger King Restaurants
1820 International Drive
McLean, VA 22102
703-356-9736

Capitol Hilton
16th and K Sts. N.W.
Washington, DC 20036
202-393-1000

Clydes Restaurant Group
3236 M St. N.W.
Washington, DC 20007
202-333-9180

Double Tree Hotel—National Airport
300 Army Navy Drive
Arlington, VA 22202
703-892-4100

Grand Hyatt
1000 H St. N.W.
Washington, DC 20001
202-582-1234

Guest Services
3055 Prosperity Ave.
Fairfax, VA 22031
703-849-9300
Restaurants, hotels, business dining services.

Holiday Inn Capitol
550 C St. S.W.
Washington, DC 20024
202-479-4000

Hotel management: more than puttin' on the Ritz

With a little more than two years' experience in the hotel business, Nancy Nachman landed a job as sales manager for the Ritz-Carlton Hotel. We asked her for an overview of the hospitality industry.

"If you want to move up quickly," says Nancy, "this is the industry to be in. Some people stay with the same organization for most of their careers. But I'd say that the average is probably around five years with any given company. People are frequently calling and making job offers.

"I studied hotel management and general

business. But you can't just walk out of college and into a middle-management job. I started as a receptionist at the Ritz-Carlton. Then I became a secretary. I don't know anyone who hasn't paid dues for a year or two. If you are interested in food or beverages, you might start out as a dining room assistant. Essentially, you'd be doing secretarial work—typing up menus or contracts. You really have to learn the business from the bottom up.

"In sales you move from secretarial to a full-fledged sales position. I was a sales representative before I was promoted to manager. The next step might logically be director of sales or marketing, where I'd be responsible for advertising and marketing strategies, developing budgets, etc. Then, you might go on to general manager.

"I'd say the competition is about average—not nearly as fierce as advertising. Earning potential is pretty good too, depending on, of course, the size of the hotel, and the city you're in. You start out low, but every time you move up, you get a hefty raise, or ought to." ■

Hyatt Regency on Capitol Hill
400 New Jersey Ave. N.W.
Washington, DC 20001
202-737-1234

Hyatt Regency Crystal City
2799 Jefferson Davis Highway
Arlington, VA 22202
703-418-1234

JW Marriott
1331 Pennsylvania Ave. N.W.
Washington, DC 20004
202-393-2000

Key Bridge Marriott
1401 Lee Highway
Arlington, VA 22209
703-524-6400

Marriott Corp.
10400 Fernwood Road
Bethesda, MD 20817
301-380-9000
One of largest owner/operators of hotels, restaurants, fast food and food service companies in the world.

Marriott Crystal Gateway
1700 Jefferson Davis Highway
Arlington, VA 22202
703-920-3230

McDonald's Corp.
3015 Williams Drive
Fairfax, VA 22031
703-698-4000
Regional office.

McLean Hilton
7920 Jones Branch Drive
McLean, VA 22102
703-847-5000

Omni Shoreham
2500 Calvert St. N.W.
Washington, DC 20008
202-234-0700

Quality Inns International
10750 Columbia Pike
Silver Spring, MD 20901
301-593-5600

Radisson Mark Plaza Hotel
5000 Seminary Road
Alexandria, VA 22311
703-845-1010

Ritz-Carlton Hotel
2100 Massachusetts Ave. N.W.
Washington, DC 20008
202-835-2100

Roy Rogers of Washington
1634 I St. N.W.
Washington, DC 20006
202-638-0431

Sheraton Premiere at Tyson's Corner
8661 Leesburg Pike
Vienna, VA 22182
703-448-1234

Sheraton Washington Hotel
2660 Woodley Road N.W.
Washington, DC 20008
202-328-2000

Stouffer Mayflower Hotel
1127 Connecticut Ave. N.W.
Washington, DC 20036
202-347-3000

Vista International
1400 M St. N.W.
Washington, DC 20005
202-429-1700

Washington Hilton and Towers
1919 Connecticut Ave. N.W.
Washington, DC 20009
202-483-3000

Westfields International
14750 Conference Center Drive
Chantilly, VA 22021
703-818-0300
The Westin Hotel
24th and M Sts. N.W.
Washington, DC 20037
202-429-2400

EMPLOYERS, CATERERS:

B&B Caterers
7041 Blair Rd. N.W.
Washington, DC 20012
202-829-8640

Bluefield Gourmet Caterers
401 Reisters Town Road
Baltimore, MD 21208
301-206-3099

Design Cuisine Caterers
2659 S. Shirlington Road
Arlington, VA 22206
703-979-9400
Sue Fischer Caterers
2080 Viers Mill Road
Rockville, MD 20851
301-251-9070

La Fontaine Bleu
7963 Annapolis Road
Lanham, MD 20706
301-731-433

Martin's Crosswinds
7400 Greenway Center Drive

Greenbelt, MD 20770
301-474-8500

Occasions Caterer
1110 Congress St. N.W.
Washington, DC 20002
202-546-7400

Paris Caterers
12260 Wilkins Ave.
Rockville, MD 20852
301-530-5402

Ridgewell's Caterers
5525 Dorsey Lane
Bethesda, MD 20816
301-948-9170

Smokey Glen Farm
16407 Riffleford Road
Gaithersburg, MD 20878

Windows Catering
1101 Wilson Blvd.
Arlington, VA 22209
703-527-3121

Human Services

For more information about human services as a career, you can write to:

PROFESSIONAL ORGANIZATIONS:

Center for Human Services
5530 Wisconsin Ave.
Chevy Chase, MD 20815

National Association of Social Workers
750 1st St. N.E.
Washington, DC 20002

PROFESSIONAL PUBLICATIONS:

Children and Youth Services Review
The Non-Profit Times
Social Work in Health Care

DIRECTORIES:

Directory of Agencies (National Association of Social Workers, Silver
    Spring, MD)
National Directory of Children and Youth Services (Marion Peterson,
    Longmont, CO)
National Directory of Private Social Agencies (Croner Publications, Queens,
    NY)

EMPLOYERS:

American Cancer Society
1825 Connecticut Ave. N.W.
Washington, DC 20009
202-483-2600

American Diabetes Association
1660 Duke St.
Alexandria, VA 22314
703-549-1500

American Heart Association
2233 Wisconsin Ave. N.W.
Washington, DC 20007
202-337-6400

American Kidney Fund
6110 Executive Blvd.
Rockville, MD 20852
301-881-3052

American Lung Association
475 H St. N.W.
Washington, DC 20001
202-682-5864

American Red Cross
17th and D Sts. N.W.
Washington, DC 20006
202-737-8300

Arthritis Foundation
1901 Ft. Meyer Drive
Arlington, VA 22209
703-276-7555

Big Brothers of the National Capitol Area
1320 Fenwick Lane
Silver Spring, MD 20910
301-587-4315

Big Sisters of the Washington Metropolitan Area
4000 Albermarle St. N.W.
Washington, DC 20016
202-244-1012

Boy Scouts of America
9190 Wisconsin Ave.
Bethesda, MD 20814
301-530-9360

Boys and Girls Clubs of Greater Washington
1320 Fenwick Lane
Silver Spring, MD 20910
301-587-4315

Catholic Charities
P.O. Box 10038
Washington, DC 20018
202-526-4100

Cystic Fibrosis Foundation
6931 Arlington Blvd.
Bethesda, MD 20814
301-951-4422

Easter Seal Society
2800 13th St. N.W.
Washington, DC 20009
202-232-2342

Epilepsy Foundation of America
4351 Garden City Drive
Landover, MD 20785
301-459-3700

Family and Child Services of Washington
929 L St. N.W.
Washington, DC 20001
202-289-1510

Girl Scouts Council of the Nation's Capital
2233 Wisconsin Ave. N.W.
Washington, DC 20007
202-337-4300

Jewish Social Service Agency
6123 Montrose Road
Rockville, MD 20852
301-881-3700

March of Dimes
2700 S. Quincy St.

Arlington, VA 22206
703-824-0111

Mental Health Association of Northern Virginia
7630 Little River Tnpk.
Annandale, VA 22003
703-642-0800

Multiple Sclerosis Society
2021 K St. N.W.
Washington, DC 20006
202-296-5363

Muscular Dystrophy Association
5350 Shawnee Road
Alexandria, VA 22312
703-941-5001

National Mental Health Association
1021 Prince St.
Alexandria, VA 22314
703-684-7722

United Way of the National Capital Area
95 M St. S.W.
Washington, DC 20024
202-488-2000

Visiting Nurses Association of DC
5151 Wisconsin Ave. N.W.
Washington, DC 20016
202-686-2862

Young Men's Christian Association (YMCA)
1625 Massachusetts Ave. N.W.
Washington, DC 20036
202-232-6700

Young Women's Christian Association (YWCA)
624 9th St. N.W.
Washington, DC 20001
202-626-0700

Instruments

For more information about careers in the instrument industry, you can write to:

PROFESSIONAL ORGANIZATIONS:

Instrument Society of America
P.O. Box 12277
67 Alexander Drive
Research Triangle, NC 27709

PUBLICATIONS:

Control Engineering
Measurements and Control
Review of Scientific Instruments

DIRECTORIES:

Analytical Chemistry (American Chemical Society, Washington, DC)
Corporate Technology Directory (Corporate Technologies Information
  Service, Woburn, MA)
ISA Directory of Instrumentation (Instrument Society of America, Research
  Triangle, NC)
Optical Publishing Directory (Learned Information, Medford, NJ)

EMPLOYERS:

Beckman Instruments
8920 Rt. 108
Columbia, MD 21045
410-995-0975
Research and scientific instruments.

Commonwealth Scientific Corp.
500 Pendleton St.
Alexandria, VA 22314
703-548-0800
Contact: George Thompson, Pres.
Electrical measurement equipment.

Data Measurement Corp.
15884 Gaither Drive
Gaithersburg, MD 20877
301-948-2450
Contact: Dominique Gignoux, Pres.
Flaw-detection equipment, thickness gauges.

Dynatech Laboratories
14340 Sullyfield Circle
Chantilly, VA 22021
703-631-7800
Surgical and medical instruments.

Eurotherm Corp.
11485 Sunset Hills Road
Reston, VA 22090
703-471-4870
Digital temperature analyzers and thermocouple pyrometers.

GRC International SWL
1900 Gallows Road
Vienna, VA 22182
703-506-5000
Measuring and controlling devices.

Hunter Associates Laboratory
11491 Sunset Hills Road
Reston, VA 22090
703-471-6870
Contact: Phillip S. Hunter, Pres.
Electro-optical instruments.

Litten Applied Technology
1235 Jefferson Davis Highway
Arlington, VA 22202
703-892-3935
Contact: Bill Doyle

March—McBirney
4539 Metropolitan Court
Frederick, MD 21701
301-831-8775
Contact: Lawrence B. March, Pres.
Water current and flow meters.

Pacific Scientific
2431 Linden Lane
Silver Spring, MD 20910
301-495-7000
Particle counting instruments.

Singer Co. Link Simulation Systems Division
11800 Tech Road
Silver Spring, MD 20904
301-622-4400
Training simulators for process operators.

Survival Technology
2275 Research Blvd.

Rockville, MD 20850
301-928-1800
Contact: Jim Miller, Pres.
Injectors, syringes, monitoring equipment

VEGA
800 Follin Lane
Vienna, VA 22180
703-938-6300
Control systems, measuring, testing.

Weinschel Engineering Co.
1 Weinschel Lane
Gaithersburg, MD 20878
301-948-3434
Contact: Dr. Bruno O. Weinschel, Pres.
Precision microwave coaxial equipment, microwave-related measuring apparatus, and multiband sweep generators.

Insurance

For networking in the insurance industry and related fields, check out the following professional organizations listed in Chapter 5:

PROFESSIONAL ORGANIZATIONS:

District of Columbia Institute of CPAs
District of Columbia Life Underwriters Association

For additional information, you can write or call:

American Council of Life Insurance
1001 Pennsylvania Ave. N.W.
Washington, DC 20004
(202) 624-2000

American Insurance Association
1130 Connnecticut Ave. N.W.
Washington, DC 20036
(202) 828-7100

National Association of Independent Insurers
2600 River Road
Des Plaines, IL 60018

National Association of Life Underwriters
1922 F St. N.W.
Washington, DC 20006
(202) 331-6000

PROFESSIONAL PUBLICATIONS:

Best's Review
Business Insurance
Insurance Times
National Underwriter
Underwriter's Report

DIRECTORIES:

Best's Directory of Recommended Insurance Underwriters (A.M. Best Co., Oldwick, NJ)
Best's Insurance Reports (A.M. Best Co., Oldwick, NJ)
Insurance Almanac (Underwriter Publishing Co., Englewood, NJ)
Insurance Telephone Directories (National Underwriter Co., Cincinnati, OH)

EMPLOYERS:

AVEMCO Corp.
411 Aviation Way
Frederick, MD 21701
301-694-5700
Airline insurance.

Acacia Group: Acacia Mutual Life; Acacia National Life
51 Louisiana Ave. N.W.
Washington, DC 20001
202-628-4506
Life and annuity products.

American International Health Care
30 W. Gude Drive
Rockville, MD 20850
301-251-8600
Employer health benefits, management services.

Banner Life Insurance Co.
1701 Research Blvd.
Rockville, MD 20850
301-279-4800
Life insurance.

Commonwealth Dealers Life Insurance Co.
3869 Plaza Drive
Fairfax, VA 22030
703-385-0121
Life insurance.

Computer Sciences Corp. Health and Administrative Services Division
4601 Presidents Drive

Lanham, MD 20706
301-306-9100
Claim processors.

Government Employees Insurance Co. (GEICO)
5260 Western Ave.
Chevy Chase, MD 20815
301-986-3000
Auto, homeowners, life, property, casualty.

Mutual Life Insurance Co. of Washington
1900 L St. N.W.
Washington, DC 20036
202-296-2650
Life insurance.

Patterson Smith Associates
P.O. Box 1407
Merrifield, VA 22116
703-698-0788
Commercial insurance services.

USLICO Corp.
4601 N. Fairfax Drive
Arlington, VA 22203
703-875-3400
Property, casualty, life.

Union Labor Life Insurance
111 Massachusetts Ave., N.W.
Washington, DC 20001
202-682-0900
Life insurance.

International Organizations

Listed below are a number of the largest international organizations located in the Washington metropolitan area. Descriptions of these, as well as many others, may be found in the following directory:

DIRECTORY:

Yearbook of International Organizations (Union of International Associations, Brussels, Belguim)

EMPLOYERS:

Institute of International Finance
2000 Pennsylvania Ave. N.W.
Washington, DC 20006
202-857-3600

Inter-American Development Bank
1300 New York Ave. N.W.
Washington, DC 20577
202-623-1000

Inter-American Foundation
901 N. Stuart St.
Arlington, VA 22203
703-841-3800

International Bank for Reconstruction and Development
1818 H St. N.W.
Washington, DC 20433
202-477-1234

International Finance Corp.
1818 H St. N.W.
Washington, DC 20433
202-477-1234

International Monetary Fund
700 19th St. N.W.
Washington, DC 20431
202-623-7000

National Association of the Partners of the Americas
1424 K St. N.W.
Washington, DC 20005
202-628-3300

Organization of American States
1889 F St. N.W.
Washington, DC 20006
202-458-3459

Organization for Economic Cooperation and Development
2001 L St. N.W.
Washington, DC 20036
202-785-6323

Pan American Health Organization
525 23rd St. N.W.
Washington, DC 20037
202-861-3200

Project Hope
2 Wisconsin Circle
Bethesda, MD 20815
301-656-7401

United Nations Development Programme. Washington Office
1889 F St. N.W.

Washington, DC 20006
202-289-8674

World Health Organization. Regional Office for the Americas
525 23rd St. N.W.
Washington, DC 20037
202-861-3200

Investment Banking/Stock Brokers

To learn more about the securities industry, you can write to or call the following:

PROFESSIONAL ORGANIZATIONS:

Association for Investment Management and Research
5 Boar's Head Lane
Charlottesville, VA 22903
(804) 977-6600

National Association of Securities Dealers
1735 K St. N.W.
Washington, DC 20006

Securities Industry Association
120 Broadway
New York, NY 10271
(212) 608-1500

PROFESSIONAL PUBLICATIONS:

Barron's
Corporate Financing Week
Dun's Business Month
Finance
Financial Analysts Journal
Financial Executive
Financial World
Institutional Investor
Investment Dealers Digest
Securities Week
Wall Street Transcript

DIRECTORIES:

Corporate Finance Sourcebook (National Register, Wilmette, IL)
CUSIP Master Directory (Standard & Poor's, New York, NY)
F.A.F. Membership Directory (Financial Analysts Federation, Charlottesville, VA)
Investment & Securities Directory (American Business Directories, Omaha, NE)

Money Market Directory (Money Market Directories, Inc., Charlottesville, VA)

Nelson's Directory of Investment Research (W.R. Nelson, Port Chester, NY)

Security Dealers of North America (Standard & Poor's, New York, NY)

Who's Who in the Securities Industry (Economist Publishing, New York, NY)

EMPLOYERS:

Allied Capital Corp.
1666 K St. N.W.
Washington, DC 20006
202-331-1112
Contact: David J. Gladstone, Pres.
Venture capital.

American Capital and Research Corp.
9300 Lee Highway
Fairfax, VA 22031
703-934-3000
Venture capital.

H. Beck, Inc.
7830 Old Georgetown Road
Bethesda, MD 20814
301-951-1000
Brokerage.

Bessemer Trust Co.
1050 Connecticut Ave. N.W.
Washington, DC 20036
202-659-3330
Contact: David G. Curry, V.P.
Asset management.

Alex Brown & Sons
1440 New York Ave. N.W.
Washington, DC 20005
202-626-7000
Contact: Jim Dudley, Jr., Mgr. Dir.
Brokerage.

CRI Insured Mortgage
11200 Rockville Pike
Rockville, MD 20852
301-468-9200
Real estate investment trust.

Calvert Group
4550 Montgomery Ave.
Bethesda, MD 20814
301-951-4830

Contact: Clifton Sorrell, Jr., Pres.
Investment fund management.

Carlyle Group
1001 Pennsylvania Ave. N.W.
Washington, DC 20004
202-347-2626
Contact: Frank C. Carlucci, Vice Chairman
Acquires property and companies.

Columbia Real Estate Investments
10440 Little Patuxent Pkwy.
Columbia, MD 21044
301-964-8875

Dean Witter Reynolds
1850 K St. N.W.
Washington, DC 20006
202-862-9000
Contact: David Boyer, V.P.
Securities broker.

A.G. Edwards & Sons
5301 Wisconsin Ave.
Washington, DC 20015
202-364-1600
Contact: William Mitchell
Brokerage.

Ferris, Baker, Watts
1720 I St. N.W.
Washington, DC 20006
202-429-3500
Contact: Richard P. Sullivan, Pres.
Investment bankers.

Folger Nolan Fleming Douglas
725 15th St. N.W.
Washington, DC 20005
202-783-5252
Contact: Lee Folger
Brokerage.

Foxhall Investment Management
815 Connecticut Ave. N.W.
Washington, DC 20006
202-872-6600
Contact: John Montgomery

Fulcrum Venture Capital Corp.
2021 K St. N.W.
Washington, DC 20006

202-785-4253
Contact: C. Robert Kremp

GIT Investment Fund and Brokerage
1655 N. Ft. Meyer Drive
Arlington, VA 22209
703-528-3600
Contact: A. Bruce Cleveland, Pres.
Mutual fund.

Goldman Sachs
1101 Pennsylvania Ave. N.W.
Washington, DC 20004
202-637-3700
Contact: Judah C. Sommer
Brokerage.

Greater Washington Investors
5454 Wisconsin Ave.
Chevy Chase, MD 20815
301-656-0626
Contact: Rainer Bosselmann, Pres.
Venture capital.

Johnston, Lemon & Co.
1101 Vermont Ave. N.W.
Washington, DC 20005
202-842-5500
Contact: James H. Lemon, Jr.
Brokerage.

Kidder Peabody
919 18th St. N.W.
Washington, DC 20006
202-463-4400
Contact: Doug Black
Brokerage.

Legg Mason
1747 Pennsylvania Ave. N.W.
Washington, DC 20006
202-452-4000
Brokerage.

Merrill Lynch Pierce Fenner & Smith
1850 K St. N.W.
Washington, DC 20006
202-659-7333
Brokerage.

Paine Webber
1300 I St. N.W.

Washington, DC 20005
202-336-5000
Contact: Robert Clark
Brokerage.

Potomac Asset Management
5247 Wisconsin Ave. N.W.
Washington, DC 20015
202-364-6900
Contact: Peter Ladd Gilsey

Prudential Bache Securities
1130 Connecticut Ave. N.W.
Washington, DC 20036
202-861-4400
Contact: Danny Walsh
Brokerage.

Rushmore
4922 Fairmont Ave.
Bethesda, MD 20814
301-657-1500
Money market mutual fund.

Rymac Mortgage Investment Corp.
20251 Century Blvd.
Germantown, MD 20874
301-353-9210
Real estate investment.

Salomon Brothers
1455 Pennsylvania Ave. N.W.
Washington, DC 20004
202-879-4100
Contact: Stephen E. Bell
Brokerage.

Charles Schwab & Co.
1722 I St. N.W.
Washington, DC 20006
202-638-2500
Contact: Tom Noonan
Brokerage.

Shearson Lehman Bros.
1825 I St. N.W.
Washington, DC 20006
202-331-2500
Contact: Paul Powers II, Mgr.
Brokerage.

Smith Barney, Harris Upham
1776 I St. N.W.
Washington, DC 20006
202-862-2800
Contact: George Fellows
Brokerage.

Tucker, Anthony and R.L. Day
1300 I St. N.W.
Washington, DC 20005
202-408-4500
Contact: Robert Sampson
Brokerage.

Washington Real Estate Investment
4936 Fairmont Ave.
Bethesda, MD 21046
301-652-4300

Labor Unions

The Washington area houses many headquarters of national unions. The ones included here are of a significant enough size to warrant a reasonable staff. Remember that even those labor unions that represent blue collar workers have professional, managerial staff members who are college graduates. As with the other national organizations listed in this chapter, these unions employ accountants, computer specialists, legislative analysts, and so forth. To find out more about the unions listed below, please consult the following:

PUBLICATIONS:

Employment Alert
Labor Trends

DIRECTORIES:

Directory of National Unions and Employee Associations (U.S. Dept. of Labor, Washington, DC)
National Trade and Professional Associations (Columbia Books, Washington, DC)

EMPLOYERS:

Air Line Pilots Association
1625 Massachusetts Ave. N.W.
Washington, DC 20036
703-689-2270

Amalgamated Clothing and Textile Workers Union
815 16th St. N.W.

Washington, DC 20006
202-628-0214

American Association of University Professors
1012 14th St. N.W.
Washington, DC 20005
202-737-5900

American Federation of Government Employees
80 F St. N.W.
Washington, DC 20001
202-737-8700

American Federation of Labor and Congress of Industrial Organizations (AFL/CIO)
815 16th St. N.W.
Washington, DC 20006
202-637-5000
Many of the other unions included in this list are affiliated with the AFL/CIO.

American Federation of State, County and Municipal Employees
1625 L St. N.W.
Washington, DC 20036
202-452-4800

American Federation of Teachers
555 New Jersey Ave. N.W.
Washington, DC 20001
202-879-4400

Association of Flight Attendants
1625 Massachusetts Ave. N.W.
Washington, DC 20036
202-328-5400

Communication Workers of America
501 3rd St. N.W.
Washington, DC 20001
202-434-1100

International Association of Machinists and Aerospace Workers
9000 Machinist Place
Upper Marlboro, MD 20772
202-857-5200

International Brotherhood of Electrical Workers
1125 15th St. N.W.
Washington, DC 20005
202-833-7000

International Brotherhood of Painters and Allied Trades
1750 New York Ave. N.W.
Washington, DC 20006
202-637-0736

International Brotherhood of Teamsters, Chauffeurs, Warehousemen and Helpers of America
25 Louisiana Ave. N.W.
Washington, DC 20001
202-624-6800

International Union of Electronic, Electrical, Technical, Salaried & Machine Workers
1126 16th St. N.W.
Washington, DC 20036
202-296-1200

International Union of Operating Engineers
1125 17th St. N.W.
Washington, DC 20036
202-429-9100

Laborers' International Union of North America
905 16th St. N.W.
Washington, DC 20006
202-737-8320

National Association of Letter Carriers
100 Indiana Ave. N.W.
Washington, DC 20001
202-393-4695

National Education Association of the United States
1016 16th St. N.W.
Washington, DC 20036
202-862-4400

National Treasury Employees Union
901 E St. N.W.
Washington DC 20004
202-783-4444

Service Employees International Union
1313 L St. N.W.
Washington, DC 20005
202-898-3200

United Food and Commercial Workers International Union
1775 K St. N.W.
Washington, DC 20006
202-223-3111

United Mine Workers of America
900 15th St. N.W.
Washington, DC 20005
202-842-7280

Law Firms

For networking in law and related fields, check out the following professional organizations listed in Chapter 5:

PROFESSIONAL ORGANIZATIONS:

Alexandria Bar Association
American Bar Association/Washington Office
Arlington County Bar Association
Bar Association of the District of Columbia
Bar Association of Montgomery County
District of Columbia Bar
Fairfax Bar Association
Federal Bar Association
Federal Communications Bar Association
Federal Energy Bar Association
Law Librarians Association of Washington DC
National Bar Association
National Capital Area Paralegal Association
Trial Lawyers Association of Metropolitan Washington
Women's Bar Association of the District of Columbia

For more information, you can write or call:

American Bar Association
750 N. Lake Shore Drive
Chicago, IL 60611
(312) 988-5000

National Bar Association (minority attorneys)
1225 11th St. N.W.
Washington, DC 20001
(202) 842-3900

National Paralegal Association
P.O. Box 406
Solebury, PA
(215) 297-8333

PROFESSIONAL PUBLICATIONS:

ABA Journal
American Lawyer
The Bar News
The Complete Lawyer

Lawyers' Weekly
The Paralegal
Student Lawyer

DIRECTORIES:

ABA Directory (American Bar Association, Chicago, IL)
Directory of Local Paralegal Clubs (National Paralegal Association, Solebury, PA)
Lawyer's List (Commercial Publishing Co., Easton, MD)
Martindale-Hubbell Law Directory (Martindale-Hubbell, Summit, NJ)

EMPLOYERS:

Akin, Gump, Strauss, Hauer & Feld
1333 New Hampshire Ave. N.W.
Washington, DC 20036
202-887-4000
Headquarters: Dallas.

Arent, Fox, Kintner, Plotkin & Kahn
1050 Connecticut Ave. N.W.
Washington, DC 20036
202-857-6000

Arnold & Porter
1200 New Hampshire Ave. N.W.
Washington, DC 20036
202-872-6700

Baker & Hostetler
1050 Connecticut Ave. N.W.
Washington, DC 20036
202-861-1500
Headquarters: Cleveland.

Browstein, Zeidman and Lore
1401 New York Ave. N.W.
Washington, DC 20005
202-879-5700

Burns, Doane, Swecker & Mathis
699 Prince St.
Alexandria, VA 22314
703-836-6620

Cadwalder, Wickersham & Taft
1333 New Hampshire Ave. N.W.
Washington, DC 20036
202-862-2200
Headquarters: New York.

How to Get a Job

City of paralegals

Because of the vast number of law firms in Washington, combined with the presence of corporate counsel offices, lobbying firms with attorney staffs, the Justice Department and other government agencies, and the huge court structure, Washington is surely a dream come true for those desirous of landing a paralegal position. While many paralegals who work here do go on to law school after a few years, many continue in research or administrative positions with public interest groups.

Kathleen Norman, formerly a paralegal with the prestigious firm of Arnold & Porter, decided after finishing at Brown that she wanted to work in Washington, ideally for an organization that could use her Chinese language skills and give her some exposure to international trade work. Finding this too restrictive when actually job hunting, Kathleen thought paralegal work might be the right sort of fit.

With some advice from her mother, who is an attorney, Kathleen spent some time sorting through the *Martindale-Hubbell Law Directory* to locate those firms who actually did international trade work. She sent cover letters and resumes to about twenty-five law firms in DC and received a number of positive responses. After quite a few interviews, Kathleen accepted the position at A&P, which involved a two-year commitment required by the international trade group there.

Kathleen strongly recommends paralegal work for those who want to work for a while after college before making any permanent career choices. Paralegals have quite diverse backgrounds; some are liberal arts majors, some have concentrated in pre-law courses. She feels that the high turnover rate in paralegal work, plus the diverse types of organizations employing paralegals, give job seekers a good chance of landing a position. She also thinks that the firms benefit as well since they can take a "chance" on a liberal arts graduate, knowing they only will be around for a few years. ∎

Clifford & Warnke
815 Connecticut Ave. N.W.
Washington, DC 20006
202-828-4200

Collier, Shannon, Rill & Scott
3050 K St. N.W.

Washington, DC 20007
202-342-8400

Covington & Burling
1201 Pennsylvania Ave. N.W.
Washington, DC 20044
202-662-6000

Crowell & Moring
1001 Pennsylvania Ave. N.W.
Washington, DC 20004
202-624-2500

Cushman, Darby & Cushman
1615 L St. N.W.
Washington, DC 20036
202-861-3000

Dewey, Ballentine, Bushby, Palmer & Wood
1775 Pennsylvania Ave. N.W.
Washington, DC 20006
202-862-1000

Dickstein, Shapiro & Morin
2101 L St. N.W.
Washington, DC 20037
202-785-9700

Dow, Lohnes & Albertson
1255 23rd St. N.W.
Washington, DC 20037
202-857-2550

Epstein Becker & Green
1227 25th St. N.W.
Washington, DC 20037
202-861-0900
Headquarters: New York.

Finnegan, Henderson, Farabow, Garrett & Dunner
1300 I St. N.W.
Washington, DC 20005
202-293-6850

Frank, Bernstein, Conaway & Goldman
6701 Democracy Blvd.
Bethesda, MD 20817
301-897-8282
Headquarters: Baltimore.

Fried, Frank, Harris, Shriver & Jacobson
1001 Pennsylvania Ave. N.W.

Washington, DC 20004
202-639-7000
Headquarters: New York.

Fulbright & Jaworski
801 Pennsylvania Ave. N.W.
Washington, DC 20004
202-662-0200
Headquarters: Houston.

Gibson, Dunn & Crutcher
1050 Connecticut Ave. N.W.
Washington, DC 20036
202-955-8500
Headquarters: Los Angeles.

Ginsburg, Feldman & Bress
1250 Connecticut Ave. N.W.
Washington, DC 20036
202-637-9000

Hazel & Thomas
P.O. Box 12001
Falls Church, VA 22042
703-641-4200

Hogan & Hartson
555 13th St. N.W.
Washington, DC 20004
202-637-5600

Howrey & Simon
1730 Pennsylvania Ave. N.W.
Washington, DC 20006
202-783-0800

Jones, Day, Reavis & Pogue
1450 G St. N.W.
Washington, DC 20005
202-879-3939

Kelly Drye & Warren
2300 M St. N.W.
Washington, DC 20037
202-955-9600

Kirkland & Ellis
655 15th St. N.W.
Washington, DC 20005
202-879-5000
Headquarters: Chicago.

Kirkpatrick & Lockhart
1800 M St. N.W.
Washington, DC 20036
202-778-9000

Linowes & Blocher
1010 Wayne Ave.
Silver Spring, MD 20907
301-588-8580

McDermott Will & Emery
1850 K St. N.W.
Washington, DC 20006
202-887-8000
Headquarters: Chicago.

McGuire, Woods, Battle & Boothe
8280 Greensboro Drive
McLean, VA 22102
703-712-5000

McKenna & Cuneo
1575 I St. N.W.
Washington, DC 20005
202-789-7500

Miller & Chevalier
655 15th St. N.W.
Washington, DC 20005
202-626-5800

Morgan, Lewis and Bockius
1800 M St. N.W.
Washington, DC 20036
202-467-7000

Newman & Holtzinger
1615 L St. N.W.
Washington, DC 20036
202-955-6600

Patton, Boggs and Blow
2550 M St. N.W.
Washington, DC 20037
202-457-6000

Reed, Smith, Shaw & McClay
1200 18th St. N.W.
Washington, DC 20036
202-457-6100

Shaw, Pittman, Potts & Trowbridge
2300 N St. N.W.
Washington, DC 20037
202-663-8000

Sidley & Austin
1722 I St. N.W.
Washington, DC 20006
202-736-8000
Headquarters: Chicago.

Skadden, Arps, Slate, Meagher & Flom
1440 New York Ave. N.W.
Washington, DC 20005
202-371-7000
Headquarters: New York.

Steptoe & Johnson
1330 Connecticut Ave. N.W.
Washington, DC 20036
202-429-3000

Sutherland, Asbill & Brennan
1275 Pennsylvania Ave. N.W.
Washington, DC 20004
202-383-0100

Tuttle & Taylor
1025 Thomas Jefferson St. N.W.
Washington, DC 20007
202-342-1300

Verner, Liipfert, Bernhard, McPherson and Hand
901 15th St. N.W.
Washington, DC 20005
202-371-6000

Williams & Connolly
725 12th St. N.W.
Washington, DC 20005
202-434-5000

Wilmer, Cutler & Pickering
2445 M St. N.W.
Washington, DC 20037
202-663-6000

Winston & Strawn
1400 L St. N.W.
Washington, DC 20005
202-371-5700

**Washington Area
Paralegal
Association**

This is an extremely active organization with regard to employment services for members. It maintains a Job Bank, has published a job-hunting handbook, keeps a list of employers who hire paralegals in the Washington area, and is planning a series of workshops designed to assist members in obtaining good paralegal positions. Call (215) 297-8333 for information about this group. ■

Media: Print

For networking in the magazine and newspaper publishing industry, check out the following professional organizations listed in Chapter 5:

PROFESSIONAL ORGANIZATIONS:

**American News Women's Club
Capital Press Women
National Press Club
Washington Independent Writers
Washington Press Club
White House Correspondents Association**

For additional information, you can write to:

Audit Bureau of Circulation
900 Meacham Road
Schaumburg, IL 60173

Magazine Publishers of America
575 Lexington Ave.
New York, NY 10022
(212) 752-0055

Newspaper Association of America
11600 Sunrise Valley Drive
Reston, VA 22091

PROFESSIONAL PUBLICATIONS:

The Columbia Journalism Review
Editor & Publisher
Folio
The Writer
Writer's Digest

DIRECTORIES:

Editor & Publisher International Yearbook (Editor & Publisher, New York, NY)
Magazines Career Directory (Career Press, Inc., Hawthorne, NJ)
Magazine Industry Market Place (R.R. Bowker, New York, NY)
Newspapers Career Directory (Career Press, Inc., Hawthorne, NJ)
SNA Membership Directory (Suburban Newspapers of America, Chicago, IL)

EMPLOYERS:

Arcom, Arundel Communications
13873 Park Center Road
Herndon, VA 22071
703-471-9596
Community weekly neswpapers.

Army Times. Division of Times Journal
6883 Commercial Drive
Springfield, VA 22159
703-750-8699
Contact: James S. Doyle
Five weekly national newspapers for military market.

Broadcasting Publications
1705 DeSales St. N.W.
Washington, DC 20036
202-659-2340
Contact: Lawrence B. Taishoff
Communications industry.

Bureau of National Affairs
1231 25th St. N.W.
Washington, DC 20037
202-452-4200
Contact: William Beltz, Pres.
Newsletters, loose-leaf services, and books.

Business Publishers
951 Pershing Drive
Silver Spring, MD 20910
301-587-6300
Contact: Leonard A. Eiserer
Variety of business-related publications.

Cambridge Information Group
7200 Wisconsin Ave.
Bethesda, MD 20814
301-961-6750
Contact Robert Snyder
Scientific abstracts.

Capitol Publications
1101 King St.
Alexandria, VA 22314
703-683-4100
Contact: Richard Gibbons
Trade newsletters.

Cardiff Publications
214 Massachusetts Ave. N.E.
Washington, DC 20002
202-544-4043
Telecommunications, magazines, and newsletters.

Getting clips in DC

We asked Marianne Szegedy-Maszak, a frequently published freelance writer who works out of Washington, for some hints for would-be writers and journalists. Getting published, or getting clips as they say in the trade, is obviously the most important thing. Even if you don't get paid, or if it is for a local or community paper, published articles are necessary to show editors what you can produce.

Marianne reminds job hunters that, as far as major news organizations go, Washington is usually the place where successful writers end up, not where they begin their careers. Gaining experience at trade magazines, community papers, out-of-town newspapers and news services, in-house publications and public interest group newsletters should be useful and may eventually lead to other jobs.

For freelancers, affiliation with the Washington Independent Writers group (see Chapter 5) is essential, not only for their formal benefits, such as job lines and lower insurance rates, but for meeting other writers and making the contacts that are so critical in this city. Always be willing to help out with a referral, Marianne suggests, because you might need one yourself for that next assignment. ■

Carroll Publishing Co.
1058 Thomas Jefferson St. N.W.
Washington, DC 20007
202-333-8620
Contact: Thomas E. Carroll
Directories.

Computer Age
3918 Prosperity Ave.
Fairfax, VA 22031
703-573-8400

Contact: Charles Bailey
Editorial material for newspapers.

Congressional Information Service
4520 East-West Highway
Bethesda, MD 20814
301-654-1550
Contact: Paul Massa
Reference materials.

Congressional Quarterly
1414 22nd St. N.W.
Washington, DC 20037
202-887-8500
Contact: Neil Skene, Editor
Legislative-monitoring publications.

Crain Communications
529 14th St. N.W.
Washington, DC 20045
202-662-7200
Contact: Paul Merrion
Trade magazines.

Current Newspapers
5125 MacArthur Blvd.
Washington, DC 20016
202-244-7223
Free, bi-weekly community newspapers.

DCI Publishing
717 N. St. Asaph St.
Alexandria, VA 22314
202-549-0004
Contact: Peter Labovitz
Community newspapers.

Editorial Projects in Education
4301 Connecticut Ave. N.W.
Washington, DC 20008
202-364-4114
Publishes *Education Week* for teachers nationwide.

Fairchild Publications
1333 H St. N.W.
Washington, DC 20005
202-682-3200
Contact: Susan Watters
Trade magazines.

F-D-C Reports
5550 Friendship Blvd.

Chevy Chase, MD 20815
301-657-9830
Contact: Wallace Werble
Regulatory-monitoring publications.

Federal Publications
1120 20th St. N.W.
Washington, DC 20036
202-337-7000
Contact: James Tomes
Regulatory-monitoring publications.

Gannett Co.
1100 Wilson Blvd.
Arlington, VA 22234
703-284-6000
Newspapers.

Gazette
P.O. Box 2410
Merrifield, VA 22116
703-204-2800
Contact: Erik Fatemi
Community newspapers.

Journal Newspapers. Times Journal Co.
2720 Prosperity Ave.
Fairfax, VA 22034
703-560-4000
Contact: C.F. McClughan
Community newspapers.

King Publishing Group
627 National Press Building
Washington, DC 20045
202-638-4260
Trade magazines.

Kiplinger Washington Editors
1729 H St. N.W.
Washington, DC 20006
202-887-6400
Contact: Austin H. Kiplinger, Publisher
Newsletters.

Reed Travel Group
1156 15th St. N.W.
Washington, DC 20005
202-293-5510
Trade magazines.

Official Airline Guides
1010 Vermont Ave. N.W.
Washington, DC 20005
202-393-2775
Travel publications.

Phillips Publishing
7811 Montrose Road
Potomac, MD 20854
301-340-2100
Contact: Thomas L. Phillips
Newsletters.

Staff Directories
P.O. Box 62
Mt. Vernon, VA 22121
703-739-0900
Contact: Ann L. Brownson, Publisher
Directories.

United Press International
1400 I St. N.W.
Washington, DC 20005
202-898-8000
News service.

Warren Publishing
2115 Ward Court N.W.
Washington, DC 20037
202-872-9200
Contact: Albert Warren, Editor
Communications industry publications.

Washington Post Co.
1150 15th St. N.W.
Washington, DC 20071
202-334-6000
Newspaper and magazines.

Office Supplies and Equipment

For more information about the office products industry, you can write to:

PROFESSIONAL ORGANIZATION:

National Office Products Association
301 N. Fairfax St.
Alexandria, VA 22314

PROFESSIONAL PUBLICATIONS:

Modern Office Technology
The Office
Office Automation Report
Office Products Dealer

DIRECTORIES:

Geyer's "Who Makes It" Directory (Geyer-McAllister Publications, New York, NY)
NOPA Directory (National Office Products Association, Alexandria, VA)
Product Buying Guide & Industry Directory (Office Products Dealer, Hitchcock Publishing, Wheaton, IL)

EMPLOYERS:

George Allen Co.
5646 3rd St. N.E.
Washington, DC 20011
202-269-9500

Andrews Office Products
401 Hampton Park Blvd.
Capitol Heights, MD 20743
301-499-1500

Baltimore Stationery
2524 Kirk Ave.
Baltimore, MD 21218
301-470-7090

Bell & Howell
4350 Fair Lakes Court
Fairfax, VA 22033
703-222-5100

Benjamin Office Supply
10792 Tucker St.
Beltsville, MD 20705
301-937-3500

Boise Cascade Office Products
7125 Thomas Edison Drive
Columbia, MD 21046
301-621-3456

Chasen's Business Interiors
901 N. Pitt St.
Alexandria, VA 22314
703-684-1161

Desks & Furnishings
1160 Rockville Pike
Rockville, MD 20852
410-792-2729

M.S. Ginn Co.
5620 Ager Road
Hagerstown, MD 20782
301-853-3000

Jacobs Gardner
4350 Kenilworth Ave.
Hyattsville, MD 20781
301-779-3700

Guernsey Office Products
4311 Walney Road
Chantilly, VA 22021
703-968-8200

Logetronics
7001 Loisdale Road
Springfield, VA 22150
703-971-1400

Ricoh Corp.
1700 N. Moore St.
Arlington, VA 22209
703-527-6561

Southern Office Supply
13868 MetroTech Drive
Chantilly, VA 22021
703-378-2728

Staples, Inc.
1133 20th St. N.W.
Washington, DC 20036
202-331-8843

Chas. G. Stott & Co.
9301 Largo Drive West
Landover, MD 20785
301-499-5800

3M
8301 Greensboro Drive
McLean, VA 22102
703-734-0300

Xerox Corp.
1616 N. Ft. Meyer Drive

Arlington, VA 22209
703-527-6400

Political Consultants

This is probably an industry unique to Washington. It has no real directories, professional organizations, or publications, other than the general news and political magazines that cover the day-to-day workings of the electoral system. The firms listed below are of sufficient size to support several campaigns simultaneously, yet they are not especially large. They are included here primarily because this industry is important to the Washington scene. Keep in mind that their staff requirements are not large and, in fact, are driven by the election cycles.

EMPLOYERS:

Bailey & Associates
282 N. Washington St.
Falls Church, VA 22046
703-237-2188
GOP.

Black Manafort Stone & Kelly
211 N. Union St.
Alexandria, VA 22314
703-683-6612
GOP.

Bond, Donatelli
1414 Prince St.
Alexandria, VA 22314
703-684-5991
GOP.

Carmen Group
2100 Pennsylvania Ave. N.W.
Washington, DC 20037
202-785-0500
GOP.

Cassidy and Associates
700 13th St. N.W.
Washington, DC 20005
202-347-0773
Both parties.

Dearrdourff & Associates
7799 Leesburg Pike
Falls Church, VA 22043
703-237-2188
GOP.

Doak Shrum and Associates
1000 Wilson Blvd.
Arlington, VA 22209
703-522-8910
Democratic Party.

Elections Research Center
5508 Greystone St.
Chevy Chase, MD 20815
301-654-3540
Both parties.

Greer, Margolis, Mitchell & Associates
2626 Pennsylvania Ave. N.W.
Washington, DC 20037
202-338-8700
Democratic Party.

Peter D. Hart Research Associates
1724 Connecticut Ave. N.W.
Washington, DC 20009
202-234-5570
Democratic Party.

Hickman Brown Research
1350 Connecticut Ave. N.W.
Washington, DC 20036
202-659-4000
Democratic Party.

The Kamber Group
1920 L St. N.W.
Washington, DC 20036
202-223-8700
Both parties.

The Keefe Company
444 N. Capitol St. N.W.
Washington, DC 20001
202-638-7030
Both parties.

Eddie Mahe, Jr. & Associates
900 2nd St. N.E.
Washington, DC 20002
202-842-4100
GOP.

John P. Sears
2021 K St. N.W.
Washington, DC 20006

202-331-3300
GOP.

Mark Siegel & Associates
1030 15th St. N.W.
Washington, DC 20005
202-371-5600
Democratic Party.

Squier-Eskew Nappe Ochs Communications
511 2nd St. N.E.
Washington, DC 20002
202-547-4970
Democratic Party.

Viguerie Company
7777 Leesburg Pike
Falls Church, VA 22043
703-356-0440
GOP.

Wexler, Reynolds, Harrison, Fuller & Schule
1317 F St. N.W.
Washington, DC 20004
202-638-2121
Both parties.

Wirthlin Group
1363 Beverly Road
McLean, VA 22101
703-556-0001
GOP.

Printing

For networking in printing and graphic arts, check out the following organizations listed in Chapter 5:

PROFESSIONAL ORGANIZATIONS:

Graphic Arts Institute of Greater Wshington
Printing Industry of Metropolitan DC

For more information, you can write to:

National Association of Printers and Lithographers
780 Palisade Ave.
Teaneck, NJ 07666

National Composition and Prepress Association
100 Daingerfield Road
Alexandria, VA 22314

Technical Association of the Graphic Arts
P.O. Box 9887
Rochester, NY 14623

PROFESSIONAL PUBLICATIONS:

American Printer
Graphic Arts Monthly
Printing News

DIRECTORIES:

Graphic Arts Blue Book (AF Lewis, New York, NY)
Graphic Arts Monthly Buyer's Guide/Directory Issue (Cahners Publishing, New York, NY)
Printing & Graphic Arts Buyer's Guide (Boca Raton, FL)
Who's Who in Typesetting (National Composition Association, Arlington, VA)

EMPLOYERS:

Alexandria Drafting Co.
6440 General Greenway
Alexandria, VA 22312
703-750-0510
Contact: Mark Turcotte

Balmer, Inc.
5130 Wilson Blvd.
Arlington, VA 22205
703-528-9000
Contact: James A. O'Hare, Pres.

Byrd Prepress
5408 Port Royal Road
Springfield. VA 22151
703-321-8610
Contact: Sonya Pendleton

Composition Systems
6320 Castle Place
Falls Church, VA 22044
703-237-1700
Contact: George Scott, Pres.

Craftsman Press
3401 52nd Ave.

Bladensburg, MD 20710
301-277-9400
Contact: Anthony d'Agrosa

EV Services
649 N. Horner's Lane
Rockville, MD 20850
301-424-3300

Editor's Press
6200 Editor's Park Drive
Hyattsville, MD 20782
301-853-4900
Contact: Kenneth F. King, Pres.

Falconer Security Printers
9005 Red Branch Road
Columbia, MD 21045
301-730-8705
Contact: Bob Redic, Pres.

Federal Lithographics
6011 Blair Road N.W.
Washington, DC 20011
202-726-4522
Contact: Ralph C. Williams, Pres.

Goodway Graphics
6628 Electronic Drive
Springfield, VA 22151
703-941-1160
Contact: Robert Perotti, V.P.

Insta Print
9418 Annapolis Road
Lanham, MD 20706
301-459-9784

Judd's
1500 Eckington Place N.E.
Washington, DC 20002
202-635-1200
Contact: Tom Manning, Pres.

Keuffel & Esser
2620 Wilson Blvd.
Arlington, VA 22201
703-524-9000

Master Print
8401 Terminal Road

Newington, VA 22122
703-550-9555

McArdle Printing
800 Commerce Drive
Upper Marlboro, MD 20772
301-390-8500
Contact: Joseph Fautozzi, Pres.

S & S Graphics
1143 Taft St.
Rockville, MD 20850
301-340-7777

Specialties Bindery
4815 Lawrence St.
Hyattsville, MD 20781
301-699-8800
Contact: Ronald Ridgeway, Pres.

Stephenson Printing
5731 General Washington Drive
Alexandria, VA 22312
703-642-9000

Suburban Printing & Publishing
5380-A Eisenhower Ave.
Alexandria, VA 22304
703-370-5800
Contact: Samuel A. Dickens, Pres.

Public Interest Groups

There are many public or national interest groups located in the Washington metropolitan area. While many of these are essentially one-or-two person offices, a number of them are sizable organizations with large staffs. Listed below are examples of this latter type. To find descriptions of these, as well as the smaller groups, please consult the following directories:

DIRECTORIES:

Good Works: A Guide to Social Change Careers (Center for Study of
    Responsive Law, Washington, DC)
Public Interest (National Affairs, Washington, DC)

EMPLOYERS:

Action on Smoking and Health
2013 H St. N.W.

Washington, DC 20006
202-659-4310

Alliance for Justice
600 New Jersey Ave. N.W.
Washington, DC 20001
202-662-9548

American Association of Retired Persons
601 E St. N.W.
Washington, DC 20049
202-434-2277

American Cancer Society
1875 Connecticut Ave.
Washington, DC 20009
202-483-2600

American Civil Liberties Union
122 Maryland Ave. N.E.
Washington, DC 20002
202-544-1681

American Council of the Blind
1155 15th St. N.W.
Washington, DC 20005
202-467-5081

American Nuclear Energy Council
410 1st St. S.E.
Washington, DC 20003
202-484-2670

American Heart Association
2233 Wisconsin Ave. N.W.
Washington, DC 20007
202-337-6400

American Jewish Congress
2027 Massachusetts Ave. N.W.
Washington, DC 20036
202-332-4001

American Legion
1608 K St. N.W.
Washington, DC 20006
202-861-2700

Americans for Democratic Action
1625 K St. N.W.
Washington, DC 20006
202-785-5980

Amnesty International
304 Pennsylvania Ave. S.E.
Washington, DC 20003
202-544-0200

Center for Auto Safety
2001 S St. N.W.
Washington, DC 20009
202-328-7700

Center for National Security Studies
122 Maryland Ave. N.E.
Washington, DC 20002
202-544-1681

Children's Defense Fund
25 E St. N.W.
Washington, DC 20001
202-628-8787

Committee for National Health Insurance
1757 N St. N.W.
Washington, DC 20036
202-223-9685

Common Cause
2030 M St. N.W.
Washington, DC 20036
202-833-1200

Congress Watch
215 Pennsylvania Ave. S.E.
Washington, DC 20003
202-546-4996

Conservative Caucus
450 Maple Ave. E.
Vienna, VA 22180
703-938-9626

Consumer Federation of America
1424 16th St. N.W.
Washington, DC 20036
202-387-6121

Defenders of Wildlife
1244 19th St. N.W.
Washington, DC 20036
202-659-9510

Democratic National Committee
430 S. Capitol St. S.E.

Washington, DC 20003
202-863-8000

Environmental Defense Fund
1875 Connecticut Ave. N.W.
Washington, DC 20009
202-387-3500

Environmental Law Institute
1616 P St. N.W.
Washington, DC 20036
202-328-5150

Greenpeace U.S.A.
1436 U St. N.W.
Washington, DC 20009
202-462-1177

Handgun Control
1225 I St. N.W.
Washington, DC 20005
202-898-0792

League of Women Voters
1730 M St. N.W.
Washington, DC 20036
202-429-1965

National Abortion Rights League
1101 14th St. N.W.
Washington, DC 20005
202-408-4600

National Alliance of Business
1201 New York Ave. N.W.
Washington, DC 20005
202-289-2888

**National Association for the Advancement of Colored People
(NAACP)**
1025 Vermont Ave. N.W.
Washington, DC 20005
202-638-2269

National Audubon Society
666 Pennsylvania Ave. S.E.
Washington, DC 20003
202-547-9009

National Organization for Women
1000 16th St. N.W.

Washington, DC 20036
202-331-0066

National Rifle Association
1600 Rhode Island Ave. N.W.
Washington, DC 20036
202-828-6000

National Taxpayers Union
713 Maryland Ave. N.E.
Washington, DC 20002
202-543-1300

National Trust for Historic Preservation
1785 Massachusetts Ave. N.W.
Washington, DC 20036
202-673-4000

National Wildlife Federation
1400 16th St. N.W.
Washington, DC 20036
202-797-6800

Nature Conservancy
1815 N. Lynn St.
Arlington, VA 22209
703-841-5300

Planned Parenthood Federation
2010 Massachusetts Ave. N.W.
Washington, DC 20036
202-785-3351

Public Citizen
2000 P St. N.W.
Washington, DC 20036
202-833-3000

Republican National Committee
310 1st St. S.E.
Washington, DC 20003
202-863-8500

SANE/FREEZE
1819 H St. N.W.
Washington, DC 20006
202-862-9740

Sierra Club
408 C St. N.E.
Washington, DC 20002
202-547-1141

Special Olympics
1350 New York Ave. N.W.
Washington, DC 20005
202-628-3630

Union of Concerned Scientists
1616 P St. N.W.
Washington, DC 20036
202-332-0900

United Way of America
701 N. Fairfax St.
703-836-7100

Vietnam Veterans of America
1224 M St. N.W.
Washington, DC 20005
202-628-2700

Wilderness Society
900 17th St. N.W.
Washington, DC 20006
202-833-2300

World Wildlife Fund
1250 24th St. N.W.
Washington, DC 20037
202-293-4800

Real Estate Developers and Brokers

For information about real estate as a career, you can write or call:

PROFESSIONAL ORGANIZATIONS:

Building Owners and Managers Association
1201 New York Ave. N.W.
Washington, DC 20005
(202) 223-9669

National Association of Realtors
430 N. Michigan Ave.
Chicago, IL 06011
(312) 329-8200

PROFESSIONAL PUBLICATIONS:

National Real Estate Investor
Real Estate News
Realty and Building

DIRECTORIES:

National Real Estate Investor Directory (Communication Channels,
    Atlanta, GA)
National Roster of Realtors (Stanats Communications, Cedar Rapids, IA)

EMPLOYERS, DEVELOPERS:

Blake Construction
1120 Connecticut Ave. N.W.
Washington, DC 20036
202-828-9000

Boston Properties
500 E St. S.W.
Washington, DC 20024
202-646-7600

Bresler & Reiner
401 M St. S.W.
Washington, DC 20024
202-488-8800

Oliver T. Carr Co.
1700 Pennsylvania Ave. N.W.
Washington, DC 20006
202-624-1700

Coakley & Williams
7500 Greenway Center Drive
Greenbelt, MD 20770
301-345-9730

Donohoe Companies
2101 Wisconsin Ave. S.W.
Washington, DC 20007
202-333-0880

Federal Realty Investment Trust
4800 Hampden Lane
Bethesda, MD 20814
301-652-3360

Hazel-Peterson
12500 Fair Lakes Circle
Fairfax, VA 22033
703-352-3000

JBG Associates
1250 Connecticut Ave. N.W.
Washington, DC 20036
202-364-6200

**Development's two
career paths**

Bobby Smith, who works for one of Washington's smaller real estate development firms, suggests that entry-level positions fall into two categories: engineering, requiring technical abilities and background, and business, where expertise in finance, accounting, leasing, etc., is essential. While he himself combines the two, with degrees in both enginnering and business, Bobby feels that most of the larger firms tend to compartmentalize these two functions, with executives working in both areas only at the higher echelons of the firm.

Bobby also thinks that it is important for anyone approaching real estate development firms for employment to do some homework. Find out about current projects, know where firms fits into the overall construction picture and who the major players are before the interview. ∎

International Developers
901 N. Stuart St.
Arlington, VA 22203
703-558-7300

Kaempfer Company
1150 18th St. N.W.
Washington, DC 20036
202-331-4300

Alan I. Kay Companies
4520 East-West Highway
Bethesda, MD 20814
301-652-4288

Lerner Corp.
11501 Huff Court
Bethesda, MD 20895
301-984-1500

Marriott Corp.
Marriott Drive
Bethesda, MD 20058
301-380-9000

Oxford Development
7316 Wisconsin Ave.
Bethesda, MD 20814
301-654-3100

Quadrangle Development
1001 G St. N.W.

Washington, DC 20001
202-393-1999

Rouse Co.
10275 Little Patuxent Pkwy.
Columbia, MD 21044
301-992-6000

Charles E. Smith Companies
2345 Crystal Drive
Arlington, VA 22202
703-920-8500

Spaulding & Syle
2000 Corporate Ridge
McLean, VA 22102
703-749-3800

Trammell Crow
1001 30th St. N.W.
Washington, DC 20007
202-337-1025

Washington Corp.
5550 Friendship Blvd.
Chevy Chase, MD 20815
301-657-3640

Washington Real Estate Investment Trust
4936 Fairmont Ave.
Bethesda, MD 20814
301-652-4300

West Group
1600 Anderson Road
McLean, VA 22102
703-356-2400

Western Development
3000 K St. N.W.
Washington, DC 20007
202-965-3600

Wilco Construction
7811 Montrose Road
Potomac, MD 20854
301-279-7000

EMPLOYERS, BROKERS:

Century 21
1951 Kidwell Drive

Vienna, VA 22180
703-821-3121

Coldwell Banker
1953 Gallows Road
Vienna, VA 22182
703-556-6100

Coldwell Banker Commercial
1650 Tyson's Blvd.
McLean, VA 22102
703-734-4700

Long & Foster
11351 Random Hills Road
Fairfax, VA 22030
703-359-1500

McClain-Wilson
1906 R St. N.W.
Washington, DC 20009
202-332-3131

Mount Vernon Realty
1700 Diagonal Road
Alexandria, VA 22314
703-739-3100

Prudential
7830 Old Georgetown Road
Bethesda, MD 20814
301-718-7200

Shannon & Luchs
8003 Woodmont Drive
Bethesda, MD 20814
301-986-9292

Shannon & Luchs Commercial
901 15th St. N.W.
Washington, DC 20005
202-326-1000

Recreation/Fitness

For information about recreation and related fields, you can write or call:

PROFESSIONAL ORGANIZATIONS:

Aerobics & Fitness Association of America
15250 Ventura Blvd., #310
Sherman Oaks, CA 91403
(818) 905-0040

National Recreation & Parks Association
3101 Park Center Drive
Alexandria, VA 22302
(703) 820-4940

National Sporting Goods Association
1699 Wall St.
Mt. Prospect, IL 60096
(708) 439-4000

World Leisure and Recreation Association
345 E. 46th St.
New York, NY 10017

PROFESSIONAL PUBLICATIONS:

American Fitness
Baseball Digest
Bowling Digest
Football Digest
Hockey Digest
Inside Sports
Parks & Recreation
Prime Time Sports and Fitness
Pro Football Weekly
Sporting Goods Trade

DIRECTORIES:

Directory of Information Sources in Health, Physical Education and Recreation (ERIC Clearinghouse on Teacher Education, Washington, DC)
Health Clubs Directory (American Business Directories, Omaha, NE)
New American Guide to Athletics, Sports, and Recreation (New American Library, New York, NY)
Salesman's Guide to Sporting Goods Buyers (Salesman's Guides, Inc., New York, NY)
Sporting Goods Directory (Sporting Goods Dealer, St. Louis, MO)

Sports Administration Guide and Directory (National Sports Marketing Bureau, New York, NY)
Sports Marketplace (Sportsguide, Princeton, NJ)

EMPLOYERS:

Army-Navy Country Club
2400 18th St. S.
Arlington, VA 22204
703-521-6800

Bally's Fitness Centers
2000 L St. N.W.
Washington, DC 20036
202-296-0711
Fitness facilities.

Boat America
884 S. Pickett St.
Alexandria, VA 22304
703-370-4202
Boating products and services.

Bowl America
6446 Edsall Road
Alexandria, VA 22312
703-941-6300
Bowling centers.

Bretton Woods Recreation Center
15700 River Road
Germantown, MD 20874
301-948-5497

Centre Group Limited Partnership
1 Harry S. Truman Drive
Landover, MD 20785
301-350-3400
Capital Centre arena.

Chevy Chase Club
6100 Connecticut Ave.
Chevy Chase, MD 20815
301-652-4100

Cineplex Odeon Circle
1101 23rd St. N.W.
Washington, DC 20037
202-331-7471
Theaters.

Columbia Country Club
7900 Connecticut Ave.
Chevy Chase, MD 20815
301-951-5000

Kenwood Country Club
5601 River Road
Bethesda, MD 20816
301-320-3000

Ringling Bros.
8607 Westwood Center Drive
Vienna, VA 22182
703-448-4000
Circuses.

Skyline Clubs
Crystal Gateway
1235 Jefferson Davis Highway
Arlington, VA 22209
703-979-9660

Spa Lady
1145 Herndon Pkwy.
Herndon, VA 22009
703-481-1144
Health clubs.

Sport & Health Clubs
4000 Wisconsin Ave. N.W.
Washington, DC 20008
202-362-8000

Sporting Club
8250 Greensboro Drive
McLean, VA 22102
703-442-9150

Washington Bullets Basketball
1 Harry S. Truman Drive
Landover, MD 20785
301-773-2255

Washington Capitals Hockey
1 Harry S. Truman Drive
Landover, MD 20785
301-386-7000

Washington Redskins
13832 Redskins Drive
Herndon, VA 22071
703-471-9100

Research & Development/Technical Services

Included in this section are myriad firms ranging from a full-service consulting, manufacturing, and technical research firm to a single-office R&D company offering limited expertise. All of them, regardless of size, however, operate in Washington because of the vast influence of the federal government. Many of them have only governmental clients, although there does seem to be a trend toward diversification into the private sector.

We have tried to note an area of specialization, when appropriate; however, it should be remembered that many of these companies provide extensive services in a variety of fields. You would be especially well served, particularly when contacting firms in this section, to do your research before an interview.

To find out more about working in the R&D field, you can write to:

PROFESSIONAL ORGANIZATIONS:

American Association of Small Research Companies
222 Third St.
Cambridge, MA 02142

PROFESSIONAL PUBLICATIONS:

Inside R&D
R&D Contracts Monthly
Research & Development
Research Technology Management

DIRECTORIES:

Directory of American Research and Technology (R.R. Bowker, New York, NY)
High Technology Market Place Directory (Princeton Hightech Group, Middlebush, NJ)
Membership Directory (American Association of Small Research Companies, Cambridge, MA)
Research and Development Directory (Government Data Publications, Brooklyn, NY)
Research and Development Telephone Directory (Cahners Publishing Co., Barrington, IL)
Research Centers Directory (Gale Research, Detroit, MI)

EMPLOYERS:

Advanced Marine Enterprises
1725 Jefferson Davis Highway
Arlington, VA 22202

703-979-9200
Contact: Jackie Wilson
Marine engineering.

Advanced Technology Innovations
2800 Shirlington Road
Arlington, VA 22206
703-379-5533
Computer, engineering, management science, logistics.

American Systems Corp.
2531 Jefferson Davis Highway
Arlington, VA 22202
703-418-1462
Contact: William Robert, Sr. V.P.
Engineering services.

Anadac, Inc.
2011 Crystal Drive
Arlington, VA 22202
703-685-0021
Engineering and technical services, training systems, program management for the Navy and Air Force.

Analytical Systems Engineering Corp.
5400 Shawnee Road
Alexandria, VA 22312
703-892-6000
Robert F. Reiter, V.P.

Andrulis Research
4600 East West Highway
Bethesda, MD 20814
301-657-1700
Systems development, logistics R&D, chemical defense.

Applied Management Sciences
962 Wayne Ave.
Silver Spring, MD 20910
301-585-8181
Contact: Harvey C. Byrd
Research, analysis, and management services for defense, energy, and health.

Automated Sciences Group
1010 Wayne Ave.
Silver Spring, MD 20910
301-587-8750
Contact: Arthur Holmes
Analytical studies and technical support.

Automation Research Systems
4480 King St.
Alexandria, VA 22302
703-820-9000
Contact: Albert Spaulding, Pres.

BDM International
7915 Jones Branch Road
McLean, VA 22102
703-848-5000
Contact: Philip Odeen, Pres.
Advanced technology and contract support.

Ball Corporation
2200 Clarendon Blvd.
Arlington, VA 22201
703-284-5400
Contact: Laurie Chiperfield, Dir.
Antennas, electro-optics, subsystem production, satellite instrumentation.

Betac Corp.
2001 N. Beauregard Ave.
Alexandria, VA 22311
703-824-3100
Contact: Earl F. Lockwood, Pres.
Artificial intelligence, I&W, DOD C3I systems.

Biometric Research Institute
1401 Wilson Blvd.
Arlington, VA 22209
703-276-0400
Contact: James Ogle

Biospherics
12051 Indian Creek Court
Beltsville, MD 20705
301-369-3900
Contact: Gilbert V. Levin, Pres.
Pilot waste water treatment.

Booz Allen & Hamilton
1725 Jefferson Davis Highway
Arlington, VA 22202
703-769-7700
Full-service consulting.

CACI International
1100 N. Glebe Road
Arlington, VA 22209
703-841-7800

Contact: Dr. J.P. London, Pres.
Full-service consulting.

Columbia Research Corp.
2531 Jefferson Davis Highway
Arlington, VA 22202
703-841-1445
Contact: Norman Witbeck, Pres.
Systems analysis, software, reliability configuration for ships and submarines.

DCS Corp.
1330 Braddock Place
Alexandria, VA 22314
703-683-8430
Contact: James T. Wood, Pres.
Systems engineering, operational analysis, avionics, weapon systems.

Decision-Science Applications
110 N. Glebe Road
Arlington, VA 22201
703-243-2500

Designers and Planners
2611 Jefferson Davis Highway
Arlington, VA 22202
703-418-3800
Contact: Chris Wiernicki, Pres.
Naval architecture, marine engineering, CAD ships.

Dynamics Corp.
1755 Jefferson Davis Highway
Arlington, VA 22202
703-521-3812
Contact: Walter Trzaskoma

Dyncorp
2000 Edmund Halley Drive
Reston, VA 22091
703-264-0330
Contact: Daniel Barrister
Services include operating military bases, missile test ranges, aviation, and electronic overhaul.

EG&G Washington Analytical Services
2341 Jefferson Davis Highway
Arlington, VA 22202
703-418-3000
Contact: Dick Scales, Dir.

Electrospace Systems
1725 Jefferson Davis Highway

Arlington, VA 22202
703-979-1220
Contact: C.C. Harvell, V.P.

Beltway bandits

For years, the burgeoning number of consulting and R&D firms that operate around Washington have been called Beltway bandits because, for the most part, their offices have been located on the ring road surrounding the city. They have been considered, in this city where everyone is a skeptic, the ultimate in rip-off artists.

Actually, as more and more of these firms have gained success without adverse publicity, the term has been used less frequently. In fact, if you scan this list, you will notice that most of these firms are not, technically, along the Beltway at all. Rather, they populate huge, by Washington standards, skyscrapers in a part of Arlington known as Crystal City. ■

Engineering Research Associates
1595 Spring Hill Road
Vienna, VA 22182
703-734-8800
Contact: Paul Arnone, Pres.
Design and development of technology for computer systems.

Essex Corp.
1430 Spring Hill Road
McLean, VA 22102
703-548-4500
Contact: Harry Letaw, Jr.
Design and testing of equipment for safety and physical needs of federal government.

General Kinetics
12300 Parklawn Drive
Rockville, MD 20852
301-881-2044
Contact: David Shaw
Primary subsidiary develops computer-based security systems.

General Physics
1919 S. Eads St.
Arlington, VA 22202
703-271-7700
Contact: Elliot Needleman
Combat systems, facility engineering for the Department of Defense.

General Physics Corp.
6700 Alexander Bell Drive

Columbia, MD 21046
301-290-2300
Training, systems development for the Navy; power plant safety systems.

GRC International
1900 Gallows Road
Vienna VA 22182
703-506-5000
Research and electronics.

Greenhorne & O'Mara
9001 Edmonston Road
Greenbelt, MD 20770
301-982-2800
Structural, transportation, water resources, automated information systems.

Hadron Inc.
9990 Lee Highway
Fairfax, VA 22030
703-359-6201
Contact: Dwight Geduldig, Pres.
Telecommunications, computer, engineering services.

Halifax Engineering
5250 Cherokee Ave.
Alexandria, VA 22312
Contact: Howard C. Mills
Maintains and repairs telecom, computer, heating systems, security guard systems for the government.

IBM Systems Integration Division
6600 Rockledge Drive
Bethesda, MD 20817
301-493-8100
Designs and supports government communications network, MIS, office automation.

IIT Research Institute
4600 Forbes Blvd.
Lanham, MD 20706
301-459-3711
Contact: Thomas Bode, Pres.
Computer, defense, electronic services.

Information Spectrum
5107 Leesburg Pike
Falls Church, VA 22041
703-845-3000
Contact: Mark Green

Information Systems and Network Corp.
10411 Motor City Drive
Bethesda, MD 20817
301-469-0400
Contact: Roma Malkani, Pres.
Engineering services.

Integral Systems
5000 Philadelphia Way
Lanham, MD 20706
301-731-4233
Contact: Thomas Gough, Pres.
Development of systems for the Air Force, NASA, NOAA.

Integrated Systems
2800 Shirlington Road
Arlington, VA 22206
703-824-0700
Contact: C. Michael Gooden, Pres.

Ketron
2200 Wilson Blvd.
Arlington, VA 22201
703-558-8700
Contact: Joseph Creegan, Jr.
Operations research and systems engineering.

Logicon, Inc.
2100 Washington Blvd.
Arlington, VA 22204
703-486-3500
Contact: William B. Fender, Pres.

Mandex
8003 Forbes Place
Springfield, VA 22151
703-321-0200
Contact: Kaye Anderson
Engineering, TEMPEST.

MAR
6110 Executive Blvd.
Rockville, MD 20852
301-231-0100
Ocean and marine environmental studies, ship operations.

National Systems Management Corp.
4600 H Pine Crest Office Drive
Alexandria, VA 22312
703-941-9021
Contact: Harvey Huntzinger, Pres.
Engineering services.

National Technologies Associates
1111 Jefferson Davis Highway
Arlington, VA 22202
703-920-6720
Contact: J. Kauffmann, Pres.

Ogden Government Services
3211 Germantown Road
Fairfax, VA 22030
703-246-0200
Technical consulting.

Orbital Sciences Corp.
12500 Fair Lakes Circle
Fairfax, VA 22033
703-631-3600
Contact: David W. Thompson, Pres.

Planning Research Corp.
1500 Planning Research Drive
McLean, VA 22102
703-556-1000
Contact: Gary Kennedy
Technology-based professional services to government and industry.

Presearch
8500 Executive Park Ave.
Fairfax, VA 22031
703-876-6400
Contact: Leonard P. Gollobin
Antisubmarine and mine warfare.

Primark
8251 Greensboro Drive
McLean, VA 22102
703-790-7600
Educational and training programs in health care and financial services.

RJO Enterprises
4500 Forbes Blvd.
Lanham, MD 20706
301-731-3600
Contact: Richard J. Otero, Pres.
Engineering, transportation, electronic, telecom services.

Riverside Research Institute
1815 N. Ft. Meyer Drive
Arlington, VA 22209
703-522-2310
Contact: Wayne Smith
Engineering services

SRI International
1611 N. Kent St.
Arlington, VA 22209
703-524-2053
Contact: D. Alston
Full range of technical services.

Science Applications International Corp.
1213 Jefferson Davis Highway
Arlington, VA 22202
703-979-5910
Contact: J. Galston
Full range of technical services.

Semcor, Inc.
2711 Jefferson Davis Highway
Arlington, VA 22202
703-418-4400
Contact: Carl Mazzan
Engineering services.

Sverdrup Corp.
7799 Leesburg Pike
Falls Church, VA 22043
703-709-0040
Contact: C.N. LeTellier, V.P.
Engineering services.

Systems Planning Corp.
1500 Wilson Blvd.
Arlington, VA 22209
703-351-8200
Technical consulting.

Technology, Management & Analysis Corp.
2231 Crystal Drive
Arlington, VA 22202
703-892-9420
Contact: Jay J. Dor, Pres.

TECHPLAN Corp.
2231 Crystal Drive
Arlington, VA 22202
703-685-1111

Tracor Applied Sciences
1601 Research Blvd.
Rockville, MD 20850
301-279-4200
Contact: Bruce Hamilton
Sonar, life cycle management, combat systems integration.

VSE Corp.
2550 Huntington Ave.
Alexandria, VA 22303
703-960-4600
Contact: Donald M. Ervine, Pres.
Engineering, development, testing, and management services.

Washington Consulting Group
11 Dupont Circle
Washington, DC 20036
202-797-7800
Contact: Armando C. Chapelli, Jr.
Aviation, computer technology, education and training.

Retailers

For information on the retail industry as a career, you can write or call:

PROFESSIONAL ORGANIZATIONS:

General Merchandise Distributors Council
1275 Lake Plaza Drive
Colorado Springs, CO 80906

Manufacturers' Agents National Association
23016 Hill Creek Road
Laguna Hills, CA 92654
(714) 859-4040

National Association of Wholesale Distributors
1725 K St. N.W.
Washington, DC 20006
(202) 872-0885

National Retail Federation
100 W. 31st St.
New York, NY 10001
(212) 244-8780

PROFESSIONAL PUBLICATIONS:

Cellular Agent
Chain Merchandiser Executive
Dealerscope Merchandising
Merchandising
Store Planning
Stores
Women's Wear Daily

DIRECTORIES:

Cellular Marketing (Cardiff Publishing, Englewood, CO)
Fairchild's Financial Manual of Retail Stores (Fairchild Publications, New
    York, NY)
Nationwide Directory: Buying Offices & Accounts (Salesman's Guides, Inc.,
    New York, NY)
Sheldon's Retail Directory (PS & M, Inc., Fairview, NJ)

EMPLOYERS:

ASAP Cellular
610A South Pickett St.
Alexandria, VA 22302
703-823-9435
Cellular phones.

ATI Communications
11020 Baltimore Blvd.
Beltsville, MD 20705
301-595-4000
Cellular phones.

Auto Sound Systems
4919 Bethesda Ave.
Bethesda, MD 20814
301-654-4802
Cellular phones.

Bell Atlantic Mobile Systems
11711 A Parklawn Drive
Rockville, MD 20852
301-770-4411
Cellular phones.

Britches of Georgetown
544 Herndon Parkway
Herndon, VA 22070
703-471-7900
Specialty chain.

Cellular City
8644 Colesville Road
Silver Spring, MD 20910
301-588-8000
Cellular phones.

Cellular One
7855 Greenbelt Road
Greenbelt, MD 20770
301-220-3600
Cellular phones.

Cellular Phone Services
403 E. Gude Drive
Rockville, MD 20850
301-251-3700
Cellular phones.

Cellular Services of Washington
8501 Tyco Road
Vienna, VA 22182
703-893-3500
Cellular phones.

Computerland
7469 Old Alexandria Ferry Road
Clinton, MD 20735
301-599-1596

Cosmetic Center
8839 Greenwood Place
Savage, MD 20763
301-497-6800
Cosmetics centers.

Dart Group
3300 75th Ave.
Landover, MD 20785
301-731-1200
Crown Books, Trak Auto, Shopper's Food Warehouse.

Door Store
3140 M St. N.W.
Washington, DC 20007
202-333-8170
Furniture.

Errol's
6621 Electronic Drive
Springfield, VA 22151
703-642-3300
Video.

Greg Sound & Communication
14200 Sullyfield Circle
Chantilly, VA 22021
703-968-0260
Cellular phones.

Hechinger Co.
1616 McCormick Drive
Landover, MD 20785
301-341-1000
Do-it-yourself home centers.

Hecht Co.
685 N. Glebe Road
Arlington, VA 22203
703-358-1200
Department stores.

Kitchen Bazaar
1098 Taft St.
Rockville, MD 20850
301-424-4880
Cookware, etc.

Mohasco Corp.
4401 Fair Lakes Drive
Fairfax, VA 22033
703-968-8000
Furniture.

Nordstrom
1400 S. Hayes St.
Arlington, VA 22202
703-415-1121

JC Penney
1156 15th St. N.W.
Washington, DC 20005
202-862-4800
Department stores.

Peoples Drug Stores
6315 Bren Mar Drive
Alexandria, VA 22312
703-750-6100

Raleigh's
11160 Veersmill Road
Wheaton, MD 20902
301-942-8532
Specialty stores.

Schwartz Bros.
4901 Forbes Blvd.
Lanham, MD 20706
301-459-8000
Audio and video accessories.

Sears Roebuck & Co.
10301 Westlake Drive
Bethesda, MD 20817
301-469-4000
Department stores.

Southland Corp. Highs Division
8920 Whiskey Bottom Road
Laurel, MD 20723
301-953-2200
Dairy products stores.

Trak Auto Corp.
3300 75th Ave.
Landover, MD 20785
301-731-1200
Auto parts retailer.

USA Telecommunications
6269 Franconia Road
Alexandria, VA 22310
703-922-6000
Cellular phones.

Waxie Maxie Quality Music
Frederick Town Mall
Frederick, MD 21701
301-662-6255
Records and tapes.

Woodward & Lothrop
11th and F Sts. N.W.
Washington, DC 20013
202-879-8000
Department stores.

Think Tanks

Listed below are a number of non-profit research centers in the greater Washington area. Companies engaged in similar research, but operating in the commercial arena, may be found in the **Research & Development/Technical Services** section. For descriptions of the below organizations, as well as others, please consult the following directory:

DIRECTORY:

Research Centers Directory (Gale Research, Detroit, MI)

EMPLOYERS:

American Enterprise Institute for Public Policy Research
1150 17th St. N.W.
Washington, DC 20036
202-862-5800
Contact: Christopher C. DeMuth, Pres.
Public policy.

American Institute for Research
3333 K St. N.W.
Washington, DC 20007
202-342-5000
Contact: Dr. David A. Goslin, Pres.
R&D, evaluation services.

American Legislative Exchange Council
214 Massachusetts Ave. N.E.
Washington, DC 20002
202-547-4646
Contact: Samuel A. Brunelli, Exec. Dir.
Research and legislative analysis.

ANSER
1215 Jefferson Davis Highway
Arlington, VA 22202
703-685-1000
Contact: John Fabian

Applied Physics Laboratory/Johns Hopkins University
Johns Hopkins Road
Laurel, MD 20723
301-953-5000
Contact: Dr. Gary Smith, Dir.
Scientific research.

Armed Forces Institute of Pathology
Walter Reed Army Hospital
6825 16th St. N.W., Bldg. 54
Washington, DC 20306
202-576-2800
Consultation on pathological diagnosis.

Batelle Memorial Institute
370 L'Enfant Promenade S.W.
Washington, DC 20024
202-479-0500
Contact: K. Killingstad, Mgr.
Technological research.

Beltsville Agricultural Research Center
6305 Ivy Lane
Greenbelt, MD 20770
301-504-9403
Environmental, plant, animal, human nutrition.

Brookings Institution
1775 Massachusetts Ave. N.W.
Washington, DC 20036
202-797-6000

Contact: Bruce K. MacLaury, Pres.
Public policy.

Carnegie Endowment for International Peace
2400 N St. N.W.
Washington, DC 20037
202-862-7900
Contact: Ambassador Morton I. Abramowitz
Public policy.

Carnegie Institution
1530 P St. N.W.
Washington, DC 20005
202-387-6400
Contact: Maxine F. Singer, Pres.
Physical and biological scientific research.

Cato Institute
224 2nd St. S.E.
Washington, DC 20003
202-546-0200
Contact: Edward H. Crane III, Pres.
Libertarian public policy.

Center for Defense Information
1500 Massachusetts Ave. N.W.
Washington, DC 20005
202-862-0700
Contact: Gene R. La Rocque, Dir.
National defense research.

Center for Innovative Technology
2214 Rock Hill Road
Herndon, VA 22070
703-689-3000
Contact: A. Linwood Holton Jr., Pres.
State of Virginia sponsored effort to combine industry needs with
capabilities of the state's universities.

Center for National Policy
317 Massachusetts Ave. N.E.
Washington, DC 20002
202-546-9300
Contact: Edmund S. Muskie, Chair
Public policy.

Center for Science in the Public Interest
1875 Connecticut Ave. N.W.
Washington, DC 20009
202-332-9110
Contact: Mike Jacobson, Dir.
Consumer advocacy.

Center for Strategic and International Studies/Georgetown University
1800 K St. N.W.
Washington, DC 20006
202-887-0200
Contact: David M. Abshire
Public policy.

Center for the Study of Social Policy
1250 I St. N.W.
Washington, DC 20005
202-371-1565
Contact: Thomas Joe, Pres.
Public policy.

Center on Budget and Policy Priorities
777 North Capital St. N.E.
Washington, DC 20002
202-408-1080
Contact: Robert Greenstein, Dir.
Public policy.

Committee for Economic Development
2000 L St. N.W.
Washington, DC 20036
202-296-5860
Contact: Sol Hurwitz, Pres.
Public policy.

Conference Board/Washington Office
1755 Massachusetts Ave. N.W.
Washington, DC 20036
202-483-0580
Contact: Ellen Boyers, Dir.
Business and public affairs.

Economic Policy Institute
1730 Rhode Island Ave. N.W.
Washington, DC 20036
202-775-8810
Contact: Geoffrey Faux, Pres.
Economic policy.

Ethics and Public Policy Center
1015 15th St. N.W.
Washington, DC 20005
202-682-1200
Contact: George S. Weigel, Jr., Pres.
Public policy.

Fogarty International Center for Advanced Study in the Health Sciences
9000 Rockville Pike
Bethesda, MD 20892
301-496-1415
Contact: Dr. Phillip E. Schambra, Dir.
Division of NIH.

Goddard Space Flight Center
Greenbelt Road
Greenbelt, MD 20771
301-286-2000
Contact: John M. Klieneberg

Alan Guttmacher Institute
2010 Massachusetts Ave. N.W.
Washington, DC 20036
202-296-4012
Contact: Jeannie Rosoff, Pres.
Fertility regulation, population demographics.

Heritage Foundation
214 Massachusetts Ave. N.E.
Washington, DC 20002
202-546-4400
Contact: Dr. Edwin J. Feulner, Jr., Pres.
Public policy.

Hudson Institute
1015 18th St. N.W.
Washington, DC 20036
202-223-7770
Contact: L. Lenkowsky, Pres.
Public policy.

Hughes Medical Institute
6701 Rockledge Drive
Bethesda, MD 20817
301-571-0200
Contact: Dr. Purnell W. Choppin, Pres.
Medical research.

Human Resources Research Organization
66 Canal Center Plaza
Alexandria, VA 22314
703-549-3611
Contact: William C. Osborn, Pres.

Institute for Defense Analysis
1801 N. Beauregard St.
Alexandria, VA 22311

703-845-2000
Contact: Larry Welch, Pres.
R&D for the Defense Department.

Institute for Policy Studies
1601 Connecticut Ave. N.W.
Washington, DC 20009
202-234-9382
Contact: Susan Crowell
Public policy.

Investor Responsibility Research Center
1755 Massachusetts Ave. N.W.
Washington, DC 20036
202-234-7500
Contact: Margaret Carroll, Exec. Dir.
Business and public policy.

Joint Center for Political Studies
1301 Pennsylvania Ave. N.W.
Washington, DC 20004
202-626-3500
Contact: Eddie N. Williams, Pres.
Minority and disadvantaged involvement in governmental process.

Logistics Management Institute
6400 Goldsboro Road
Bethesda, MD 20817
301-320-2000
Contact: Robert E. Pursley, Pres.
Federally funded logistics research at the strategy and policy level.

Middle East Institute
1761 N St. N.W.
Washington, DC 20036
202-785-1141
Contact: Robert Keeley

National Academy of Engineering
2101 Constitution Ave. N.W.
Washington, DC 20418
202-334-3677
Contact: Robert M. White, Pres.

National Academy of Public Administration
1120 G St. N.W.
Washington, DC 20005
202-347-3190
Contact: Scott Fosler, Pres.
Governance problems.

National Academy of Sciences
2101 Constitution Ave. N.W.
Washington, DC 20418
202-334-2000
Contact: Dr. Frank Press, Pres.
Natural and social science issues and research.

National Center for Appropriate Technology
1212 New York Ave. N.W.
Washington, DC 20005
202-289-6657
Contact: George Turman

National Engineering Laboratory
National Institute of Standards
Gaithersburg, MD 20899
301-975-2300
Contact: Dr. John W. Lyons, Dir.
Engineering research and standards.

National Geographic Society
17 & M St. N.W.
Washington, DC 20036
202-857-7000
Explorations and research projects; publications.

National Institute on Drug Abuse
5600 Fishers Lane
Rockville, MD 20857
301-443-6480
Contact: Richard Millstein

National Institutes of Health
9000 Rockville Pike
Rockville, MD 20892
301-496-2535
Umbrella organization for many individual institutes.

National Planning Association
1424 16th St. N.W.
Washington, DC 20036
202-265-7685
Contact: Malcolm Lovell, Pres.
Long-range economic projections and research.

National Science Foundation
1800 G St. N.W.
Washington, DC 20550
202-357-9498
Contact: Dr. Walter Massey
Government agency responsible for promoting research and education
in the sciences.

Naval Research Laboratory
4555 Overlook Ave. S.W.
Washington, DC 20375
202-767-2541
Contact: Dr. Timothy Coffey, Dir.
Exploratory and applied research in physical sciences.

Population Reference Bureau
1875 Connecticut Ave. N.W.
Washington, DC 20009
202-483-1100
Contact: Dr. Thomas W. Merrick, Pres.
Population policy and studies.

Potomac Institute
1400 20th St. N.W.
Washington, DC 20036
202-331-0087
Contact: Philip Hammer
Development of human resources by expanding opportunities for minorities.

Rand Corporation
2100 M St. N.W.
Washington, DC 20037
202-296-5000
Contact: Charles R. Roll, Jr., Dir.
National security and public welfare.

Resources for the Future
1616 P St. N.W.
Washington, DC 20036
202-328-5000
Contact: Robert W. Fri, Pres.
Public policy.

SRI International
1611 N. Kent St.
Arlington, VA 22209
703-524-2053
Contact: Gerald Connolly, V.P.
Strategic studies, public policy, management sciences, etc.

Transportation Research Board
2101 Constitution Ave. S.W.
Washington, DC 20418
202-334-2934
Contact: Thomas B. Deen, Dir.
Transportation systems research.

United States Institute of Peace
1550 M St. N.W.

Washington, DC 20005
202-457-1700
Contact: Samuel Lewis, Pres.
Federally funded research organization.

Urban Institute
2100 M St. N.W.
Washington, DC 20037
202-833-7200
Contact: William Gorham, Pres.
Public policy.

Travel and Transportation

To learn more about travel and transportation, you can write or call:

PROFESSIONAL ORGANIZATIONS:

Airline Passengers of America
4212 King St.
Alexandria, VA 22302

Airline Pilots Association
1625 Massachusetts Ave. N.W.
Washington, DC 2003

American Society of Travel Agents
1101 King St.
Alexandria, VA 22314
(703) 739-2782

American Trucking Association
2200 Mill Road
Alexandria, VA 22314

Travel Industry Association of America
2 Lafayette Center
Washington, DC 20036

United States Tour Operators Association
211 E. 51st St.
New York, NY 10022

PROFESSIONAL PUBLICATIONS:

Air Travel Journal
AOPA Pilot
ASTA Travel News
Fleet Owner
Frequent Flyer

Tours & Resorts
Travel Agent

DIRECTORIES:

Moody's Transportation Manual and News Reports (Moody's Investor
    Service, New York, NY)
Travel Industry Personnel Directory (Travel Agent Magazine, New York, NY)
World Aviation Directory (McGraw-Hill, New York, NY)

EMPLOYERS:

AAA Potomac
8300 Old Courthouse Road
Vienna, VA 22182
703-222-6666
Travel agency.

American Airlines
Marketing Office
5111 Leesburg Pike
Falls Church, VA 22041
703-824-0222

Carlton Travel Network
635 Slaters Lane
Alexandria, VA 22314
703-519-9503
Travel agency.

Delta Airlines
Marketing Office
1629 K St. N.W.
Washington, DC 20006
202-296-9860

Heritage Travel
995 L'Enfant Plaza North S.W.
Washington, DC 20024
202-863-4263

Interstate Van Lines
5801 Rolling Road
Springfield, VA 22152
703-569-2121
Full service carrier.

National Railroad Passenger Corp (AMTRAK)
400 N. Capitol St. N.W.
Washington, DC 20002
202-484-7540

Ober United Travel Agency
5420 Wisconsin Ave.
Chevy Chase, MD 20815
301-654-9321

Omega World Travel
5203 Leesburg Pike
Falls Church, VA 22041
703-998-7171
Travel agency.

Cal Simmons Travel
111 Oronoco St.
Alexandria, VA 22314
703-549-8646
Travel agency.

Travel Advisers of America
1413 K St. N.W.
Washington, DC 20005
202-371-1440

Travel Resources
1700 E. Gude Drive
Rockville, MD 20850
301-424-9330
Travel agency.

Travel Services Group
1500 King St.
Alexandria, VA 22314
703-684-2777

Travelogue
1201 New York Ave. N.W.
Washington, DC 20005
202-962-3111
Travel agency.

United Airlines
22800 Davis Drive
Sterling, VA 22170
703-742-4600

USAIR
2345 Crystal Drive
Arlington, VA 22227
703-418-7000

USTRAVEL Systems
1401 Rockville Pike

Rockville, MD 20852
301-251-9450

Van Slycke and Reeside Travel
5100 Wisconsin Ave. N.W.
Washington, DC 20016
202-362-7301
Travel agency.

World Corp.
13873 Park Center Road
Herndon, VA 22071
703-834-9200
Operates World Airways and Key Airlines.

Utilities

For more information about public utilities, you can write to:

PROFESSIONAL ORGANIZATIONS:

American Public Gas Association
Box 1426
Vienna, VA 22183
(703) 281-2910

American Public Power Association
2301 M St. N.W.
Washington, DC 20037
(202) 467-2900

North American Telecommunications Association
2000 M St. N.W.
Washington, DC 20036

United States Telephone Association
900 19th St. N.W.
Washington, DC 20006

PROFESSIONAL PUBLICATIONS:

Electrical World
Electric Power & Light
Public Utilities Fortnightly
Telephony

DIRECTORIES:

APGA Directory of Municipal Gas Systems (American Public Gas Association, Vienna, VA)

Moody's Public Utility Manual and News Reports (Moody's Investor Service, New York, NY)
Sourcebook (North American Telecommunications Association, Washington, DC)

EMPLOYERS:

AES Corp.
1001 N. 19th St.
Arlington, VA 22209
703-522-0073

AT&T Communications
3033 Chain Bridge Road
Oakton, VA 22185
703-691-5000

Bell Atlantic Network Services
1310 N. Courthouse Road
Arlington, VA 22210
703-974-3000
Parent company to local telephone companies.

Chesapeake & Potomac Telephone
2980 Fairview Park Drive
Falls Church, VA 22042
703-241-6000

Communications Satellite Corp (COMSAT)
950 L'Enfant Plaza S.W.
Washington, DC 20024
202-863-6000
Communications services and products.

GTE Spacenet
1801 Research Blvd.
Rockville, MD 20850
301-251-8300
Communications networks.

Intelsat
3400 International Drive N.W.
Washington, DC 20008
202-944-6800
Intercontinental telecom carrier.

MCI Communications Corp.
1801 Pennsylvania Ave. N.W.
Washington, DC 20006
202-872-1600
Long distance telephone carrier.

Northern Virginia Natural Gas
6801 Industrial Road
Springfield, VA 22151
703-750-4440
Natural gas.

Potomac Electric Power Co.
1900 Pennsylvania Ave. N.W.
Washington, DC 20068
202-872-2000
Electric utility.

Telenet Communications Corp.
12490 Sunrise Valley Drive
Reston, VA 22096
703-689-7722
Global communications network.

US Sprint
12490 Sunrise Valley Drive
Reston, VA 22096
703-264-4000
Long distance telephone carrier.

Virginia Power
3901 Fair Ridge Drive
Fairfax, VA 22033
703-359-3000
Electric utility.

Washington Gas & Light Co.
1100 H St. N.W.
Washington, DC 20080
703-750-1000
Electric and gas.

Employers Index

D

General Index

J

L

M

N,O

P

R